THE COMPLETE
BELGIAN SHEPHERD DOG

RINGPRESS

ACKNOWLEDGEMENTS

Many thanks to the following: Lee Jiles for her historical input, her encouragement, and her assistance with contacts throughout the world. Paul England for UK history, and my friend Anne Sandberg Fallesen who wrote on the Laekenois and collated numerous photos. To Martha Hoffman, Laurie Graichen, Tom Davis and Rob and Cara Greger who all contributed to the working chapter. To Dr Malcolm Willis for his genetic input and Eddie Houston (Border Terriers) who assisted with the veterinary chapter. Helen Fletcher for her input on basic obedience training and general advice.

I am also indebted to Amanda McLaren for assistance with contacting French kennels and translations and writing about showing on the continent. Judith Clout, Liz Richardson, Marcelle King, Janet Biddlecombe, Carin Lyrhome, Marcy Spalding, Yvonne Wesley, Roz Grevitt and Janice Clifford for assistance. My thanks to all who have provided photographs, especially Riitta Tjorneryd. To Ann Smiley, my editor, who turned my scrawl into something readable. Finally, to John who has put up with me being thoroughly antisocial for a considerable period of time while I wrote and collated this book.

Published by Ringpress Books
A division of INTERPET LTD
Vincent Lane, Dorking, Surrey, RH4 3YX

Designed by Rob Benson

First Published 2002
© 2002 RINGPRESS BOOKS

ISBN 1 86054 256 5

Printed and bound in Singapore
by Kyodo Printing Co

10 9 8 7 6 5 4 3 2 1

CONTENTS

1 INTRODUCING THE BELGIAN SHEPHERD

Belgian Shepherds are unique in the world of pedigree dogs because there are four varieties, all differing in coat and colour; there is a coat type to please everyone. The glamorous Tervueren has a profuse double coat, with colours ranging from a deep mahogany to an ash blond. He has a distinct black mask, and, as the finishing touch, a mantle of black hair or overlay. The Malinois is of identical colouring, but with a short coat. The Groenendael has a long, black coat. The Laekenois is somewhat less smart, but equally distinctive with his harsh, wiry coat. This book will tell you about the history and development of each variety, and how they retain their shared characteristics as Belgian Shepherd Dogs – those elegant and noble aristocrats of the Pastoral or Herding Group.

Belgians are renowned throughout the world for their versatility. They have the ability to be a family pet, a companion, and a working partner. They work as avalanche dogs, able to locate bodies through several metres of snow, as drug dogs working for Customs, as general police dogs, and even as television soap stars. They have now become a familiar sight in canine competitions, too.

Being deeply loyal to his human family, the Belgian is often uncomfortable with strangers, and he can be possessive and protective of any member of his family or

The four varieties (pictured left to right): Laekenois, Malinois, Groenendael and Tervueren.
Photo: David Dalton.

Bright, alert and energetic, the Belgian Shepherd thrives on an active life.

property. He is a dog that loves companionship; he is easily bored, and, if he is left alone for long periods, he can become extremely destructive. He needs mental stimulation, which he will accept with ease.

Belgian Shepherds are totally different from German Shepherds, having a leaner, more chiselled head, a slighter build, and a squarer stance when viewed from the side. They differ in construction, also. An ideal Belgian has a body shape that should be square from the point of shoulder to the rump. It is not unusual for the uninitiated to be confused by their first sighting of a Belgian, and to assume this is an attractive crossbreed of Border Collie and German Shepherd, or Rough Collie and German Shepherd.

The Belgian is a very active dog and loves nothing better than free running; he is not suited to a confined town environment, as he needs space in which to exercise. In his natural environment as a herder, the Belgian would tirelessly turn around his master, keeping the sheep in check and keeping them within the limits of their pasture. This inherited trait shows today in the manner in which the Belgian, when relaxed and on a daily walk, continues to move effortlessly in circles around his owner.

ORIGINS OF THE BELGIAN SHEPHERD DOG

In the late 1800s, as the spirit of nationalism grew throughout Europe, many individuals worked to develop animals that could be identified with their own countries. In Belgium, efforts were made to determine whether there was a true shepherd dog unique to that country. In September 1891, the Club du Chien de Berger Belge (Belgian Shepherd Dog Club) was formed with this purpose in mind. A commission of club members was established, which contacted veterinarians throughout the provinces.

In November 1891, under the direction of Professor Adolphe Reul, a gathering was held at Cureghem, on the outskirts of Brussels, to examine the shepherd dogs of that area. From the 117 dogs exhibited, Professor Reul and his panel of judges concluded that, for this Brabant province, there was a consistent type of shepherd dog. They were anatomically identical, but differed in hair texture, colour, and length. What Professor Reul described was a square, medium-sized shepherd dog with well-set triangular ears and dark-brown eyes.

Following events at Cureghem, The Club du Chien de Berger Belge devoted its efforts to similar exhibitions in the other eight provinces, finding similar results. Between 1891 and 1901, when the Société Royale Saint-Hubert registered the Belgian Shepherds as a breed, efforts were directed toward developing a Standard, improving type, and exhibiting the dogs.

FIRST VARIETIES
The first Standard for the Belgian Shepherd Dog, adopted in April 1892 by

Kadour de la Quievre: The Groenendael variety was named after the Chateau Groenendael, owned by Nicolas Rose, outside Brussels. Photo: Ritta Tjorneryd.

the CCBB, separated the varieties into long-haired, short-haired, and rough-haired, with a number of colours acceptable. Between 1892 and the beginning of World War I, many kennels emerged, promoting the variety of their choice. Place names became popular as a way of identifying a variety.

By the beginning of the 20th century, the long-haired blacks became known as Groenendaels, in honour of breeder Nicolas Rose, restaurateur and owner of the Chateau Groenendael outside Brussels. The long-haired fawns became known as Tervueren, after the village where Monsieur Corbeel began breeding the variety. The short-haired fawns were called Malinois, because of the many kennels established around Malines. The fawn rough-hairs became known as Laekenois, in honour of breeder J.B. Janssen of Laeken.

As the breed developed in Belgium, between 1892 and World War I, a number of different clubs and organisations came into being. The Berger Belge Club was founded in 1898, in opposition to the Club du Chien de Berger Belge. In 1908, a second national kennel club, the Kennel Club Belge, was founded in opposition to the Société Royale Saint-Hubert, while in 1910, the Groenendael Club was established to promote that variety. In 1912, the Fédération Cynologique Internationale (World Canine Organisation) was established, with the Saint-Hubert society quickly joining it. All have played a role in the breed's development in Belgium.

REBUILDING STOCK
During World War I, Belgian Shepherd Dogs distinguished themselves on the battlefields, serving as message carriers, as ambulance dogs, and even pulling

Lady du Casa Barry: The Malinois soon established itself as the premier working dog. Photo: Ritta Tjorneryd.

machine guns. However, the war decimated the breeding stock, so, when it ended, rehabilitation had to begin.

The period between the two world wars was also a time of exportation and increasing popularity of the breed in other countries. The Malinois became the premier working dog, and the most popular of the varieties in Belgium, and has remained so. Several fine Malinois kennels came into existence, among them L'Écaillon, established by noted breed historian Felix E. Verbanck. Other notable

kennels of the time included M. Vanderkerekhove's Chalet des Glycines, M. Hanappe's Jolimont, and M. Crunelle's Pimprenelles.

In Groenendaels, the Mont-Sara kennels and the Infernal kennels were major players. In Laekenois, M. Peffer established Kennel Redoute, but, by this time, Laekenois breeding took place primarily in Holland. The Tervueren kennels were few, based primarily on the Tervueren born from Malinois after the war, and, overall, the Tervueren had become a rarity.

Immediately prior to World War II, the Société Royale Saint-Hubert recognised eight varieties of Belgian Shepherd Dog:
• Black, long-haired Groenendael
• Fawn, long-haired Tervueren
• Long-haired of other colours
• Fawn, short-haired Malinois
• Short-haired of other colours
• Fawn, rough-haired Laekenois
• Grey, rough-haired
• Rough-haired of other colours.

FCI INFLUENCE
Since World War II, the FCI has had a considerable influence over the national kennel clubs associated with it, dictating the future developments in the Belgian Shepherd breed. In 1966, the FCI Standard changed, establishing four recognised varieties – Groenendael, Laekenois, Malinois, and Tervueren.

At various times in Belgium, particularly between the two world wars, intervariety breeding has been permitted to increase and to maintain similarity between the varieties. Colour has been in contention since the foundation of the breed, and remains an issue to date. The short-haired blacks, still recognised by the Kennel Club Belge as the fifth variety, are no longer FCI-recognised. Tervueren colour also

Kehala Reason To Dream: Colour has been a subject of controversy in the Tervueren variety. Photo: Linda Collins.

remains in contention in countries affiliated to the FCI. The brindle long- and short-hairs seem to have vanished, together with the grey rough-hairs. However, given the colour genetics of the breed, they may reappear in the future.

In 1973, the Belgian kennel club ruled that cross-breeding between the different varieties was no longer allowed, except in exceptional circumstances, and then only with the permission of the Belgium breed council. Even when permission was granted, the offspring resulting from the cross-breeding could not be entered on the full register for three generations, until the outcome of colour and coat could be seen.

In 1978, the FCI recognised the following colours:
- **Groenendael:** Long-haired black
- **Tervueren:** Long-haired in all shades of red and grey with a dark overlay and a dark mask
- **Malinois:** Short-haired red to brown with a dark mask
- **Laekenois:** Rough-haired red to brown.

HOME COUNTRY BREEDING
M. Hinnekens of the Van Nekkerberg ter Leie kennel had a long association with the Kennel Club Belge before 1939. He bred Groenendaels after the war, but it is probably for the grey Tervueren that his kennel is best remembered.

The des Bonmoss kennel began in 1964, while, in the mid-1960s, Jerome Chastel produced two litters at his Thudinie kennel that were quite influential within the breed, not only in Belgium, but also in Switzerland and Italy. The L'Ouchenee kennel was established in 1967.

GROENENDAEL
In 1969, Rene Renard began breeding Groenendaels under the kennel name Pouroffe. Boscaille kennel was established in 1972, followed by the Val de l'Amblève kennel. In 1977, Anne-Marie Heraly's Maison du Bois kennel began, with her foundation bitch, Lynda du Chemin des Dames, imported from France. That same year, Domaine Ponti began breeding Groenendaels, and Norman Deschuymere began his Quievre kennel.

In 1978, M. Dohnt's Val des Artistes kennel was established, followed in 1979 by du Pays des Flandres kennel. The 1980s saw the rise of a number of new kennels devoted to Groenendaels, including Domaine des Noirs, Filamarchois, Poumyroffe, l'Ocre Noir, du

Buddy van Lana's Hof: The striking Groenendael is the third most popular variety in Belgium. Photo: Jans-Jurgen fischer.

Loriers, and Terres Bergeres. Van de Hoge Laer, primarily a Tervueren kennel, also began Groenendael production in the mid 1980s. In the 1990s, vant Sparrebos, Of the Two, Sincfal, and Pré du Vieux Pont joined the ranks of Groenendael kennels. Today, the Groenendael is the third most popular variety in Belgium, having been overtaken by the Tervueren.

TERVUEREN
After the end of World War II, few Tervueren remained in Belgium. The Ferme Termunt kennel of M. Desees produced Tervueren that could be traced back to the original foundation Tervueren couple. However, most Tervueren after the war were from Malinois or Groenendael parents, and no particular kennel in Belgium, other than Ferme Termunt, seriously focused on Tervueren until the beginning of the 1960s, when the Bonmoss, de Landas, and du Talion kennels began breeding.

By the mid to late 1960s, several more kennels had become interested in Tervueren. In 1966, Mr. Viaene began his van't Hof Melyn kennel. Val des Aubepines also began breeding Tervueren. The following year, the d'Helizanne kennel started. In 1968, Erik Desschans began breeding under the kennel name van't Hof Baheino, and, in 1973, under the name Of the Two.

In 1969, kennel Pouroffe was established. In 1972, Anne-Marie Franck's Domaine Ponti kennel began, followed in 1973 by M. Gesquiere's van het Davidshof kennel. M. Kuijlaars's van't Herent kennel began in 1978, followed by Jean-Louis Vandenbemden's van de Hoge Laer kennel in 1979. Mme De Smet's du Pomereuil kennel, and Mme Monique Gieres's van het Wouwenhof kennel, began in 1984. In the 1990s, Mas des Beautuyas, l'Ocre Noir, van't Sparrebos, Clan des Fauves, and Grimmendans kennels began breeding. Tervueren are well established in Belgium today.

MALINOIS
The de l'Assa Malinois kennel of M. Hantson rose swiftly to a prominence that lasted throughout the middle of the 1970s. M. Van Hoolandt's Bonmoss kennel, M. Van Hover's van de Molenbeek kennel, and M. Roels's van't Hofstedeken kennel can be traced to the mid-1950s. Georges van Ceulebroeck's Clos Saint-Antoine kennel, and M. Vanderlinden's van de Oewa's working kennel, began in 1958. In 1961, the du Talion kennel was established, followed in 1964 by the Belle Edita and Belle Hacienda kennels.

Jade de Mas des Lavandes: Many kennels now specialise in producing top-quality Malinois. Photo: Ritta Tjorneryd.

In 1965, Albert Vloemans's van Bouwelhei kennel began, although M. Vloemans had bred Malinois sporadically before the war. In that same year, the Mouscronnais kennel of M. Destailleur began production, with M. Hellin's Champs du Bois kennel following in 1968. In 1969, Pouroffe kennel briefly began breeding Malinois, and Yves Dambrain launched his du Maugre kennel. In 1971, Regis Lebon established his Boscaille kennel, while in 1977, the Casa du Barry kennel began, currently breeding under the Hameau Saint-Blaise kennel name.

A year later, in 1978, the Deux Pottois kennel was established. It became a strong working kennel, from which Malinois were exported to a great number of countries. In 1979, Paul Vloemans, whose father had the van Bouwelhei kennel, began breeding under the van Balderlo kennel name.

In the 1990s, the Romanin, Ardents Fauves, van de Duvetorre, and Kukay kennels also began production. Today, the Malinois remains the most popular of the varieties in Belgium, and there is an ever-growing number of kennels devoted to this variety.

LAEKENOIS
Laekenois production in Belgium continued to be sparse and sporadic until

Swedish Ch. Lacken-Vacken D'Artagnan: The Laekenois has a dedicated following.

M. Wagemans's de l'Apache kennel began, in 1966, with two Dutch imports as its foundation stock. Litters were produced annually until 1983. In 1977, Canadabos kennel began breeding, also with imports from the Netherlands, although production was brief; it was in 1982 that Evelyn Comeine started her van Kriekebos kennel, which had a great impact on the Laekenois variety. In 1985, the Filamarchois kennel also began breeding Laekenois.

The 1990s saw more kennels producing Laekenois – de Lancaument, van Balderlo, van't Hoogkwartier, van du Duvetorre, Fauves de Saline, and Nature's Best. Historically slow to develop in its country of origin, the Laekenois now has a dedicated following, and, while numbers remain few in comparison to the other varieties, the Laekenois variety is becoming steadily more popular.

BELGIAN SHEPHERDS IN BRITAIN
The Belgian Shepherd Dog came into being as a distinct breed around 1890, but it did not appear in the UK until the 1920s. The only plausible reasoning behind this is that the UK already had high-quality working and herding dogs – the Border Collie and the Bobtail. These breeds were greatly admired in Europe and were, in fact, a spur to the Continental fanciers to produce some working dogs of note.

The first signs of any Belgian Shepherd Dog variety in the UK came in the 1920s, when some Malinois were imported by their owners. However, these dogs were not bred from and no progress was made in the breed at that time. Similarly, a Malinois bitch appeared in the UK in 1945, but there were no males of that variety in the UK, and, once again, a chance to establish the breed foundered.

In between the appearances of the Malinois, the Groenendael made a brief visit to the UK, when Mrs Grant-Forbes returned to the UK in 1931, bringing two Groenendaels with her. These, however, were purely pets, and no advancement of the variety was made.

The UK then had to wait nearly 30 years until any serious attempts were made to establish the breed. In the late 1950s, a consortium consisting of eight enthusiasts, all of whom were keen Obedience competitors, tried to establish Groenendaels in the UK. The main driving force was Eric Irvine, a Chief Instructor at an Obedience club and formerly an ex-Army dog trainer. It was while on European duties that he had become so impressed with the capabilities of the Belgian Shepherd Dog.

Late in 1958, the group made plans to import unrelated Groenendael pupppies, dog and bitch, from the then-famous Des Forges Monceux kennel. In May 1959, a dog puppy, Indo des Forges Monceux, arrived at Heathrow airport, late in the evening. He was followed, several weeks later, by the bitch Inkasa des Forges Monceux. These two names were to feature prominently in many of the UK's early pedigrees, and proved in every way to be one of the finest foundations possible on which to build the future of the breed. Indo and Inkasa had two litters, one in 1960 and the other in 1962.

Of the original eight people involved in the importation of these two puppies, only one is still active in the breed today – Ann O'Shea of the well-known Zellik kennel.

GROENENDAEL
The basis of the Groenendael in Britain had now been laid, and, in 1963, a Groenendael bitch, Kaline des Chimeres,

UK, Ir Ch. Woodlyn Black Jack: Groenendaels achieved CC status in the UK in 1971. Photo: David Dalton.

was imported. Sadly, she died in 1965, but not before producing a litter the year before. Kaline was followed by a Groenendael male, Nowgly de la Baraque de Planches. He was bred by Ms Bottemanne, who, at that time, owned one of the leading kennels on the Continent.

While Nowgly was in quarantine, it was discovered that another Groenendael had passed through the same quarantine kennels earlier that year. This animal was eventually identified as Hadinga Katangais, originating from the Belgian Congo, where many dogs were taken by the occupying Belgian population. Although he was not the finest breed specimen, it was felt that he would be of great use because the gene pool was still severely restricted. After due examination by some KC-approved judges, he was given a registration status that allowed him to be used at stud. He was renamed

Noir de Rhodesia and he sired two litters. He greatly improved the temperament of the breed.

With the breed now firmly established, in 1964 a club was formed, and, with a great deal of forethought, it was called The Belgian Shepherd Dog Association. This enabled it to encompass any other varieties that might enter the United Kingdom.

In 1971, the English Kennel Club awarded Challenge Certificates to the Groenendael for the first time, allowing the breed to have Champions after winning three such awards. This saw the Groenendael removed from a rare-breed status to that of an acknowledged breed in the UK.

TERVUEREN
The next of the four varieties of the Belgian Shepherd Dog to arrive in the UK was the Tervueren. Being the most glamorous of the four varieties, with startling colour combinations and the ever-lively look that all Belgians have, the Tervueren's success was assured. The variety attracted the interest of many dog fanciers, some of whom moved over from other breeds.

The first two Tervueren puppies were imported by Eric Irvine and Ann O'Shea, who imported the puppies from Mme Muller in France. They were called Ungo de Clos St Jacques and Ula de Clos St Jacques. Ula, the bitch, was very friendly, but Ungo was more 'standoffish', and, by the time the quarantine period finished, Eric Irvine decided to sell Ungo to Eric and Yvonne Westley. Eventually, Ungo settled, achieving reasonable success in the show ring.

In May 1972, Ungo and Ula were mated, resulting in the famous Zellik 'A' litter. It included Zellik Alexis, the first

The glamorous Tervueren was quick to gain popularity among British breeders.
Photo: Russell Fine Art.

MALINOIS

The next variety to cross the Channel was the Malinois. In 1972, a bitch named Venus de la Grange Aux Cerfs entered the UK, quickly followed by a male in the following year, Vidoc de Clos des Ondes. He was followed by another male and female, in 1975, and the variety was then firmly established.

The working dog of the four varieties, the Malinois has a history of being alert, easy to train, and fearless when working with the services or police force. He has an activity level almost unsurpassed by any other dog, and it is this feature that has firmly established him as one of the premier working dogs of the world. The breed has been utilised, along with Groenendaels and Tervueren, by the police forces of the Low Countries, and, more recently, has been adopted as the major breed of the German Police Force.

grey Tervueren the UK had seen, Zellik Alexandra, winner of a CACIB (Certificat d'Aptitude au Championnat International de Beauté) on the Continent, and Zellik Artemis. Artemis was mated to a Groenendael born in quarantine, Quentin de la Baraque de Planches, and this was the first intervariety mating of a Groenendael to a Tervueren carried out in the UK – a direct result of an application made to the Kennel Club by the Belgian Shepherd Dog Association of Great Britain for interbreeding between the two long-coated varieties. It was felt that the gene pool was too small, and intervariety mating was a way to increase it for both varieties.

Five years on, the club applied for a continuation of matings between Tervueren and Malinois, and also between Malinois and Laekenois, for the same reasons as the first application. This was continued for a number of years.

Lanaeken Standout At Sabrefield: The Malinois has been adopted as the major breed of the German Police Force.

14

LAEKENOIS

The last to arrive was the Laekenois, five of which were imported between 1979 and 1983. Sadly, this breeding base never became fully established. The Laekenois, both in the UK and on the Continent, has struggled to keep up a breeding programme and to sustain sufficient interest to make any real progress.

By a short time after the end of World War II, numbers of the Laekenois variety were reduced to almost zero. The limited gene pool resulted in the Laekenois developing a 'heavier' look than the other three varieties. This was a problem for a considerable period of time, despite evidence to suggest that efforts were made to increase the Laekenois gene pool by introducing a similar breed with which to cross-mate the variety. It was only when an outstanding male, Champion Opium van Kriekebos, sired puppies to various bitches of outstanding quality and type, that the Laekenois variety began to improve. Today, it is making real progress.

THE 'ONE BREED' RULE

The popularity of all four varieties of Belgian Shepherd Dog grew steadily in the UK. By the middle of the 1980s, even the Laekenois had established its presence firmly. However, the English Kennel Club was always unhappy with matings between varieties, and, in 1994, it decided that all Belgian Shepherd Dogs

would be shown in the ring as one breed, not one breed with four distinct varieties. This proved to be a massive mistake, with breeders of each variety losing heart; breeding reached a virtual standstill. The only variety not to sustain serious damage was the Tervueren.

By 1999, the Kennel Club realised what was happening, and approached the Northern Belgian Shepherd Dog Club and the Belgian Shepherd Dog Association, asking them to ballot their members. The result was to revert to the old status of four varieties, shown separately, with no intervariety matings. The Kennel Club accepted the result, and the first show of this kind was Crufts 2000.

The future of the Belgian Shepherd Dog looks very rosy, particularly as the UK's quarantine laws have now been relaxed. This, of course, allows British breeders of Continental breeds to import new bloodlines with far greater ease.

THE FRENCH INFLUENCE

As France shares its northern border with Belgium, it is not surprising that French breeders have participated in the development of the Belgian Shepherd. The earliest French kennel to play an important role was the Bois de la Deule Malinois kennel, established by M. Georges Danna of Lille. This was founded in 1903, with the male Bergeot, and the female Mirza, both from M.

Cloetens's kennel in Belgium. In 1907, Danna added Fleche II, from Mme Bertrand's Belgian kennel, and began serious breeding of the variety. In 1917, Louis Fernier's Chrysanthemes kennel began production with the Belgian imports Valda, Fricki, and Kita des Postes, the last two being offspring of Ch. Fram du Bois de la Deule. In 1922, Mlle Parseval began her Sommervieu kennel, based on the Belgian imports Flup, Fina, and Colette. In 1925, the Belgian imports Nichotte du M'nu Bos and Miarka de la Croix-Bleue were added to the kennel.

KENNELS

While some Groenendaels were imported into France in the first decade of the 20th century, and some were used by police forces in the early 1900s, it was not until after World War I that several major kennels were established. Mme Charlot's de la Louvre kennel began in 1917, with the male Athos III, and the female Theba de la Tour. In 1920, Mme Charlot imported Toby d'Hoyaux from Belgium and he became the major stud dog. Her 1923 litter produced Eric de la Louvre, from Toby d'Hoyaux and Souck du Progres. Toby was exported to the United States, where he earned his Championship. In 1925, the kennel's last litter was an intervariety litter by the Belgian import Tervueren Minox, and the Groenendael Erka de la Louve, a littermate to Eric.

In 1921, Ladiane, from Piratin de l'Enfer and Feda, was imported by Marcel Lachevre, who began producing Groenendaels under the des Barricades kennel name in 1923. The first litter, from Brigo Brigand du M'nu Bos and Ladiane, produced French Champion Belle des Barricades. A repeat breeding, the following year, produced Fr. Ch. Pitou des Barricades, the foundation stud for the Chemin des Dames kennel of M. Dusoulier, and his daughter, Jacqueline. This kennel was to dominate French breeding of Groenendaels for 60 years, with many of its dogs becoming the foundation stock for kennels in France, Belgium, Italy, the Netherlands, and Switzerland. Mme Jacqueline Aubry-Dusoulier eventually retired in 1988.

In 1922, M. Baudouin began his de la Sente kennel, using Fr. Ch. Digo, and Rapine de la Selection, an import from Robert Henry's kennel in Belgium.

The Étoile Blanche kennel of Mme Battut began breeding in 1930. The foundation bitch was Champion Manon de la Sente. In 1932, Banjo des Diables Noirs was imported from Belgium to add to the stock. This kennel produced a number of outstanding Groenendaels, which are still found in extended pedigrees today. The last Étoile Blanche litter was whelped in 1950.

In 1931, the Abbé Livergnage began his Planche Neuve kennel, having acquired Missya du Saphora from the Maison-Blanche kennel. Planche Neuve produced litters throughout the 1950s, although it is Jaste de Planche Neuve, a granddaughter of Anick and Ch. Manon de la Sente, born in 1935, that is most remembered as an ancestor of the Tervueren Willy de la Garde Noire.

In 1934, the Comtesse de Lambilly began her Beaux Sillons kennel, with Helsa de l'Étoile Blanche as the foundation bitch. A few Tervueren litters had been bred in France before 1939, but there were no fawn descendants in existence after the war, nor were any Laekenois registered in France. Malinois had been in France since the beginning of the 20th century, but the major interest was in Groenendaels.

16

S.R. Happy Dream de la Clairiere Aux Louves.

Since World War II, the most dramatic changes have occurred with the Malinois and Tervueren varieties. Starting with only a handful of Malinois and a few Tervueren from Groenendael parents born after World War II, the Malinois is today the most popular variety in France, with the Tervueren the second most popular. The Groenendael, most popular before the war, is now third. Laekenois arrived in France in the late 1960s, and, after a tentative beginning, now have several kennels devoted to their production.

TERVUEREN
In 1945, at a meeting of the Club des Amateurs Français du Chien de Berger Belge, Gilbert Fontaine addressed the club on the possibilities of breeding the Tervueren variety. The following year, Fontaine imported two Tervueren littermates from Belgium, Unique and Unica, but he was unable to find a suitable male until the club was notified of two male Tervueren born in a litter of

Groenendaels at the Garde Noire kennel. The fawn, Willy de la Garde Noire, from Samy du Mordant and Ura du Chemin des Dames, was chosen to enter Fontaine's Clos Saint-Clair kennel. This male became the most popular Tervueren stud dog of his day, and he was the major contributor to the re-emergence of the Tervueren variety. Clos Saint-Clair produced litters until 1961, and it is noted for such dogs as Ami, Djinn, Fiam, and Kactus du Clos Saint-Clair.

GROENENDAEL
Mme Charlotte Muller's Clos Saint-Jacques kennel, begun in 1947 as a Groenendael producer, acquired two Tervueren in 1978. These were Witan de la Garde Noire, younger brother of Willy, and Walhalla de Sang Bleu. In 1949, Xilene du Clos Saint-Clair entered the kennel. The Clos Saint-Jacques kennel produced both Groenendaels and Tervueren throughout the 1970s, among them the outstanding Braise, Faune, Gin, Kama, Matelot, and Phidias du Clos Saint-Jacques.

The Clos Saint-Clair and Clos Saint-Jacques kennels were the major stimulus for the establishment of other kennels devoted to the Tervueren, including Mme Le Moro's Cledeville kennel, Mme Lacarriere's Clos du Cher, Mme Renée Demillier's Hauts de Bievre, and Dr Yves Surget's Bois du Tot kennel. In the 1970s, the Parc de Pathyvel and the Sart des Bois kennels were established, followed in the 1980s by Condivicnum, Clairiere aux Louves, and Grande Lande. In the 1990s, a number of newer kennels were established, assuring that the Tervueren variety will not fade.

No history of the Groenendael would be complete without mentioning the Chemin des Dames kennel and its great

Nelson de Kenatier.

contributions to the breed both before and after World War II. Mme Aubry not only produced some outstanding subjects, but she also carefully guided the development of the Tervueren in France until her retirement in 1988. Willy du Chemin des Dames, born in 1948, and Yale, born in 1950, were outstanding stud dogs used by a variety of kennels. Fiesta du Chemin des Dames became the foundation bitch for the Parc de l'Hay kennel of Emile Charneau. Demon du Chemin des Dames, born in 1954, and Joujou in 1960, were also outstanding stud dogs. Joujou was exported to Switzerland, where he played a major role. He was also the sire of Mick de Iamara, a bitch that entered the Chemin des Dames kennel, where she produced RE Onix du Chemin des Dames in 1965. Onix became the major sire of his era. Bred to Vega du Chemin des Dames, born in 1972, he produced, among others, Lann-Morian, the grey Leslie, who entered the Sart du Bois kennel of Dr Denis Descamps, and Lynda du Chemin des Dames, foundation

for Mme Heraly's Maison du Bois kennel in Belgium. The last litter, in 1988, produced Dandy du Chemin des Dames, another popular sire. This kennel, dedicated to the Groenendael for more than half a century, has had a tremendous influence on the breed, not only through the dogs produced, but also in the guidance and direction given.

MALINOIS
Malinois production in France was slow to start after World War II. Alexandre Charbonnel's Ventadour kennel was established in 1948, founded with Nello de la Sommervieu, and, later, Cora des Fontainis and Lady de Chennevelles. The kennel produced a number of Champions of beauty; it was noted for quality, and it was the foundation for many other kennels.

Ranie de Ventadour, producer of many excellent working dogs, entered the Mas des Lavandes kennel of Mme Auriant, whose breeding programmes dominated the shows through the 1980s. The Mas des Lavandes kennel provided the basis for the Loups Mutins kennel, the Mas de la Galandie kennel of Mme Berton-Sarlat, and the Val de Scarpe kennel, which, in turn, influenced the Douce Plaine kennel through Palma du Val de Scarpe, the dam of RE Vagner de la Douce Plaine. There are numerous working Malinois kennels now in existence in France, many devoted to the French ring sport.

LAEKENOIS
French interest in the Laekenois variety was limited, until, in 1967, Dutch import Charles Winston van Elina's Home was mated with the Groenendael Ines du Parc de l'Hay. The subsequent litter produced SR Quina-Quarteronne. Bred to her sire, Quina-Quarteronne produced Rejane du

Valkohoampan Athene.

Parc de l'Hay, and he, in turn, produced Toscane du Parc de l'Hay. Toscane was the dam of Iambo du Parc de l'Hay.

Parc de l'Hay then returned to breeding long-haired Belgians, while the l'Orchidee Noir kennel continued, albeit briefly, to breed Laekenois. The Malinois, Undine de la Blaise, entered the kennel, mating the Dutch Laekenois, Gaston van de Middachten. This mating produced two litters in 1976. Currently, the Tangi Morgane kennel is also breeding Laekenois, with two imports from the Bois Chablis kennel in Belgium.

INTERVARIETY BREEDING
France is a far larger country than Belgium, and has many more kennels devoted to Belgian Shepherds. The Club Français du Chien de Berger Belge is a large, powerful organisation. Intervariety breeding, with the breeding commission's permission, has always been permitted. The ruling that grey Tervueren cannot obtain a CAC/CACIB is ignored, simply because it is considered illogical

genetically. The ruling was never approved by the French commission to the FCI.

BELGIANS IN THE US
A small notice in the January 1908 edition of the American Kennel Club's Gazette mentioned that five additional Belgian Sheepdogs had been added to the NYC police force, to work with an American-bred one. This is the first information about the beginnings of Belgians in US. The American Kennel Club studbooks supply additional clues for many of the following years. Finally, a breed club was formed, and articles about Belgian Shepherd Dogs began to appear in the AKC's Gazette in the middle of the 1920s.

Two Malinois and two Groenendaels were imported from Belgium and registered in the AKC's 1911 studbooks as German Sheepdogs, with the affix Belgian given to their names. By 1912, the AKC assigned the name Belgian Sheepdogs to the breed, although no details were given about variety, only of colour. One, named Belgian Blackie, a Malinois registered with Saint-Hubert as Blackor, became an early AKC Champion of the breed.

Prior to the World War I, only a few Malinois and Groenendaels arrived, and a few offspring from two litters (one Malinois, one Groenendael) were also registered. The AKC studbooks included a three-generation pedigree for the imports, which were descendants of the finest dogs in Belgium at that time.

EARLY IMMIGRANTS
Initially, Belgian Shepherds had been imported by individuals who had emigrated from Belgium. This trend continued throughout the 1930s and the early 1940s, but, over time, other people became interested in the breed. After World War I, a Canadian kennel also

BIS Am. Ch. Rolin Ridge's Fourteen Karat: The Groenendael was the first variety to make an impact in the USA.

influenced the breed's development in the US. Georges Domus, living in Montreal, but originally from Belgium, bred under the name Belgium Kennel, with a number of his Groenendael stock being bought by Americans. The Groenendael littermates, Jet and Marco, and their younger sister, Pearl of Belgium, were from Domus' kennel. These dogs earned their Championships in the US in the mid-1920s. The progeny of another import, Fracasse de l'Enfer, also left their mark on American history.

Oliver Page of Pittsburgh imported Cesar from the Select kennels of Robert Henry in Belgium. Cesar was listed in the 1923 AKC studbook as a German Shepherd, wolf-grey with a black saddle. He was later re-registered as a sable-and-fawn Belgian Sheepdog. His pedigree was Malinois, and there has been ongoing debate as to whether he was a Malinois or a Tervueren.

Cesar was one of the foundation dogs for Oliver Page's kennel. He also used the black La Terrible Lionne, a daughter of the Groenendael imports Dick des Batards and Marca de Ranst. Many of today's American-bred Groenendaels trace their ancestry back to Cesar and La Terrible Lionne. However, Oliver Page's kennel was short-lived, most of his dogs played no role in the continuing history of the breed.

In the decade following World War I, imports from Belgium were not registered with the Société Royale Saint-Hubert, instead being registered with the Kennel Club Belge or the Berger Belge Club. Some dogs were not registered with any organisation.

In Belgium, a number of returning soldiers became trainers of Belgian ring dogs and police dogs. Others became breeders, selling dogs to the US and Canada, where little was known about the ancestry of individual dogs. This was the case with the dogs from Domus, as well as the sire and dam of La Terrible Lionne. Early photos show larger and coarser Groenendaels than was the norm in Europe at that time.

THE FIRST AMERICAN STANDARD
The 1920s were a prosperous time for Belgian Shepherds in America. Interest was high, and imports were brought in and bred. In that decade, a Belgian Sheepdog Club of America was established, and a Standard was drawn up and accepted by the AKC. This Standard recognised three varieties of Belgian Sheepdogs: the Groenendael (with acceptable colours listed as black, fawn, or any other colour), the Malinois (brindled fawn or fawn were acceptable), and the Gris Cendre (a rough-coat with acceptable colours of grey or fawn).

A 1925 AKC Gazette article, written by Florida-based Malinois breeder Walter Mucklow, mentions that there was at least one Laekenois in the country at that time. However, the article supplies no additional information. A similar state of affairs existed with the Tervueren. It is known that several Tervueren were imported, and that Tervueren were born in Groenendael litters, but the word Tervueren was never mentioned in any records. It is also interesting to read the breed columns of the Gazette of the 1920s, where authors mention that they have heard of the Malinois, but have never seen one. The Groenendaels were the most well known, and, by 1926, the breed was ranked 42nd in popularity out of 100 breeds recognised by the AKC.

THE BREED'S DECLINE
The 1929 stock market crash, and the Great Depression that followed, had a marked effect on everyone and everything, including Belgian Shepherd Dogs. During the 1930s, they dropped to 97th in AKC registrations and the BSCA was dissolved. A handful of Malinois and Groenendaels were imported in those years, and we can trace some current Groenendael pedigrees back to these dogs, but the imported Malinois left no trace.

The Groenendael Erex, produced by an early breeding of Emile Boudart (Mont-Sara kennel in Belgium), was imported to the US and used at stud. Faquin of Scheld, Djil des Lilas Mauves, Moto du Mont-Sara and Minora, all from Belgium, and Hadji du Chemin des Dames from France, continued to contribute to the development of the Groenendael in the US during this time. Generally, however, very few Belgian Shepherd breeders and oweners were left.

By the early 1940s, August Goris, originally from Belgium, had established the Beldome Groenendael kennel on Long Island, with Moto du Mont-Sara and Minora as his foundation stock. Cecile Lutz was breeding Groenendaels in Pennsylvania, crossing older lines (produced by Fracasse de l'Enfer and Oliver Page) with newer imports and their offspring. Wilmont O'Keefe, in Wisconsin, was breeding from stock provided by Goris and Lutz. Eva Lewis, in Massachusetts, used Djil des Lilas Mauves, and Lisette III (the daughter and granddaughter of Erex), with the remaining quarter of the pedigree tracing back to Oliver Page's breeding.

The Malinois Sudo des Arbousiers was imported and registered in the 1942 AKC stud book, but it seems that no progeny were produced. No Tervueren were registered in the 1940s. During World War II, a few American-bred Groenendaels were registered.

REGENERATION
In 1949, a group new to the breed obtained AKC permission for the second and current BSCA. These people, centered primarily in Indiana, owned Groenendaels descended from the early 1920s lines and 1930s imports. The AKC Standard of the time still recognised the Groenendael (of the many colours), and the Malinois, but the Gris Cendre had been dropped by 1948 (without one rough-hair ever being registered by the AKC).

By 1953, the BSCA was publishing a monthly newsletter and gaining new members. One individual, who changed his future by joining the newly-energised club, was Rudy Robinson, from Wheaton, Illinois. After establishing his Candide kennel in 1949, Rudy began importing a number of Groenendaels from Belgium, France, and Italy. He bred Belgians and helped to ensure their growing popularity by writing about them in his columns and advertisements in all-breed magazines. The owners of older lines were unhappy with this, viewing the imports as inferior, but the new lines did very well at the National Specialties.

In 1950, the Malinois Xlyoidine du Chaos was imported in whelp. Malinois had returned to the US, but only just. In 1953, Rudy Robinson, Bob and Barbara Krohn, and Marge Coyle imported three Tervueren from the Clos Saint-Jacques kennel in France, with more following in the next few years from the Clos Saint-Clair kennel. In 1956, two Laekenois were imported from Holland, and AKC registration was requested.

AKC/UKC Ch. Avonlea Forget Me Not: The Malinois has emerged as the most popular variety in the US.

SEPARATE BREEDS

By 1958, several intervariety breedings had occurred between Tervueren and Groenendaels, with one intervariety breeding between Laekenois and Malinois. BSCA membership had grown to 95 by this time, but only a few Tervueren owners and breeders belonged; there were still few Tervueren in the US. Two members of the club were noted as owning Malinois.

By 1958, the AKC had rejected applications to register the Laekenois variety. Consequently, no Laekenois owners were BSCA members. The 'old guard' (1949 BSCA founders and followers) wanted only Groenendaels to be accepted as Belgian Sheepdogs. They were horrified by intervariety breedings, and wanted the other varieties to be excluded. The AKC received a great number of complaints, and, in April 1958, they sent out an opinion survey to the membership, asking for opinions on intervariety breedings and show procedures (all varieties were shown

together at that time). Although less than half the membership responded, in July of that year the AKC board ruled that, based upon the opinion poll, the varieties would be separated into breeds, effective from June 1959. Malinois and Groenendaels were required to have a three-generation, same-variety pedigree for importation, while the Malinois, being few in numbers, were put in the Miscellaneous Group. The Laekenois were not recognised, and the registrations of the Groenendaels from the intervariety breedings were pulled.

After the 1959 split into separate breeds, the BSCA became the Groenendael-only club. The American Belgian Tervuren club was founded in 1960 (Tervueren is spelled Tervuren in the US). A Malinois club was formed, which, today, is known as the American Belgian Malinois Club. Between 1959 and 1979, the Tervueren grew in numbers. This was largely due to the dedication of owners and breeders, who were enjoying the new-found luxury of being able to import any Tervueren, regardless of ancestry. In 1980, however, the AKC imposed the three-generation rule on the Tervueren.

Malinois registrations picked up, and, in 1973, the Malinois were moved from the Miscellaneous Group to the Working (today the Herding) Group. The Laekenois have re-arrived in the US, and, although they number less than 100, two breed clubs have been formed to promote this variety. Currently, the Laekenois breed clubs are seeking AKC recognition as a separate breed.

In 1991, the United Belgian Shepherd Association was formed and affiliated with the United Kennel Club. This association views the Belgian Shepherds as one breed with four varieties. It has a Standard similar to the FCI, and it uses critiques at all shows. Continental breed specialists have judged the National shows since 1993, giving seminars on type, and recommendations about where improvements are needed. It is a growing organisation and an interesting alternative to the American Kennel Club and its shows.

On June 12th 1995, the AKC lifted the three-generation ruling on imports for all breeds. This has spurred importations, and it has also complicated the Belgian 'separate breeds' dilemma, with import littermates registered as two different breeds, along with half-siblings and cousins, etc.

THE CURRENT SCENE
Currently, the Malinois is the most popular variety in terms of yearly AKC registrations, followed by the Groenendael (called the Belgian Sheepdog) and the Tervueren. Herding, Flyball, and Agility are now popular activities for many Belgians and their owners, with the Malinois still excelling at Schutzhund and the various ring sport groups that are now active.

Belgian Shepherds working in the fields of search and rescue, service, and assistance, are becoming more common. It is not unusual for a local police force to have one or more Malinois, and a number of Malinois are used in the US armed forces.

Since the 1959 split into separate breeds, there have been several attempts at reunification. To date, these have not been passed in the AKC breed clubs with enough percentage of support. More individuals seem to favour one breed, but the opposition to intervariety breeding is still strong.

Through the Internet, e-mail, and breed-specific books, there is more knowledge in the US about Belgian Shepherds today than at any time in the past. More people are travelling to Europe to see National Specialties, to meet other breeders and enthusiasts, and to breed to the Continental dogs. More people are importing than at any time in the past. More are also willing to tackle breed-specific health problems. Breeders are no longer as isolated and quite as 'in the dark' as some of them felt they were in the past, but they say they still have much to learn.

Ula Van de Duvetorre: Flyball is one of the many canine disciplines enjoyed by Belgian Shepherds.

2 CHOOSING A BELGIAN SHEPHERD

For the majority of people, their first contact with a Belgian Shepherd is through a picture in a book, although Belgians are increasingly being used in television work. However, whether the dogs have been cast as wolves or as mongrels, it is unlikely that the viewer is aware that what they have seen is an example of this magnificent breed.

To see a Belgian in the flesh for the first time is a different story. Almost without exception, the initial meeting will turn your head and leave a lasting impression, even if it is no more than to comment on the graceful balance of elegance and power, the intelligent persona, or simply the general presence that the dog commands. That first meeting may be further enhanced by close physical contact, especially if the dog has a friendly, outgoing nature and is well behaved. On these occasions, the onlooker's interest is often matched by the Belgian's naturally assured inquisitiveness, giving rise to an initial instinct that says – 'I want one of those dogs!'.

What the new person does not see is the hours of socialising, training, and general management that have gone into refining and encouraging the natural breed characteristics to produce this perfect pet. However, the majority of people who

Jairouck de la Fureur du Crepuscule: The eye-catching Belgian Shepherd has instant appeal, but think carefully before you take on a puppy. Photo: Amanda McLaren.

enthuse following their initial encounters with the breed, subsequently choose not to own a Belgian Shepherd of their own. This generally stems from a realisation of the degree of responsibility that accompanies ownership, and usually follows contact with a recognised breeder or experienced owner, either of whom will honestly apprise the prospective new owner of all the aspects, good and bad, which are associated with this breed of dog.

OWNERSHIP RESPONSIBILITIES
Belgian Shepherds have an average life span of 12 to 15 years. During this time, the owner will invest a considerable amount of time, energy, and money in their dog. For this reason, you should think long and hard, even if you have previously owned other breeds of dog, before letting your heart rule your head and rushing out to buy a Belgian puppy.

For households that have neither children nor pets, the thought of a puppy may fill them with joy, but there are many practical considerations that have to be given great thought. For the houseproud, the initial enthusiasm and excitement over the arrival of a new puppy can quickly turn to horror as the cuddly bundle grows up, and both its required input and output increases accordingly.

The gregarious party person should consider potential ownership carefully, because lack of freedom is part of owning any dog. On finishing work at night, having to go home to feed and exercise your dog as the priority, when you would rather be going out with colleagues to the pub, can severely dampen your social life. Impulse weekends away from home can become a hazy memory – who will look after the dog in the absence of his trusted owner? Kennelling is expensive, and few hotels welcome pets.

Do you or other members of your household work full-time? Will the dog be left for more than four hours on his own? Does the addition of a dog fit the social and domestic pattern of the household, and, if so, will all members (particularly children) willingly accept the additional share of responsibility?

Does anyone in the household suffer from asthma, or other allergies? The fine, downy undercoat of a Belgian can exacerbate these problems, although it is likely that such symptoms will also preclude ownership of many other breeds. A Belgian will have a major moult twice a year, when they lose what appears to be every hair on their body. In addition, they also shed some hair on a daily basis, and their coat can trap a considerable amount of dust.

Finally, a word to those who have previously owned, or recently lost, a Belgian Shepherd, especially if he had been with you for many years. Think long and hard before jumping in and getting another puppy. Your old dog will have been well behaved, used to a routine, and he probably required less exercise in his latter years. Equally, you would have known all the likes, dislikes, and foibles of your friend. Ask yourself, are you ready to cope with a young, boisterous puppy and all that a puppy entails? Perhaps, instead, you should consider a rescue dog or an older dog.

Most breeders will hesitate about letting a new or inexperienced dog owner have a Belgian puppy. Experience shows that, when it comes to juggling a job, a family, and running a household, the dog ends up well down the list of priorities.

PUPPY DAMAGE
Pale, plain carpets show dog hair from any

An active puppy is bound to get up to mischief.

angle, as do fabric furnishings, and, until the puppy is completely house-trained, every urine stain will serve to provide an additional reminder of the latest member of the household. Even if the owner is in the fortunate position of being able to be with their dog all day, there will still be occasions, shopping for example, when the dog needs to be left alone – and the bored Belgian can be exceedingly destructive.

The smallest exposed thread on a carpet can be pulled apart. Exposed wood, be it a table leg, a kitchen kickboard, or the spars of a chair, tend to be at exactly the right height for puppies to chew on. Mail (but with some discernment – important mail is preferable to the junk variety), papers left lying around, or magazines that can be reached from available surfaces, all will be chewed up into a mash.

HOUSEHOLD APPLIANCES
It is at this stage that the owner should realise that the choice of household appliances is equally significant if a long and successful relationship is to be sustained. For example, the choice of vacuum cleaner becomes important. Can it cope with dog hair? Does it become blocked easily, and, if so, can it be easily cleaned? Are the motors sufficiently powerful to cope with greater use than recommended by the manufacturer? Think also of the washing machine. Is it capable of the more frequent use imposed on it by welcoming muddy pawprints? Can the filter discern between flick, fluff, or flying dog hair?

GARDENS AND CARS
Gardens need to be made secure so that the dog cannot escape, and unwanted dogs cannot enter. The Belgian shows a natural exuberance for gardening, assisting with the digging, and contributing to the design of the garden's architecture. He favours a cratered moonscape type of landscape, which may lead you to reject costlier purchases at garden centres.

Cars must also be considered, as a Belgian is a happy traveller, preferring to be with his master than to remain at home. However, while he will make himself comfortable in the back seat of any saloon, mud and hair will soon adhere to the upholstery. The majority of owners quickly convert to estate or hatchback types of vehicle.

THE ACTIVE OWNER
Belgian Shepherds do not suit an owner who enjoys a sedentary lifestyle. They require considerable exercise and need a minimum of one hour a day free-running. Is there open park or heath land nearby, where there is no danger of the dog being a nuisance to livestock or people? As an owner, are you prepared to be out in all weathers with your dog, even when it is pouring with rain and you do not feel like

Make sure your garden is secure and well fenced before your puppy arrives home.

it, or when you would rather be lying in the sun topping up a tan? You may be lucky, being the owner of a garden large enough to allow your dog to run freely. However, you should be prepared for your lawn taking on the appearance of a mud bath.

For owners with a large garden, it is still important to take the dog out to exercise elsewhere, providing him with mental stimulation and socialisation. The owner who regularly takes their dog away from the immediate environs of the home is frequently rewarded: your dog will appreciate the stimulating exercise, which will help to ensure his fitness and his health; you will be given many opportunities to make new acquaintances with admirers of the breed; and you will develop a relationship with your Belgian that is built on loyalty and harmony.

BUYING YOUR BELGIAN

So you still want a Belgian Shepherd? The committed owner should never be tempted into an impulse buy; after all, your dog should be sharing the next twelve years or so with you and he will be part of your family. As an indication, the owner should give the same degree of consideration to obtaining a dog that a young couple would give to planning a family.

PUPPY FARMS

Do not be tempted by the cute face in the pet shop window or by the nicest-looking of several litters that may be available at a puppy farm. Both forms of these commercial pet-procurement premises have received a very bad press during the last few years, and, in the UK, the government is currently taking an interest in looking for ways in which they can be regulated.

PET BREEDERS

The buyer should be wary of the pet owner whose bitch has had a litter because someone has advised that it is good for the bitch to do so. Although these litters are usually well reared, such owners do not necessarily have the specialist knowledge of the small show kennels. You will have no guarantee that the puppies are healthy, or that they are good examples of the breed.

Your national kennel club will provide a list of breeders, including those with puppies for sale, but beware – anyone who registers a litter of pedigree puppies and pays the appropriate fee is eligible to be included in this list, and it is no guarantee of quality.

SMALL SHOW KENNELS

Your national kennel club can provide a list of breed clubs and contact telephone numbers. These may be a preferred route, since most clubs will be able to recommend a breeder from a show kennel who has puppies available in your area.

27

Do your research thoroughly and make sure you find a breeder that has a reputation for producing good, sound stock.

If you want a particular bloodline, you may have to wait a considerable time to collect your puppy, and you may need to be prepared to travel some distance. The small show kennel does not seek to multiply the breed for profit, but to try to improve it by breeding out the weaknesses and enhancing the strengths. The breeder's aim is to achieve perfection, and it is their knowledge of many other members of the breed that makes them such an excellent source of advice, and probably the best provider of a puppy for a novice owner. Any small profits that are made from the sale of a litter, taking into account stud fees, veterinary fees, and the cost of food, are quickly ploughed back into the spiralling costs of campaigning a show dog around the country.

The breeder's true reward is not financial; instead, it lies in seeing the dog they have bred considered by other experts to be a superior specimen in health, temperament, construction, and looks, and to be the best among his peers. Usually, such breeders will have an in-depth knowledge of the breed and the line(s) that they own, having lived with several generations of that line. Furthermore, the breeder can often show you other dogs from the same family, which will give you an indication of the temperament your puppy will develop.

Be patient. Many people decide they want a puppy immediately, without thinking ahead to future commitments, such as holidays. Ideally, there should be a breeder due to have a litter with timing that suits your circumstances. Beware of newspaper adverts that offer puppies for sale, and, on phoning up, you discover they have a litter of eight, all of which are available immediately. The experienced breeder will have puppies booked before the bitch is mated, and they usually have a waiting list.

BREEDER'S QUESTIONS

Do not be surprised, when you contact a breeder, to be interrogated about why you want a puppy. Furthermore, if you live some distance from the breeder, do not take it as an insult if the breeder arranges a home check (when someone experienced in the breed calls at your house and assesses you and your home's suitability). Rather than taking offence, draw confidence from the fact that you are obviously dealing with a responsible person who is ensuring that you are the right person for their puppy.

The breeder will not only ask what sex and colour (if applicable) you are interested in purchasing, but will want to know if you want to show your dog, if you wish to compete in Obedience competitions, or if you simply want a companion. The breeder will have been closely watching the puppies since they were born, trying to determine their character, and, ultimately, their show potential, so it is unlikely that they would part with the best of the litter to a pet home. Given the breeder's motives for having a new litter, it is quite reasonable to assume that the breeder will keep the most promising of the litter. Only the rest will be available for sale.

Most breeders will sell each available puppy at the same price. However, if you require your dog as a companion only, some breeders may offer you a puppy at a reduced price. The reason for this is that the breeder may think the puppy is unsuitable for showing and breeding due to some minor imperfection, such as size, markings, or colour. In agreeing the reduced price, the breeder may elect to retain the kennel club registration certificate, so that the dog cannot be bred from, which will help to ensure the future quality of the breed. These dogs can make super pets, since the imperfections are in the eye of the breeder, are aesthetic only, and do not affect the health, character, or general wellbeing of the dog.

YOUR QUESTIONS
Before visiting the breeder for the first time, it is well worth making a list of questions you want to ask about rearing a young Belgian. Take the list with you, as it is almost guaranteed that, in the excitement of viewing the puppies, you will forget most of the questions until you are on the journey home. Ask about parental health checks, ask about any history of hereditary problems in the lines, and, if you are in any doubt, ask to see health certificates. Both parents should have been X-rayed for hip dysplasia (see Chapter Ten). Eye tests should have been carried out to ascertain if the bitch has suffered from juvenile cataract, or any

other eye problems, and the registration certificate should be endorsed accordingly. Do not listen to excuses about the line being healthy with no need for checks to be carried out. Tests are expensive, but necessary, and any breeder who is concerned for the wellbeing of the puppies, and the future of the breed in general, will not breed from untested animals.

Check the bitch's temperament, as this will give a good indication of what the puppy's will be. Some breeders and exhibitors have their dog's character assessed (see Chapter Seven), and, although it is not mandatory, it is a guide to the temperament of the progeny. Ask to see the breeder's other dogs; do they appear to be in good condition, is the environment in which the puppies are being reared clean? The breeder should be willing to offer help and advice should problems arise at a later date with your dog. He or she should also be prepared to take back a puppy, if, for any reason, he is later found to be unsuitable.

The breeder will want to know what plans you have for your Belgian Shepherd.
Photo: Amanda McLaren.

VIEWING THE LITTER

You have found a breeder who has puppies available. Ideally, you should have viewed the puppies on several previous occasions, from the ages of two weeks onwards. Puppies change daily, and, for this reason, most breeders like to make their own choice of puppy as late as possible, usually at seven weeks. Hopefully, by this age, the breeder will be able to give some guidance as to how the finished puppy may look, as well as giving an indication of his character.

However, even experts get it wrong, and choosing a show-quality puppy can be a complete lottery. Many an ugly duckling has been sold as a pet, only to have the breeders kick themselves when he turns into a stunning adult, never to grace the show ring.

VIEWING WITH CHILDREN

Wear old clothes when visiting the puppies; they do not respect designer clothes and tend to head for the nearest shoelaces or hemlines. If you have a family and you are visiting the puppies for the first time, or, if you are still undecided as to whether a Belgian is for you or not, leave the children at home. Once children get a hint of the idea, they tend to pressurise their parents. It can be difficult to concentrate on those important questions (for both the purchaser and the owner), and it also becomes very hard to make a rational choice when viewing an adorable puppy with young children pleading with you. Make up your own mind whether you want one of this litter, and then ask the breeder's permission to bring the children next time.

ASSESSING THE PUPPIES

Always telephone the breeder in advance to arrange a suitable time to view the puppies. At the age of six weeks, a puppy's day revolves around sleep. There is nothing so disappointing as viewing a heap of snoozing puppies that have fed, played, fallen into an exhausted sleep, and are not due to wake up for another hour.

The breeder will ask you what you are looking for in a puppy, and he is likely to ask questions about your lifestyle. While you assess the puppies, the breeder will assess whether you are an acceptable future owner for a puppy. He will try to match you with a suitable puppy. For example, a dominant puppy may try to take over from a submissive owner, and the submissive puppy may not be suitable for an active household full of children.

If you want a companion pet, and you are lucky enough to have a choice, study the puppies carefully. Go for the puppy that is confident, but not arrogant. If you have a choice, go for a personal touch, such as a white marking on the chest or a

Arrange a convenient time to go and view the litter.

Handle the puppies and watch them playing together so that you can assess temperament.

hand, palm-side up, between the puppy's front legs, so that your fingers are between his legs while your palm supports his rib cage. With your other hand supporting his bottom, hold the puppy snugly against your body. Hold him securely; puppies can wriggle at incredible speed and they are easily dropped. The breeder will no doubt be hovering nearby, protectively, making sure you are confident handling the puppy. The puppy should be relaxed, and not tense or worried at being handled. If he feels tense and uncomfortable, you are either holding him incorrectly, or he has not been socialised properly.

The puppy's skin should be loose over his body, and his ribs should have a good covering of fat. Dewclaws (the spare claw situated a short way up the leg) will have been removed on the back legs, and many breeders remove them from the front legs, also. The puppy's coat should feel clean and free from parasites.

prettier expression. Do not be tempted to go for the sad puppy sitting by himself in the corner. The Belgian puppy should be inquisitive and happy to come out to investigate strangers. He should be wary of unaccustomed noises, but not sufficiently to shy away from them. Try gently clapping your hands or slapping the floor, to see which puppies take notice. Should they hear a loud noise, like a metal feeding dish being accidentally dropped, it is normal for them to be startled, but they should immediately recover from the fright and go to investigate the source of the noise. If they cannot cope with a fright in their own nest, how will they cope with the outside world?

Ask the owner if you may handle the puppies. Pick up the puppy by placing a

SHOW QUALITY

If you want a puppy to work in Obedience competitions or working trials, ask the breed club if they can recommend someone who can advise on puppy aptitude testing. If you want a show dog, you should do some research into the breed and the breeder. Does the breeder show? Does he have a kennel name (known as an affix)? Do not be impressed if he does, as anyone can purchase a name from the kennel club and pay an annual sum to retain it. Has he been showing for many years, and is he well known and established? Have any puppies bred by him been successfully exhibited? Many people fail to realise that the number of Champions in a pedigree will not guarantee the quality of the puppy. Quality mated to quality should produce the same, but nature has a wry sense of humour.

If you are satisfied by the breeder's knowledge, and you have explained to him that you want to show the puppy, the breeder should help you to pick out what he believes to be a show-quality puppy. After all, it is doing the breeder no favours if you are showing a substandard dog he has bred. Remember, the dog will have the breeder's affix at the front of his pedigree name for all to see; if the dog is clearly not a show specimen, it could prove highly embarrassing.

Watch the puppies playing. A good show puppy not only needs an extrovert temperament, but he also needs to possess an attitude of 'look at me'. He will probably be dominant with his siblings. These puppies will be well known to the breeder as they are usually the ones who are constantly getting into mischief and have a look of 'so, what are you going to do about it?'

ASSESSING POTENTIAL
Pick up the puppy and stand him on a

table or solid surface. The body should be 'square' when viewed from the side: the length from the point of shoulder to the buttocks should equal the height at the withers. The puppy should have a good depth of chest, and his rib cage should feel well sprung and not flat-sided. The body should look balanced, without exaggeration.

Check the topline from the side view. It should be straight and firm and not like a sway-backed old horse. Run your fingers down the backbone and down the tail. The tail should be free from kinks and the tip of it should reach down to the puppy's hocks.

The male puppy should have two testicles, preferably descended into the scrotum. If, at six weeks of age, the puppy's testicles have not descended, do not be concerned. However, they should have done so by the time you collect the puppy (see Chapter Ten).

At this age, the head looks short, without the muzzle definition that comes with age. Ask the breeder to show you the puppy's 'bite' or teeth placement. The top jaw should snugly overlap the bottom jaw (scissor bite). Although a level (edge to edge) bite is permitted, a scissor bite in a puppy would be more desirable. Puppies lose their milk teeth at around four months of age. When the new teeth grow in, you will have some indication of how the mouth will develop. However, during the growth period, up to one year of age, the mouth can change drastically. An undershot (bottom teeth protrude in front of the upper jaw) or overshot (upper teeth protrude over the lower jaw) mouth are major faults, and a dog with these faults is not worth exhibiting.

Eye shape is important because it gives the dog his expression. Look for an almond-shaped eye, which is neither

The breeder will stand the puppy and will help you to evaluate conformation.

It takes many years of experience to spot a puppy with show potential.

sunken into the head nor protruding. Eye colour can change, so look for an eye colour that is very dark brown. At the six-week stage, ears are still soft and will not be erect. When playing with the puppy, roll him on his back so that he is looking up at you. In this position his ears will fall into place, giving you some idea of his adult ear placement. The ears should be triangular, not too large, and set high on the head.

Put the puppy back on the floor and watch him move around. He should move freely, with his feet pointing forward and not turned out. His elbows should fit snugly against his body when he moves around. Note how the puppy carries his

tail when he is playing with a toy. At this age the tail is still being used for balance, and it is acceptable for the tail to be carried above the level of the puppy's topline, although it should not be curled over his back like a husky.

Although choosing a show puppy can be likened to a lottery, one thing cannot be stressed strongly enough: follow the advice of the breeder. If the breeder is relatively inexperienced, try the owner of the stud dog, as he, too, will want only the most superior of specimens produced by his dog to grace the show ring.

PAPERWORK AND FORMALITIES
The purchase price of the puppy should

33

have been agreed at the outset. The breeder should have a pedigree certificate written out for you to take with your puppy. This will be endorsed by the breeder, who will sign a declaration certifying the pedigree to be correct to the best of his knowledge.

DIET SHEETS AND WORMING
The breeder should have discussed the puppy's diet with you, and should put this in writing in the form of a diet sheet. It is useful to obtain a copy of this prior to taking your puppy home, giving you a chance to purchase suitable food in advance. If the breeder has reared the puppies on a food that it is not readily available, he should give you sufficient samples of the food to last for a few days. Quantities of food for a single puppy can be very difficult to judge, so ask to be shown the right quantity by the breeder.

The puppies will have been treated for worms on several occasions, usually every two weeks, starting between two and three weeks of age. Ask when they were last wormed, as your vet will want to know.

THE JOURNEY HOME
Think about where the puppy will travel in the car on the journey home. Some dogs hate cars, and, like children, they can become car-sick. It is important to start correctly. If you have an estate car or hatchback, do not put the puppy in the back without restraints. Even on a short journey he can be thrown about and will consequently be sick. I find it easier to place the puppy on someone's lap, on the

The breeder will give you details of diet and worming procedure.

back seat, where he can be held close and comforted. Get a friend to come with you. The puppy is less likely to be sick if you place him in the vehicle so that he is unable to see the motion of the car. Have a supply of old towels and newspapers handy, just in case. After a few minutes of curiosity, the puppy usually falls asleep. Travel crates or cages are also suitable for dogs to travel in, but make sure they cannot be thrown around by the movement of the car. This does not happen so much with motorway driving, but it can occur on twisty country roads.

3 *PUPPY CARE*

U ntil the moment when you take your puppy home, he has lived in a secure world, where his meals came either from his mum or from a friendly human, whose voice was probably the first thing he heard. This world was safe, with interesting visitors and food provided at regular intervals. Now that your puppy has been uprooted from this secure world, you will need to provide him with a new, equally secure world. Your puppy's old way of life should become a distant memory as he begins exploring and living life in his own world.

When you arrive home, having collected your puppy, take him out to the garden, to the place you want him to use as his toilet. He will probably have slept during the journey, and he will have an immediate need to urinate. This spot should be near to the back door, so it is accessible for the puppy and in a position for you to see when the puppy performs.

PUPPIES AND ADULT DOGS
Give the puppy the chance to explore the house and the garden at his own pace. If you have other dogs in the household, allow them to meet the puppy in the garden. Put the adult dogs on a lead, so they cannot charge at the puppy and

Changing homes is a big trauma for a puppy. This seven-week-old youngster went on to become Ch. Belamba Mostly French. Photo: Linda Collins.

frighten him – he is, after all, a stranger in their territory. It is unusual for an adult dog to attack a puppy, but it is not unheard of. In the first few weeks, never leave the puppy with adult dogs unsupervised. Some adult dogs do not appreciate being hounded and nipped by a curious puppy desperate to play. Also, the adult dog may be slightly jealous of the attention-seeking new rival, or longing for some peace and quiet.

HOUSE-TRAINING

Once you have fed the puppy, or when he wakes up, take him outside immediately. You do not have time to watch the end of a television programme, or to finish a telephone call; a puddle will await you if you try. Each time you take the puppy to the toilet area, use an associated word such as "Busy" or "Hurry up" followed by verbal praise when the puppy obliges. It is not dissimilar to potty-training a child; it can be time-consuming and frustrating. It takes a watchful owner to spot when the puppy looks uncomfortable and is looking for a place to go.

Some people advocate placing the puppy on newspaper, initially letting him become accustomed to performing on newspaper. Over time, the newspaper is moved nearer to the door, and then outside, until the dog gets the message. However, I tried this once and found that the puppy, by then about five months old, would search the house until he found a piece of paper (usually that day's unread newspaper) and urinate on that.

THE PUPPY'S BED

Find a quiet area in the house for the puppy's bed. Do not buy expensive dog beds for puppies as they usually end up with a serrated edge when the puppy is teething and desperate for anything to

chew. A large cardboard box, with the sides cut down, is adequate and costs nothing to replace. The bed's location should be draught-free and secure. It is important to position the bed where the puppy can see out into the room, but somewhere that it will not be in full sun in the owner's absence. Spread newspaper in the vicinity of the bed, so that, if accidents occur, they are easily cleaned up.

Some owners use cages or indoor kennels. These can be very successful, helping with house-training and minimising a puppy's destructive impact. Encourage the dog to use the cage as a refuge, by leaving the door open and adding comfy bedding and some favourite toys. As long as the cage is not used as a 'sin bin', the puppy soon realises that it is his own comfortable and secure area.

THE FIRST NIGHT

At bedtime on the first night, make sure the puppy is tired, put him in his bed, turn out the lights, and leave the room. It is normal for the puppy to cry, or even to howl – after all, he is missing his litter mates – but he should settle down and sleep eventually. The noise is pitiful, but woe betide the owner who, feeling sorry for the puppy, takes him into their bedroom, or, even worse, into their bed. The puppy will be delighted to have a human companion to snuggle up to, a face to lick, or someone to play with, and he will expect to sleep there from then on. The following night, if returned to his own bed, the howls will be even worse. The puppy quickly learns that, if he makes enough noise, the humans will come running! The moral is not to give in, in the first place.

INOCULATIONS

Take your puppy to the vet to be checked

over within 48 hours of purchase. Some vets run an appointment schedule, while others have a general surgery time in which patients queue to be seen. If the vet uses the latter system, do not wait in the waiting room with all the other dogs. Explain that your puppy is here for his first inoculations and wait in the car until your turn. Other dogs within the waiting room usually go to see a vet when they are unwell, and your puppy is very vulnerable. He could easily take home more than an inoculation card!

The vet will check the puppy's general health and listen to his heart and lungs, as well as checking the puppy for parasites, dirty ears, etc. There are several inoculation programmes available, most consisting of two injections, one at 8 weeks and the second at 12 weeks. During this period, the puppy should be prevented from mixing with other dogs, and, ideally, he should not be allowed to walk in places where other dogs (apart from your own) have access. Vaccination is necessary to provide protection against diseases that are life-threatening, such as distemper, hepatitis and parvovirus. Vaccination is the only proven method of protection against these diseases, and it should be topped up by regular boosters.

FEEDING

The breeder will have advised you about the type and brand of food on which the puppy has been reared. Make sure that you have several days' supply ready for the new puppy. Stainless steel dishes are easier to use for feeding, as opposed to plastic ones that are easily chewed.

Fill a bowl of clean water and make sure that this is available at all times. Many puppies seem to delight in paddling in, or tipping over, their water bowls; generally, a heavy-bottomed ceramic bowl is most suitable as a water bowl.

The type of dog food you give to your puppy will largely depend on the breeder's advice. Try to avoid anything that looks like muesli and can usually be seen, largely undigested, in the faeces. Some breeders advocate a natural diet, consisting largely of raw meat, bones, carbohydrates and vegetables. Although this can be very successful, it takes time to prepare, and many people find their time is at a premium.

If you are feeding a complete diet, remember that the diet is complete – it requires no additional vitamins, minerals or any other additives. Although these meals can be enhanced by adding meat or vegetable stock as a gravy, they do not

A complete diet can become unbalanced by adding supplements.

A Belgian Shepherd may not be exuberant, but he should be completely confident in all situations.

require additional tins of meat. Irreparable damage can be caused to young dogs by overdoing supplements such as calcium, which are not necessary if your dog is on a complete food.

It is not uncommon for a puppy to lose his appetite within the first few days of leaving his mother. While he was with the litter, there was competition for food and for mum's attention. This all changes with the new home, where routines are different and life is full of adventure. If the puppy shows a lack of interest in his food, it may be because he is overtired. Alternatively, the meals may have been given too close together, or excess quanitities may have been given in the last meal.

If the puppy refuses the food, leave it in the dish for 10 minutes and then throw it away – food spoils easily and puppies have delicate tummies. Do not pander to the puppy, trying to tempt his appetite by adding meat or other treats, until a regular feeding pattern has been established.

FADDY EATERS

Belgian Shepherds can have an annoying habit of turning into exceedingly faddy eaters, to the point of becoming anorexic. This usually happens within the first nine months and it drives the worried owner to distraction. The dog shows no interest in food whatsoever, turning up his nose at anything, be it prime steak or best sausage. At their best, such dogs reluctantly take the morsel of offered food, giving the owner a withering look and dissecting it as if it was poisonous. The owner, in desperation, tries other brands of dog food, which the dog eats with gusto for the first day before refusing all food, again, a few days later.

I had one such Belgian, and I had tried everything, from expensive appetite enhancers to parma ham – anything to get her to eat. I despaired every time a judge commented on her skinny

There is a lot for puppies to learn and experience before they are ready to venture into the outside world.

backbone. She was 18 months old when a new puppy came to join us. She watched with horror as he tore into the food she had yet again disregarded, and the competition forced her to eat again. I find that the presence of other dogs tends to encourage fussy eaters to eat things they do not really want, rather than to give up food to their kennelmates.

If you have a single dog, the above strategy will not help. One solution is to refuse to give in, insisting the dog eats what is provided, rather than pandering to his whims. Unless a dog is unwell, or suffering from a psychological disorder, he is unlikely to refuse food to the point where he becomes desperately hungry or at risk of endangering his health.

THE 'WARY' BELGIAN

The UK Breed Standard for the Belgian Shepherd describes the breed's temperament as "wary, neither timid, nervous, nor aggressive." For years, defensive owners have used the excuse of 'wary' for poor temperament and antisocial dogs. Most Belgians are not exuberant with strangers, but they should be comfortable with visitors coming to the house, and with meeting strangers in the street.

Go to any gathering of Belgian Shepherd enthusiasts and you can spot the so-called 'wary' Belgian, usually looking miserable, with his tail tucked firmly between his legs, shying away from a kind hand or an unfamiliar object. These dogs are no pleasure to live with – the owner can seldom relax, waiting for the dog to react. Nothing is as embarrassing as having a large Belgian Shepherd peering out from behind his owner at the horror of a stranger asking for directions when out for a walk. To prevent this happening, your dog must be socialised.

SOCIALISATION

Although some owners have sufficient land to exercise their dog without meeting the general public, homes such as these are rare. Even dogs living in rural surroundings will meet postmen and strangers.

To some extent, your puppy's breeder should have ensured that you take home a well-socialised puppy, content with being handled, and comfortable with unfamiliar people. However, the breeder is limited by the amount of time the puppy resides in his care. The remaining responsibility for socialisation belongs to the puppy's new owner.

Most problems begin when the puppy is approximately 14 weeks old. At this time, prior to his second inoculation, the puppy is normally restricted to his owner's property. The majority of vets recommend that the puppy is kept in for several days after the final inoculation. By the time the puppy has had the all-clear to be taken out, he will be 14 weeks old, and he will have been socially restricted during this time.

From the time a puppy opens his eyes, at nearly 3 weeks old, to the time he is 14 weeks old, a puppy goes through a period of maximum growth, physically and mentally. Between 8 and 10 weeks, he will be naturally fearful, and should be handled gently and respectfully by all concerned. A puppy brought up in a kennelled environment, where he has been handled very little and has had minimal contact with humans, will often remain shy of people, particularly if he does not go to his new home before 14 weeks of age. He is also likely to be fearful in stressful conditions.

As soon as you have had the puppy checked by the vet, and the first inoculation has been given, take your puppy out of the confines of familiar territory for some socialisation. Carrying him in your arms, go to places where you know you will meet people, such as the shopping centre, the post office, or the school run. Few people can resist a cute puppy, and many will stop and make a fuss of the pup. This is very important; the puppy is seeing people at eye level while still having the security of his owner's arms. Aim to take the puppy out on a daily basis. As the puppy grows, he will become heavy, and these socialisation periods may make you feel as if you have been at circuit training, but it is good for your upper arms!

FIRST RELATIONSHIPS

Allow the puppy some respite after his first inoculation, giving him a few days of peace and quiet before inviting visitors to meet this new addition to the household. This gives the puppy a chance to learn the routine of the house and to explore his new surroundings. The puppy should be happy to meet people in what should now be a comfortable environment, and he should be content to be handled.

If the puppy is worried or nervous around visitors, ask them to ignore the puppy completely, warning them especially not to make eye contact (the puppy will perceive this as threatening). Eventually, natural curiosity should take over, and even the most nervous youngster should venture out to have a sniff of these strange people. Do not, under any circumstances, allow the visitor to pursue the puppy around the room in an attempt to catch or cajole him. This will make the pup panic, reinforcing his fear of strangers. If the puppy is nervous of being handled by strangers, it is worth carrying a pocketful of treats and encouraging the person fondling the

puppy to give one of them. This will encourage the puppy's natural curiosity.

Although you must socialise the puppy, take care not to put him on the ground when you are in areas where strange dogs have access. When the puppy is still suckling milk from his mother he receives natural immunity through the milk. The period between leaving his mother and completing the inoculation programme can be dangerous, as germs and diseases spread easily and the puppy is very vulnerable.

THE SECOND PHASE

Once the puppy has completed his inoculation programme, and he is old enough to go out into the world, take him out as much as possible, and at least on a daily basis, in addition to his daily exercise. Find a local pub that allows dogs, and sit there with the puppy once or twice a week. In these situations, a lot of people will come over and talk to the puppy, often offering him treats. The puppy soon learns to relax and soak up the atmosphere.

Other places that can be useful are town centres. Sit down on a bench and watch the world go by – in parks, at train stations and car boot sales – in fact, anywhere where there are plenty of people. If the puppy is uncomfortable in these situations, do not reassure him if his discomfort appears to be without cause. Doing so encourages the development of a vicious circle, where the pup wonders why you are reassuring him and becomes even more worried. It is better to adopt a policy of almost ignoring a puppy (but still giving plenty of praise) unless circumstances dictate otherwise.

If you have an older, steadier or 'bomb-proof' dog, it can help a worried puppy to be accompanied by the older dog for the

Fannyhill's Olivia D'Equinox: When you take your puppy out, give him the opportunity to sit and absorb new situations at his own pace.

first few occasions. However, if your older dog is likely to react in a negative way to anything, take the puppy on his own, as puppies can pick up bad habits just as easily as good ones.

PUPPY PLAYGROUPS
Contact your vet and your local dog clubs and find out if any of them hold 'puppy playgroups' which are designed for pups who have just completed their vaccinations. Puppies are encouraged to play together for short periods, so that the trainer is able to assess dominant or aggressive puppies and advise the owners accordingly. As the puppy gains

confidence, handlers are encouraged to swap puppies, so they become accustomed to being handled by strangers for short intervals, before being returned to their owners.

THE LEARNING CURVE
Socialisation does not finish when the puppy reaches 6 months of age. Some puppies appear well settled and confident at 6 months, but may reach a second crisis period between the ages of 12 and 18 months. For this reason, socialisation must be a continuous learning curve until the dog is at least 2 years old. It is interesting to note that laid-back, relaxed people usually have dogs with similar temperaments. The reverse is also true. Relax, enjoy your dogs, and do not take life too seriously!

EXERCISE
There are no hard-and-fast rules regarding exercise for a Belgian Shepherd puppy. Every breeder will give a different answer, and what works for one owner will not work for another. Take advice from your breeder and use your common sense.

Between 8 and 12 weeks, puppies require very little exercise. They expend their energy in short, frantic bursts of activity before collapsing in a deep sleep, and their exercise should reflect this. By the time they have had their second inoculation, the owner is usually desperate to get them out and about as their energy level increases.

Initially, a 15-minute outing is ample, and your youngster will come home and fall into a deep sleep. Do not 'road-walk' young dogs; that is, do not take them for long walks, on the lead, on a pavement or a hard surface. This can put an unnatural strain on the pup's joints, which are still developing.

To begin with, your puppy will get all the exercise he needs playing in the garden.

As soon as you are taking the puppy out, accustom him to being let off the lead. Much of his exercise should consist of games, which also stimulate the mind. Throwing a ball or toy for the puppy not only teaches him basic obedience, but it also increases the bond between him and you. I also find it useful to play a game of 'hide and seek' with my youngsters. It teaches them to use their noses to find me, discourages them from wandering away, and it also encourages them to come when called. I develop this game further with my adult dogs. If they go round a corner or out of sight, I dive into the undergrowth and wait to be found. It is a great game, enjoyed by all!

If you have several dogs, it is best not to exercise the puppy with them. The adult dog is much faster than the puppy and tends to run for longer periods without stopping. Puppies can damage themselves with such strenuous exercise, trying to keep up with the pack. Some adult Belgians also have a habit of bowling puppies over when they are trying to run with them – the adults think that this is a great game, putting puppies in their place. Although some breeders will advocate that puppies should not be given free exercise until they are at least six months old, a young Belgian has tremendous energy and needs to expend it, otherwise he can be absolute hell to live with, possibly becoming extremely destructive as he finds other ways to expend that pent-up energy. Exercise must be ruled by common sense; never attempt to push a puppy too hard. If a puppy seems unusually tired after a walk, he has probably overdone things.

COLLARS AND LEADS

The experienced owner will be well aware of what sort of lead and collar they like to use, but, for the novice, the huge choice can be confusing. Rolled-leather collars, with soft leather leads, are a good choice. Chain leads, even with a leather handle, can be uncomfortable on your hands if you have to shorten the lead when pulling the dog towards you. Choke chains can be lethal in the wrong hands, so get an expert to show you how to use them properly. Choke chains and other chain-type collars also tend to tear the neck hair on a Belgian Shepherd, leaving an unsightly mark that takes months to regrow. Use pliable leads that are kind to your hands, and strong and durable. For badly-behaved dogs, which insist on pulling their owners wherever they want to go, there are several specialist leads that act as head collars or body harnesses and prevent the dog from having total control.

SEPARATION
In an ideal world, owners would have unlimited time to spend with their dogs. In reality, however, with the demands of modern life and the need for most people to work, few have this luxury. Although the older dog may be used to a routine and may be content to be left for several hours, try this with a puppy and you can guarantee a wrecked house and irate neighbours complaining about the howling.

A dog is a pack animal, and one of the things that humans enjoy is the fact that a dog likes your company and accepts you for what you are. The dog does not appreciate "won't be long" or "back soon". Instead, he sees a blank door separating him from his humans. Frustrated by this, the dog usually vents his irritation on the barrier keeping him separated – the door – or he throws back his head, lets his natural instinct take over, and howls for attention. The owner may not be aware of this until angry neighbours start to complain. The noise factor may be separate from, or accompanied by, the destruction of anything and everything.

Dogs initially vent their frustration on items that smell strongly of their owner, but anything within reach can be destroyed. Bedding, mail, skirting boards, furniture, and books are all favourites. The dog can become so stressed that he will urinate and defecate in large quantities. Even worse, the chewing of household materials may lead to frequent bouts of diarrhoea.

Some dogs will settle with no fuss. This is usually because the owner has taken the time to teach the dog that, although the human may go away, he always returns. Teaching a dog not to rely on human companionship starts with puppy training, and may be as simple as creating a barrier, such as a door, between you and the puppy for a few minutes each day, building up to longer separations over time. Initially, the puppy may cry, but he will usually settle and fall asleep after a short period. It is also a good idea to keep a large supply of interesting toys that will prevent the puppy from getting bored.

CRATES, CAGES AND PENS
Some people use cages or crates for their young puppies. While these can be a useful tool when house-training, it is cruel and unacceptable to leave a dog shut in a cage for hours at a time. Providing that a cage is never used as a punishment area, a dog will enjoy the relative security that it offers. However, I find it equally beneficial to invest in a puppy pen. This is made up of galvanised panels and can be purchased to suit any size.

A dog that is well fed and sufficiently exercised is more likely to settle when the owner departs than a dog that is desperate to expend some energy. Make little fuss of the dog prior to leaving the house and complete your normal routine, leaving with no prolonged farewells. Most dogs can be left for up to four hours; beyond that, expect to return to a mess.

4 LIVING WITH A BELGIAN SHEPHERD

By nature, the dog is a pack animal, and, in the wild, he would have a pack leader. Your puppy looks to you for leadership, and he should eagerly accept the rules you lay down. Most problems start when the dog is not given this leadership or guidance, and, when he reaches canine puberty, like any teenager, he will think he knows better than you!

A young puppy is cute, and many people fail to discipline the youngster, allowing him to jump up, or to climb on them when they are sitting, etc. As the dog grows, the owner's enthusiasm can diminish – an adolescent Belgian Shepherd becomes a real handful. There is nothing more annoying than to be dressed smartly to go out somewhere (usually in light colours), when an unruly Belgian with muddy paws comes hurtling towards you, leaping up to greet you and covering your midriff with a clear reminder of the recent walk or exercise in the garden.

Never give treats from the table, and, if family and guests alike stick to this rule, you will not have the embarrassment of a Belgian drooling expectantly at the table, annoying guests.

COMMANDS
Discipline must be instilled from the outset, but it should be done using a 'softly softly' approach, and, as with all training, fully supported by a praise and reward basis. The basic commands of "Come", "Sit", "Down" and "Stay" are necessary for modern life and can prevent your dog from being involved in accidents.

The Belgian Shepherd is a quick learner. He is eager to please and he enjoys short, informal training sessions. Incorporate these into your daily routine, making the

It is never too early to start basic training.

dog sit before his dinner is put down on the floor, or before his lead is put on. Belgian Shepherds are sensitive and require careful handling; training needs to be simple and consistent. If you are unsure of how to train your dog, contact your local dog clubs (your vet will advise you where to find them). Most clubs use rewards and praise to train dogs – praising your dog works far better than constantly chastising him for misdemeanours. Although handlers may aspire to go on and compete in other disciplines such as Agility or open Obedience, nothing can be successfully undertaken without the basics.

"COME"

It is not unknown for young Belgians to find life much more entertaining away from their owner. When let off the lead, many a Belgian will run to the other end of the park to play with other dogs, returning only when ready. This can be exceedingly frustrating, as it usually happens when you are pressed for time and already stressed. When your dog reappears, the temptation is to scold him for running off, but this is the worst response to make.

Dogs do not think like humans. If you punish your dog for running off, he will, instead, link the punishment with his return, making him even less likely to return to you when you call. It is better to teach your puppy the "Come" command, calling the dog enthusiastically and opening your arms by way of welcome, rewarding him with a treat or with praise, and making a big fuss of him when he returns to you. Repeat this again and again throughout the walk, so that the dog does not associate returning to you with the end of his fun.

"SIT"

Training should be started as soon as the puppy has settled into his new home, usually after a few days. Pick a quiet time, when the puppy can concentrate. Use a really juicy treat, such as cooked liver, or cheese. It is important that the treat is nice and smelly to attract the dog, but no larger than your little fingernail, as you will need to hold quite a few of them in one hand. During this session, you will be using four aids: food, voice commands, hand signals, and petting.

It is easier, in the initial sessions, to go down to the puppy's level. Pinch a treat between your thumb and index finger. Get your puppy interested in it, without letting him eat it, and just raise the treat slightly above the dog's nose, towards his eyes. As the puppy's head follows the treat, gravity should take over, forcing the dog into a sitting position. As soon as that happens, give the puppy the command "Sit" and give him the treat as a reward.

Use a tasty treat to lure your puppy into the Sit.

Then, run your other hand down the puppy's back in a slow caress.

To get the puppy to Sit from the Down position (see below), put another treat in front of his nose and raise it slowly above his head. As he lifts his front end into the Sit, give the command "Sit" and reward him with the treat and a caress. Repeat this procedure a few times, but end before the puppy becomes bored.

"DOWN"

With your puppy in a sitting position, place a treat close to his nose, and lower it to the floor, just in front of the pup's front feet. With the puppy's attention on the treat, slowly draw the treat along the floor. The puppy should follow it with his feet and go into a Down. Give the command "Down", and let the puppy eat the treat as a reward. Once again, slowly caress your other hand along your puppy's back.

Do the "Sit" and "Down" exercises several times a day, encouraging all the family to join in. This is a particularly good idea if you have children, as the

Lower the treat , and your puppy will follow it, going into the Down position.

puppy must realise that he has to obey the smaller members of the family as well as the adults. Within a few days, the puppy should be very conversant with this training, and, gradually, the treats can be withdrawn. The other aids, such as praise and the caress, remain. Treats may still be given sporadically – when the puppy has responded extremely quickly, for example.

"STAY"

Once the puppy understands "Sit" and "Down", use treats to teach him to Stay. Command your puppy to sit, and then tell him "Stay". Hold the treat where the puppy can see it, and, after a count of three, give him the treat. Run your hand down the puppy's back while he is still sitting, and then introduce the release command, which lets the puppy know that you have finished with that exercise. Use the command "That will do" and then deliberately move the puppy from the spot. Turn a small circle with the puppy and start again. Build this up slowly, over a few days, until the puppy can hold a Sit-Stay for about 20 seconds before he attempts to move away.

If, when you first take one step away from the puppy, he tries to follow you, quickly step back to him before he can move from the Sit. If you are successful, give him a treat while he is still sitting, caress him, and then release him from the Sit. The object is for the puppy to learn to stay while the owner with the treat walks away and then returns. The puppy quickly learns that, if he wants the treat, he has to stay when told to do so, and the treat will return to him. Build up the distance slowly, but always return to the puppy's side. Never call the puppy out of a Stay.

Once the puppy is proficient at the Sit-Stay, teach the Down-Stay in the same way.

LEAD-TRAINING

Some Belgians will attempt to pull on the lead, dragging the owner along like an anchor. This can be easily remedied by teaching basic heelwork.

Lead-training is best started in the garden, before the pup is of an age to go out for a walk. Once he is used to a collar, attach a light lead and accustom him to trailing it behind him. If he tries to chew on the lead, gently distract him with a toy or a treat. After doing this a few times, pick up the end of the lead and gently encourage the puppy to follow you and to walk with you. If he rushes in front of you, change direction quickly, so that the pup has to catch up with you. When he is level with you, produce a treat at his nose level and encourage him to walk a few steps by your side. Then reward his actions with the treat.

When you have mastered this in the garden, with plenty of directional changes, it is time to go out into the big world. Do not be in a hurry to go straight to the park. Directional changes help to keep the puppy by your side, instead of leading the way; remember who is supposed to be in control – you! You should decide where you go, and which way you move when you get there. Do not let the pup begin to pull on the lead, and you will have a dog that is a pleasure, not a pain, to walk with. However, if the problem persists, a type of head collar or shoulder harness can be used to control the dog.

CAR-TRAINING

Dogs that jump out of cars have developed a dangerous habit. Dogs have been killed doing this. It also shows an unforgivable lack of discipline. The simplest solution is to teach your dog to Stay – it could save his life.

If your dog is in the habit of leaping

With the help of a treat, the puppy's initial reluctance is overcome, and he is happy to walk on the lead.

straight out of a car, try opening the car door very slowly, and, just as the dog is about to leap out, quickly shut the door in his face. Repeat this, and the dog should soon learn that it is better to wait until the door is opened fully. When you reach in to take hold of the dog, make him Sit and Stay until he is totally relaxed, and only then invite him out.

An alternative method is to enlist a helper. The helper restrains the dog, in a Sit or Down position, while you repeatedly open and close the car door. Eventually, the dog should learn that an open car door does not necessarily mean that he is about to leave the vehicle. If you have no helper, attach a lead to the dog's collar and tie a loose knot at the handle end of the lead. Then shut the lead in the door, with the knot on the outside to prevent it being pulled through. This enables you to take hold of the lead, and so control the dog as you open the door. By restraining the dog, to prevent him from leaping out, you establish control.

TRAINING AND CHILDREN

Never allow your Belgian to chase children, even in a game with your own family. In today's world of litigation – contacting the police first and asking questions second – a dog can be destroyed if the person concerned has reasonable grounds to fear that a dog may injure them. Although your dog may be used to playing with your own family, a strange child running away from him can be a temptation beyond resistance, with tragic consequences.

Never leave children and dogs unsupervised, especially children that do not belong to the household. If your puppy attempts to put his mouth around a child's arm, or if he tries to jump at children, teach the children to cross their arms, to protect their hands and arms, and to shout "No!" at the puppy. Children should also be taught the basic commands, so that they can keep the dog under some control.

GROOMING

Belgians do not require hours of grooming to keep their coat in top condition. The adult coat is made up of two types – the fluffy, downy undercoat, which provides insulation, and the longer topcoat, which is waterproof.

No expensive grooming equipment is required for Belgian coat care. The basic grooming kit needs to consist of no more than a slicker brush (curved or straight), a 'pin' or bristle brush, and a metal comb. Pin brushes come in many variations, but the ones with metal 'bobbles' on the end of the pin tend to rip out too much undercoat. If possible, try out several types of brushes to see which suits your dog best. Dog combs are essential for teasing out the feathering on the Belgian's front legs, and the combs with two types of teeth, one being coarser than the other, tend to work the best.

Start with your dog relaxed on the floor beside you, and wait until he is tired and content. A tired puppy is less likely to fight against you, and it is almost impossible to groom a hyperactive puppy that wants to chew all the equipment, including you! Using a pin or bristle brush, brush the hair along the pup's back, following the direction of the hair. When the puppy is relaxed with this, move to the chest area, again following the direction of the hair. Work your way down to the front legs, followed by the back legs. Most dogs are initially uncomfortable about having their trousers and tail brushed, and may try to wriggle, gnaw the brush or otherwise distract you.

Children and dogs can have great relationships, but it is important to supervise interactions.

However, you must persevere, until your puppy accepts the situation.

Once the puppy is comfortable with a light brushing, go back to the neck and back area, gently brushing the coat against the direction of the hair, so that it stands on end. When the puppy is completely relaxed, place your other hand at the bottom of the trousers, so that you lift up the hair. This should allow you to place the brush near the skin and then groom back towards you. The slicker should be used on the trousers and tail, but brush gently – the metal teeth can be sharp. As the feathers grow, use the comb on the front legs and behind the ears.

As your dog matures, he should become used to grooming, and you may like to progress to grooming on a grooming table. Not only does this save your back, but it also has the added benefit of accustoming the dog to standing on the table until you tell him he is released. Most dogs learn the routine quickly, and will happily stretch out and snooze while you work on their coat. If, at first, your dog seems unwilling to stay on the grooming table, you can purchase a metal arm, which can be clamped to the table. You can tie your dog to the arm, leaving you with both hands free to groom. However, never leave a dog unattended like this, as he could easily attempt to jump off, strangling himself in the process.

When grooming your Belgian, take the opportunity to become familiar with the feel of his body. Grooming is an ideal opportunity to check for any lumps, tumours, or other indications that your Belgian is not fully fit. Also check his nails and feet for damage. Your Belgian's feet can become very sore in the winter if you are exercising him on main roads that are sprayed with salt to prevent ice. Like humans, nails can easily split and cause great pain to the dog. If your dog still has dewclaws on the front legs (some breeders have these removed), make sure they are kept short. In extreme cases, the dewclaws can become so long they grow back into the leg.

MOULTING

Twice a year, your Belgian will decide that you do not do enough housework and will shed most of his hair. During this period, which lasts for several weeks, your dog will lose all of his undercoat and some of the topcoat. The first sign is tufts of undercoat appearing between the topcoat. The tufts will lift off neatly. Parting the coat, especially down the flanks, will show the undercoat clumping together.

In bitches, the moult is dominated by hormones, and, although there are many food preparations and additives on the market, the only successful remedy is time. A bitch's cycle works in such a way that, if she was mated, she would be in full coat from the time of giving birth until her puppies were five weeks old. This is because the increased body heat generated by the full coat helps milk production to reach its peak.

Although it is normal for the Belgian to shed his coat twice a year, he may also 'blow' his coat. During a normal shed, the Belgian loses his undercoat only – the topcoat of guard hairs is replaced continually, so that the dog still has a protective coat, but it is thinner than normal. The dog will have the appearance of being shaved, with thin wisps of topcoat left behind the ears, feathers and trousers. 'Blowing' the coat is usually stress-induced, and it means that both the undercoat and the guard hairs fall out. This often happens if the dog has had a general anaesthetic.

PUPPY GROOMING

It is important to accustom your puppy to grooming from an early age.

The pup must learn to accept all-over handling. Here, he is having his ears checked.

The paws are picked up, one at a time, to examine the pads and the nails.

Remember to check teeth and gums on a regular basis.

BATHING

I do not bath my Belgians unless they have rolled in something disgusting. However, during a moult, the remaining coat may feel greasy, and, with an older dog, dandruff can be seen. Bathing the coat loosens dandruff, making it easier to groom out when the coat is dry. Some owners of show dogs purchase a 'blaster' to assist with drying. This is an extremely powerful hairdryer, but without the heating element. The blown air is excellent for removing dead undercoat and dirt, and, with a little practice, the dog pays no attention to the noise it makes. When bathing your dog, always use a specialist dog shampoo. Shampoo designed for human hair is too strong and strips all the natural oils from the coat.

THE NEUTERED COAT

Once a dog has been neutered, hormonal changes occur. These can affect the dog's coat very noticeably. Both neutered dogs and bitches exhibit the same tendencies, with the undercoat becoming thicker and woollier, and the featherings becoming more pronounced. Instead of the dog having a natural moult twice a year, he remains in full coat throughout the year. Consequently, the coat requires much more work, particularly the undercoat, which will matt unless it is combed several times a week. I regularly use a comb on these coats, to strip out the undercoat and to let the skin breathe. Some people take to trimming these coats on older dogs, so that the hair is more manageable. A rake comb, which has bladed teeth, is essential for getting through the trousers and long feathering of a neutered dog's coat.

FEEDING

As your puppy matures into adulthood, check the protein level in his food and tailor it accordingly. Active working dogs, dogs living outside, and lactating bitches, all require a high protein intake. However, the average family pet requires less protein in his diet.

As your dog ages, reassess his protein levels once again. You would not feed your geriatric grandparent an athlete's diet and the same applies to your dog. The older dog may also suffer with digestive problems, just like older people. Split your dog's food into two smaller meals.

If you have any concerns about your dog's diet, or if you need advice, contact your vet.

DOMINANT BEHAVIOUR

It is as much instinct for a puppy to find 'his place' in his new, human family as it is for him to breathe when he is newborn. The dominant puppy will force his way on to the bitch's most productive teats between the hind legs. As a result of this, he will gain weight faster than the rest of the litter. As the puppy's senses start developing, and he becomes mobile, he will play games with the rest of his litter. These games teach him the skills he will need later in life. The games consist of wrestling, chasing, 'hide and seek', and, most important to the dominant dog, games of strength and possession. Watch any litter of puppies at play and it becomes apparent which is the dominant puppy. He (or occasionally she) will play with a toy until he takes possession of it. He will then lie down with the toy and guard it. As this game is played often, he will become more interested in showing his littermates that he is the boss.

As the weaning process is undertaken, the dominant puppy will often eat his fill before his siblings, growling at them and keeping them away until he is finished. By the time the dominant puppy is ready to

ADULT GROOMING

Work through the coat with a bristle brush.

Check the nails, and trim if necessary.

A comb will be needed on the feathering.

If tartar has accumulated on the teeth, it can be removed with a tooth scaler.

Work out a programme of training and socialisation so that your puppy becomes well integrated in his human family.

go to his new home, he is already confident of his strength, and his place in 'his pack'.

TAKING HOME THE DOMINANT PUPPY

When the dominant puppy arrives at his new home, he will work out the pecking order of the household by observing household procedure. In the puppy's eyes, he has simply left one pack and joined another. New and inexperienced owners rarely notice the puppy asserting himself until it becomes a problem.

The puppy soon learns that, when family meals are being prepared, if he paces the floor, nudges or paws his owner, and looks pleadingly at his food bowl, the normal response from the owner is to feed him immediately. The puppy may not be that hungry, but he is conditioning his owners to feed him first – reinforcing, in the puppy's mind, that he is the most important member in this new 'pack'.

The dominant puppy will enjoy playing games with members of the family, and he will especially love 'tug-of-war' games – the harder you pull, the harder he will fight back. This game then expands, until, by four months, he may start to growl playfully during these games. Often, this is unwittingly encouraged by the owners, who lavish praise and make growling noises back. The game finishes when the puppy has had enough and stalks off with the toy, refusing to play anymore or to give up his toy. The puppy sees these games of strength as challenges, and, as they always end with him having possession of the toy, he thinks he has won. He has also learnt that it is acceptable to growl at his owners, as no punishment was forthcoming. Both these results reinforce the puppy's perception that he is pack leader.

UNCO-OPERATIVE BEHAVIOUR

By five months of age, the dominant puppy will be obsessed with showing 'his pack' how strong he is. He will also have found out where his owners' bedroom is, if he did not work his way in there while he was still a very young puppy. His next move will be to take over in the bedroom. If he is allowed to sleep in the bed he may growl in his sleep if his owner nudges him or turns over in bed.

A development of the bedroom scenario involves the chairs and sofas in the house. The usual behaviour is for the puppy to immediately jump into a chair vacated by a family member who leaves the room. Although there are other chairs available, the puppy will want that particular one, again reinforcing his ownership of it. He may also try to 'share' a chair, stretching and pushing until the obliging owner moves to another chair.

Try to move the dominant dog, from either your bed or your chair, and he will go completely limp, becoming a dead weight, and almost impossible to shift. Taking this a step further, the dog may growl or snap at the person trying to move him. The person steps back in horror and shock that their wonderful 'cute' puppy has just snapped at them. If they attempt again to move him they will do so warily. The dog will instantly recognise their nervousness, and, on the second attempt, he may only growl, but he will not move. Guess who has won?

Normally, these encounters give the dog the go-ahead to make the next step in an attempted take-over. He will push through the doorway in front of his owners. In his mind he is pack leader, and, therefore, he must be seen to lead.

AGGRESSION

Many dog owners fail to realise that their dog is becoming overly dominant until it is too late. Often, the problem only becomes apparent after some sort of confrontation. Stairs are a favourite place for such a confrontation. The dog will race upstairs to arrive at the top before his owners. He will then turn around and 'eyeball' his owners as they approach. The dog will not move from this position of his own accord, and, if he is pushed, he may become aggressive.

The dominant dog will rarely lie on his back next to humans or other dogs, because doing so is an act of submission. The dominant dog will only come to you when he feels like doing so. Generally, the dominant dog is likely to be thoroughly objectionable.

The dominant dog may also take great delight in showing his dominance over you at the local dog club, with typical behaviour being the breaking of the "Stay" command, followed by a backing away from his owner, barking loudly. The owner is mortified at this public display and will do anything to lessen his embarrassment. From the dog's point of view, he has disobeyed a command, and, in standing there barking, he is showing his authority over his owner. As the owner moves towards the dog, desperately trying to coax him into co-operating, the dog's dominant status is further reinforced.

CURING DOMINANCE

Once your dog has reached the above level of dominance, physical punishment cannot be used to correct his behaviour. Direct physical confrontation is more likely to make matters worse, and, in some cases, it may result in serious injury if the dog decides to retaliate using his claws or teeth. Instead, behavioural methods need to be applied. If you are unsure of how to tackle this problem, take advice from your breeder or from your vet. In some cases, you may be referred to an animal behaviourist.

The best way of avoiding dominance issues in your home is to prevent them from arising in the first place. Right from the beginning, reinforce your puppy's position in the family – at the bottom of the pack. When he is relaxing, roll him on his back and gently rub his tummy. The dominant dog will fight against this, as he is exposing the vulnerable parts of his body to attack. However, do not give up. It is much easier to accustom your dog to this display of subservience while he is a puppy. By the time he is an adult, his position should be sufficiently reinforced that he will adopt the pose willingly.

Do not challenge your dog to games of strength or speed – he will usually win, whatever his age. Never attempt tug-of-war games with a dominant dog, or get into any situation that you are unable to control. My husband lost the respect of my first Groenendael when she refused to come in from the garden at about 12 weeks of age. He decided to chase and catch her, which, of course, she thought was a great game. Some time later, he came back into the house, thoroughly frustrated, sending me to retrieve the puppy, which I managed to do with one whistle. For the rest of her life, Inca considered that I was pack leader, she my second-in-command, and my husband barely existed.

If your dog suffers from temporary deafness, beat him at his own game. If he runs off in one direction, call him, then turn and run in the opposite direction. He will soon get the message. If your dog is determined to race up the stairs and challenge you at the top, change your direction so you are not confronting him, or, if he growls when you attempt to move him from your favourite chair, do not let him get up there in the first place.

Your dog should learn that humans go through doors first, and dogs that barge past tend to have doors shut in their faces. Teaching basic-obedience exercises, such as those described earlier in the chapter, will also help to reinforce who is the 'boss' in the relationship.

INVOLVING THE FAMILY
Most people's natural instinct is to minimise contact between the dog and the people over whom he is most domineering. However, this only encourages the dog further. The person who has the most trouble with the dog should take over the dog's care, becoming the main supplier of everything the dog needs, including food, water, praise, and affection. This person must be able to get the dog to obey basic commands, but should initially avoid the "Down" command, as the dominant dog will perceive this as being submissive. Other family members should totally ignore the dog, so that he looks on that one family member as his sole provider. If in doubt, seek professional advice.

Your dog will be about four years old before you hopefully accomplish what you set out to achieve – to have a well-behaved, well-mannered pet to be proud of. By that time, you will have forgotten the wallpaper that had to be replaced, the new shoes that were chewed, and the endless standing in the dark in a freezing garden telling an uninterested puppy to hurry up. You may even be contemplating a second companion and starting the cycle again. Do persevere. It is well worth it in the long run.

5 THE BREED STANDARDS

The official Breed Standard gives breeders and judges a 'blueprint' of how a Belgian Shepherd should look. It describes the ideal dog that breeders should attempt to produce, highlighting the points that judges should look for in the show ring. In this section we will look at the three Standards for the Belgian Shepherd Dog: the UK Standard, the AKC Standard, and the FCI Standard.

Until 1994, the UK Standard classified the Belgian Shepherd Dog by the four varieties. Since 1995, the dogs have been registered as the Belgian Shepherd breed, with the variety shown in brackets on the registration certificate. From 2000, however, the Belgian has been once again classified according to variety, with Challenge Certificates for both Groenendael and Tervueren.

In the US, the American Kennel Club (AKC) does not recognise the Laekenois variety. The other varieties are named as Belgian Sheepdog (Groenendael), Belgian Tervuren (Tevueren – note the different spelling), and Belgian Malinois (Malinois).

In the US, dogs may also be registered with the United Kennel Club (UKC). The UKC Standard has not been reproduced in this chapter as it is very similar to the FCI Standard. Unlike the AKC Standard, the UKC Standard recognises the Laekenois variety.

THE UK BREED STANDARD

GENERAL APPEARANCE: Medium-sized dog, well proportioned, intelligent, attentive, hardy and alert. (Four varieties: Groenendael, Tervueren, Malinois and Laekenois.)

UK Ch. Zodiac Of Questernberg At Jalus: Groenendael breed record holder, winner of 40 CCs. Photo: Pearce.

CHARACTERISTICS: With fine proportions and proud carriage of head, conveying an impression of graceful strength. Not only a sheepdog but a guard dog.

TEMPERAMENT: Wary, neither timid, nervous nor aggressive.

HEAD AND SKULL: Head finely chiselled, long but not excessively so. Skull and muzzle roughly equal in length, with, at most, a slight bias in favour of muzzle, giving the impression of a balanced whole. Skull of medium width in proportion to length of head, forehead flat, centre line not very pronounced; in profile, parallel to imaginary line extending muzzle line. Muzzle of medium length tapering gradually towards nose. Nose black, well-flared nostrils. Moderate stop. Arches above eyes are not prominent, muzzle finely chiselled under eyes. Cheeks spare, quite flat but well muscled.

EYES: Medium size, neither protruding nor sunken, slightly almond shaped, preferably dark brown; black-rimmed eyelids. Direct, lively and enquiring look.

EARS: Distinctly triangular appearance, stiff and erect, set high, moderate length with external ear well rounded at base.

MOUTH: Wide, lips thin textured, very firm, strongly pigmented. Strong, white teeth firmly set in well-developed jaws. Scissor bite, i.e. upper teeth closely overlapping the lower teeth and set square to the jaws. Pincer bite tolerated.

NECK: Very supple. Neck slightly elongated, well muscled and without dewlap, broadening slightly towards shoulders. Nape very slightly arched.

FOREQUARTERS: Withers distinct, strongly boned throughout, with wiry, powerful muscle structure. Shoulder blades long and oblique, firmly attached, flat, forming such angle with humerus as to enable elbows to work easily. Forelegs long, well muscled, parallel. Pasterns strong and short. Carpus clearly defined. Dewclaws permissible.

BODY: Body powerful but elegant. In males, length from point of shoulders to point of buttocks approximately equal to height at withers. In females the same, slightly longer permissible. Chest deep and well let down. Ribs moderately well sprung. Upper line of body straight, broad and powerfully muscled. Belly moderately developed, neither drooping nor unduly cut up, continuing lower line of chest in a graceful curve. Rump very slightly sloping, broad but not excessively so. Skin springy but quite taut over whole body. All external mucous membranes highly pigmented.

UK Ch. Domburg Reve d'Amour.
Photo: Linda Collins.

HINDQUARTERS: Well muscled and powerful. Good but not excessive angulation; hocks well let down. Viewed from behind, legs parallel. Dewclaws to be removed.

FEET: Toes arched, very close together, soles thick and springy with large dark claws. Forefeet round. Hindfeet slightly oval.

TAIL: Tail firmly set, strong at base, of medium length. When at rest, it hangs down, with tip slightly bent backwards at level of hock; when moving, it should lift accentuating curve towards tip, never curled, nor bent to one side. Tip may be carried slightly higher than topline.

GAIT/MOVEMENT: Brisk, free and even.

COAT: There are three distinct coat types:
• Groenendael/Tervueren: Outer coat long, straight and abundant. Texture of medium harshness. Not silky or wiry. Undercoat extremely dense. Hair shorter on head, outside of ears, and lower part of legs. Opening of ear protected by hair. Hair especially long and abundant, ruff-like around neck, particularly in males. Fringe of long hair down back of forelegs, long and abundant hair evident on hindquarters and tail. Males longer-coated than females.

• Laekenois: Harsh, wiry, dry, and not curly. Any sprinkling of fluffy-fine hair in locks in rough-coats is undesirable. Length of coat about 6 cms (2.5 inches) on all parts of body. Hair around eyes, but not to obscure them. Muzzle hair not so long as to make head appear square or heavy. Tail not plumed.

• Malinois: Hair very short on head, exterior of ears and lower parts of legs. Short on rest of body, thicker on tail and around neck, where it resembles a ridge or collar, beginning at base of ear and extending to throat.
Hindquarters fringed with longer hair. Tail thick and bushy. Coat thick, close, of good, firm texture with woolly undercoat, neither silky nor wiry.

No variation in these types is acceptable.

COLOUR: The acceptable colours relate directly to coat type:
• Groenendael: Black, or black with limited white as follows: small to moderate patch or strip on chest, between pads of feet and on tips of hind toes. Frosting (white or grey) on muzzle.

• Laekenois: Reddish fawn with black shading, principally on muzzle and tail.

• Tervueren: All shades of red, fawn, grey with black overlay. Coat characteristically double-pigmented, wherein tip of each light-coloured hair is blackened. On mature males this blackening especially pronounced on shoulders, back and rib sections. Black mask on face, not extending above line of eyes, and ears mostly black. Tail should have a darker or black tip. Small to moderate white patch or strip permitted on chest, between pads of feet and on tips of hind toes. Frosting (white or grey) on the muzzle. Beyond the age of 18 months, a washed out colour, or colour too black, undesirable.

• Malinois: As Tervueren.

SIZE: Ideal height: dogs 61 to 66 cms (24 to 26 inches); bitches 56 to 61 cms (22 to 24 inches). Weight in proportion to size.

FAULTS: Any departure from the foregoing points should be considered a fault and the seriousness with which the fault should be regarded should be in exact proportion to its degree.

NOTE: Male animals should have two apparently normal testicles fully descended into the scrotum.

Reproduced with kind permission of the Kennel Club. Revised March 1993.

THE AMERICAN KENNEL CLUB BREED STANDARDS

The AKC has different Standards for each of the three varieties that it recognises. It does not recognise the Laekenois variety.

THE BELGIAN SHEEPDOG (GROENENDAEL)

GENERAL APPEARANCE: The first impression of the Belgian Sheepdog is that of a well-balanced, square dog, elegant in appearance, with an exceedingly proud carriage of the head and neck. He is a strong, agile, well-muscled animal, alert and full of life. His whole conformation gives the impression of depth and solidity without bulkiness. The male dog is usually somewhat more impressive and grand than his female counterpart. The bitch should have a distinctly feminine look.

Faults: Any deviation from these specifications is a fault. In determining whether a fault is minor, serious, or major, these two factors should be used as a guide: 1. The extent to which it deviates from the Standard. 2. The extent to which such a deviation would actually affect the working ability of the dog.

SIZE, PROPORTION, SUBSTANCE: Males should be 61 to 66 cms (24 to 26 inches) in height, and females 56 to 61 cms (22 to 24 inches), measured at the withers. Males less than 57.25 cms (22.5 inches) or more than 70 cms (27.5 inches) in height, and females less than 51 cms (20 inches) or more than 62.75 cms (25 inches) in height, shall be disqualified. The length, measured from point of breastbone to point of rump, should equal the height. Bitches may be slightly longer. Bone structure should be moderately heavy in proportion to height so that he is well balanced throughout and neither spindly or leggy nor cumbersome and bulky. The Belgian Sheepdog should stand squarely on all fours.

SIDE VIEW: The topline, front legs, and back legs should closely approximate a square.

HEAD: Clean-cut and strong, overall size should be in proportion to the body.

EXPRESSION: Indicates alertness, attention, readiness for activity. Gaze should be intelligent and questioning.

EYES: Brown, preferably dark brown. Medium size, slightly almond shaped, not protruding.

EARS: Triangular in shape, stiff, erect, and in proportion to the head in size. Base of the ear should not come below the centre of the eye. Ears hanging (as on a hound) shall disqualify.

SKULL: Top flattened rather than rounded. The width approximately the same, but not wider than, the length. Stop moderate.

MUZZLE: Moderately pointed, avoiding any tendency to snipiness, and approximately equal in length to that of the top skull. The jaws should be strong and powerful.

BIS winner Am. Can. Ch. Sumerwynd A Smyle For Awhile.
Photo: The Standard Image.

NOSE: Black, without spots or discolored areas. The lips should be tight and black with no pink showing on the outside.

TEETH: A full complement of strong, white teeth, evenly set. Should not be overshot or undershot. Should have either an even bite or a scissor bite.

NECK, TOPLINE, BODY: Neck: Round and rather outstretched, tapered from head to body, well muscled, with tight skin. Topline: The withers are slightly higher and slope into the back, which must be level, straight, and firm from withers to hip joints. Chest: Not broad, but deep. The lowest point should reach the elbow, forming a smooth, ascendant curve to the abdomen.

ABDOMEN: Moderate development. Neither tucked up nor paunchy. The loin section, viewed from above, is relatively short, broad and strong, but blending smoothly into the back. The croup is medium long, sloping gradually.

TAIL: Strong at base, bone to reach hock. At rest, the dog holds it low, the tip bent back level with the hock. When in action he raises it and gives it a curl, which is strongest toward the tip, without forming a hook. Cropped or stump tail shall disqualify.

FOREQUARTERS: Shoulder: Long and oblique, laid flat against the body, forming a sharp angle (approximately 90 degrees) with the upper arm. Legs: Straight, strong and parallel to each other. Bone oval rather than round. Development (length and substance) should be well proportioned to the size of the dog. Pastern medium length, strong, and very slightly sloped. Feet: Round (cat footed), toes curved close together, well padded. Nails strong and black, except that they may also be white to match white toe tips.

HINDQUARTERS: Legs: Length and substance well proportioned to the size of the dog. Bone oval rather than round. Legs are parallel to each other. Thighs: Broad and heavily muscled. The upper and lower thigh bones approximately parallel to the shoulder blade and upper arm respectively, forming a relatively sharp angle at stifle joint. The angle at the hock is relatively sharp, although the Belgian Sheepdog does not have extreme angulation. Metatarsus medium length, strong and slightly sloped. Dewclaws, if any, should be removed. Feet: Slightly elongated. Toes curved close together, well padded. Nails strong and black, except that they may be white to match white toe tips.

COAT: The guard hairs of the coat must be long, well fitting, straight and abundant. They should not be silky or wiry. The texture should be a medium harshness. The undercoat should be extremely dense, commensurate, however, with climatic conditions. The Belgian Sheepdog is particularly adaptable to extremes of temperature or climate. The hair is shorter on the head, outside of the ears, and lower part of the legs. The opening of the ear is protected by tufts of hair.

ORNAMENTATION: Especially long and abundant hair, like a collarette, around the neck; fringe of long hair down the back of the forearm; especially long and abundant hair trimming the hindquarters, the breeches; long, heavy and abundant hair on the tail.

COLOR: Black. May be completely black, or may be black with white, limited as follows: Small to moderate patch or strip on forechest. Between pads of feet. On tips of hind toes. On chin and muzzle (frost may be white or gray). On tips of front toes allowable, but a fault. Disqualification: Any color other than black, except for white in specified areas. Reddening due to climatic conditions in an otherwise correct coat should not be grounds for disqualification.

GAIT: Motion should be smooth, free and easy, seemingly never tiring, exhibiting facility of movement rather than a hard driving action. He tends to single track on a fast gait;

the legs, both front and rear, converging toward the centre line of gravity of the dog. The back line should remain firm and level, parallel to the line of motion, with no crabbing. He shows a marked tendency to move in a circle rather than a straight line.

TEMPERAMENT: The Belgian Sheepdog should reflect the qualities of intelligence, courage, alertness and devotion to his master. To his inherent aptitude as a guardian of flocks should be added protectiveness of the person and property of his master. He should be watchful, attentive, and always in motion when not under command. In his relationship with humans, he should be observant and vigilant with strangers, but not apprehensive. He should not show fear or shyness. He should not show viciousness by unwarranted or unprovoked attack. With those he knows well, he is most affectionate and friendly, zealous of their attention, and very possessive.

DISQUALIFICATIONS: Males less than 57.25 cms (22.5 inches) or more than 70 cms (27.5 inches), and females less than 51 cms (20 inches) or more than 57.25 cms (22.5 inches) in height. Ears hanging (as on a hound). Cropped or stump tail. Any color other than black. Viciousness.

THE BELGIAN TERVUREN

GENERAL APPEARANCE: The first impression of the Belgian Tervuren is that of a well-balanced, medium-sized dog, elegant in appearance, standing squarely on all fours, with proud carriage of head and neck. He is strong, agile, well muscled, alert and full of life. He gives the impression of depth and solidity, without bulkiness. The male should appear unquestionably masculine; the female should have a distinctly feminine look and be judged equally with the male. The Belgian Tervuren is a natural dog and there is no need for excessive posing in the show ring. The Belgian Tervuren reflects the qualities of intelligence, courage, alertness and devotion to his master. In addition to his inherent ability as a herding dog, he protects his master's person and property without being overtly aggressive. He is watchful, attentive and usually in motion when not under command. The Belgian Tervuren is a herding dog, and faults which affect his ability to herd under all conditions, such as poor gait, bite, coat, or temperament, should be particularly penalised.

SIZE, PROPORTION, SUBSTANCE: The ideal male is 61 to 66 cms (24 to 26 inches) in height and female 56 to 61 cms (22 to 24 inches) in height, measured at the withers. Dogs are to be penalised in accordance to the degree they deviate from the ideal. Males less than 58.5 cms (23 inches) or more than 61.25 cms (26.5 inches) or females less than 53.25 cms (21 inches) or more than 63.25 cms (24.5 inches) are to be disqualified. The body is square; the length measured from the point of the shoulder to the point of the rump approximates the height. Females may be somewhat longer in body. Bone structure is medium in proportion to height, so that he is well balanced throughout and neither spindly and leggy, nor cumbersome and bulky.

AKC/UKC Ch. Domburg Talk Of The Town.

HEAD: Well chiselled, skin taut, long without exaggeration.

EXPRESSION: Intelligent and questioning, indicating alertness, attention and readiness for action.

EYES: Dark brown, medium sized, slightly almond shaped, not protruding. Light-yellow or round eyes are a fault.

EARS: Triangular in shape, well cupped, stiff, erect, height equal to width at base. Set high, the base of the ear does not come below the centre of the eye. Hanging ears, as on a hound, are a disqualification.

SKULL AND MUZZLE: Measuring from the stop are of equal length. Overall size is in proportion to the body, top of skull flattened rather than rounded, the width approximately the same as, but not wider than, the length. Stop: Moderate. The topline of the muzzle is parallel to the topline of the skull when viewed from the side. Muzzle moderately pointed, avoiding any tendency towards snipiness or cheekiness.

JAWS: Strong and powerful.

NOSE: Black, without spots or discolored areas. Nostrils well defined.

LIPS: Tight and black, no pink showing on the outside when mouth is closed.

TEETH: Full complement of strong, white teeth, evenly set, meeting in a scissor or a level bite. Overshot and undershot teeth are a fault. Undershot teeth, such that contact with the upper incisors is lost by two or more of the lower incisors, is a disqualification. Loss of contact, caused by short centre incisors in an otherwise correct bite, shall not be judged undershot. Broken or discolored teeth should not be penalised. Missing teeth are a fault.

NECK, TOPLINE, BODY: Neck: Round, muscular, rather long and elegant, slightly arched and tapered from head to body. Skin well fitting with no loose folds. Withers accentuated. Topline: Level, straight and firm from withers to croup. Croup medium long, sloping gradually to the base of the tail. Chest not broad without being narrow, but deep; the lowest point of the brisket reaching the elbow, forming a smooth ascendant curve to the abdomen. Abdomen: Moderately developed, neither tucked up nor paunchy. Ribs well sprung but flat on the sides. Loin section viewed from above is relatively short, broad and strong, but blending smoothly into the back.

TAIL: Strong at the base, the last vertebra to reach at least to the hock. At rest, the dog holds it low, the tip bent back level with the hock. When in action, he may raise it to a point level with the topline, giving it a slight curve, but not a hook. Tail is not carried above the back line nor turned to one side. A cropped or stump tail is a disqualification.

FOREQUARTERS: Shoulders: Long, laid back 45 degrees, flat against the body, forming a right angle with the upper arm. Top of the shoulder blades roughly two thumbs width apart. Upper arms should move in a direction exactly parallel to the longitudinal axis of the body. Forearms: Long and well muscled, legs straight and parallel, perpendicular to the ground. Bone oval rather than round. Pasterns short and strong, slightly sloped. Dewclaws may be removed. Feet: Rounded, cat footed, turning neither in nor out, toes curved close together, well padded, strong nails.

HINDQUARTERS: Legs: Powerful without heaviness, moving in the same pattern as the limbs of the forequarters. Bone oval rather than round. Thighs broad and heavily muscled. Stifles: Clearly defined, with upper shank at right angles to hip bones. Hocks: Moderately bent. Metatarsus short, perpendicular to the ground, parallel to each other when viewed from the rear. Dewclaws are removed. Feet: Slightly elongated, toes curved close together, heavily padded, strong nails.

COAT: The Belgian Tervuren is particularly adaptable to extremes of temperature or climate. The guard hairs of the coat must be long, close fitting, straight and abundant. The texture is of medium harshness, not silky or wiry. Wavy or curly hair is undesirable. The undercoat is very dense, commensurate, however, with climatic conditions. The hair is short on the head, outside the ears, and on the front part of the legs. The opening of the ear is protected by tufts of hair.

ORNAMENTATION: Consists of especially long and abundant hair, like a collarette around the neck, particularly on males; fringe of long hair down the back of the forearm; especially long and abundant hair trimming the breeches; long, heavy and abundant hair on the tail. The female rarely has as long or as ornamented a coat as the male. This disparity must not be a consideration when the female is judged against the male.

COLOR: Body rich fawn to russet mahogany with black overlay. The coat is characteristically double pigmented wherein the tip of each fawn hair is blackened. Belgian Tervuren characteristically becomes darker with age. On mature males, this blackening is especially pronounced on the shoulders, back and rib section.

Blackening in patches is undesirable. Although allowance should be made for females and young males, absence of blackening in mature dogs is a serious fault. Washed-out predominant colour, such as cream or gray is to be severely penalised. Chest is normally black, but may be a mixture of black and gray.

A single white patch is permitted on the chest, not to extend to the neck or breast. Face has a black mask and the ears are mostly black. A face with a complete absence of black is a serious fault. Frost or white on chin or muzzle is normal. The underpants of the body, tail, and breeches are cream, gray, or light beige. The tail typically has a darker or black tip. The tips of the toes may be white. Nail color may vary from black to transparent. Solid black, solid liver, or any area of white, except as specified on the chest, tips of the toes, chin and muzzle, are disqualifications.

GAIT: Lively and graceful, covering the maximum ground with minimum effort. Always in motion, seemingly never tiring, he shows ease of movement rather than hard driving action.

He single tracks at a fast gait, the legs both front and rear converging toward the centre line of gravity on the dog. Viewed from the side he exhibits full extension of both fore- and hindquarters. The back line should remain firm and level, parallel to the line of motion.

His natural tendency is to move in a circle, rather than a straight line. Padding, hackneying, weaving, crabbing and similar movement faults are to be penalised according to the degree to which they interfere with the ability of the dog to work.

TEMPERAMENT: In his relationship with humans he is observant and vigilant with strangers, but not apprehensive. He does not show fear or shyness. He does not show viciousness by unwarranted or unprovoked attack. He must be approachable, standing his ground and showing confidence to meet overtures without himself making them. With those he knows well, he is most affectionate and friendly, zealous for their attention and very possessive.

DISQUALIFICATION: Males less than 58.5 cms (23 inches) or more than 67.5 cms (26.5 inches), or females less than 53 cms (21 inches) or more than 62.25 cms (24.5 inches). Hanging ears, as on a hound. Undershot teeth, such that contact with the upper incisors is lost by two or more of the lower incisors. A cropped or stump tail. Solid black, solid liver or any area of white except as specified on the chest, tips of toes, chin and muzzle.

THE BELGIAN MALINOIS

GENERAL APPEARANCE: The Belgian Malinois is a well-balanced, square dog, elegant in appearance with an exceedingly proud carriage of head and neck. The dog is strong, agile, well muscled, alert, and full of life. He stands squarely on all fours, and, viewed from the side, the topline, forelegs, and hindlegs closely approximate a square. The whole conformation gives the impression of depth and solidity without bulkiness. The male is usually somewhat more impressive and grand than his female counterpart, which has a distinctly feminine look.

SIZE, PROPORTION, SUBSTANCE: Males are 61 to 66 cms (24 to 26 inches) in height; females are 56 to 61 cms (22 to 24 inches); measurement to be taken at the withers. Males less than 58.5 cms (23 inches) or more than 68.5 cms (27 inches), and females less than 53.25 cms (21 inches) or more than 63.5 cms (25 inches) are to be disqualified. The length, measured from the point of the breastbone to the point of the rump, should equal the height, but bitches may be slightly longer. A square dog is preferred. Bone structure is moderately heavy in proportion to height so that the dog is well balanced throughout and neither spindly or leggy nor cumbersome and bulky.

HEAD: The head is clean cut and strong without heaviness; overall size is in proportion to the body. The expression should indicate alertness, attention and readiness for activity, and the gaze is intelligent and questioning. The eyes are brown, preferably dark brown, medium size, slightly almond shaped, not protruding. Eye rims are black. The ears approach the shape of an equilateral triangle and are stiff, erect, and in proportion to the head in size. The outer corner of the ear should not come below the centre of the eye. Ears hanging like a hound, or semi-prick ears, are disqualifications. The top of the skull is flattened, rather than rounded, with the width approximately the same as the length, but no wider. The stop is moderate. The muzzle is moderately pointed, avoiding any tendency to snipiness, and approximately equal in length to topskull. The planes of the muzzle and topskull are parallel. The jaws are strong and powerful. The nose is black without discolored areas. The lips are tight and black, with no pink showing on the outside. The Belgian Malinois has a full complement of strong, white teeth, that are evenly set and meet in a scissor or level bite. Overshot and undershot bites are a fault. Overshot and undershot bites, in which two or more of the upper incisors lose contact with two or more of the lower incisors, is a disqualification. One or more missing teeth is a serious fault.

NECK, TOPLINE, BODY: The neck is round and of sufficient length to permit the proud carriage of the head. It should taper from the body to the head. The topline is generally level. The withers are slightly higher and slope into the back which must be level, straight, and firm from withers to hip joint. The croup is medium long, sloping gradually. The body should give the impression of power without bulkiness. The chest is not broad but

Am. Ch. Diadem Primo Royal Mascot. Photo: Rich Bergman.

is deep, with the lowest point reaching the elbow. The underline forms a smooth ascendant curve from the lowest point of the chest to the abdomen. The abdomen is moderately developed, neither tucked up nor paunchy. The loin section, viewed from above, is relatively short, broad and strong, and blends smoothly into the back. The tail is strong at the base, the bone reaching to the hock. In action, it is raised with a curve, which is strongest towards the tip, without forming a hook. A cropped or stump tail is a disqualification.

FOREQUARTERS: The forequarters are muscular without excessive bulkiness. The shoulder is long and oblique, laid flat against the body, forming a sharp angle with the upper arm. The legs are straight, strong and parallel to each other. The bone is oval rather than round. Length and substance are well in proportion to the size of dog. The pastern is of medium length, strong, and very slightly sloped. Dewclaws may be removed. The feet are round (cat footed) and well padded with the toes curved close together. The nails are strong and black, except that they may be white to match white toe tips.

HINDQUARTERS: Angulation of the hindquarters is in balance with the forequarters; the angle at the hock is relatively sharp, although the Belgian Malinois should not have extreme angulation. The upper and lower thigh bones should be approximately parallel to the shoulder blade and upper arm respectively. The legs are in proportion to the size of the dog; oval bone rather than round. Legs are parallel to each other. The thighs should be well muscled. Dewclaws, if any, should be removed. Metatarsus are of medium length, strong and slightly sloped. The hind feet may be slightly elongated, with toes curved close together and well padded. Nails are strong and black except that they may be white to match toe tips.

COAT: The coat should be comparatively short, straight, hard enough to be weather resistant, with dense undercoat. It should be very short on the head, ears, and lower legs. The hair is somewhat longer around the neck where it forms a collarette, and on the tail and backs of the thighs. The coat should conform to the body without standing out or hanging down.

COLOR: The basic coloring is a rich fawn to mahogany, with black tips on the hairs giving an overlay appearance. The mask and ears are black. The underparts of the body, tail and breeches are lighter fawn, but washed-out fawn colour on the body is a fault. Color should be a consideration not a finishing point, not to take precedence over structure or temperament. The tips of the toes may be white, and a small white spot on the breastbone/sternum is permitted, not to extend to the neck. White markings, except as noted, are faulted.

GAIT: The movement is smooth, free and easy, seemingly never tiring, exhibiting facility of movement rather than a hard driving action. The Belgian Malinois single tracks at a fast gait, the legs, both front and rear, converging toward the centre line of gravity, while the topline remains firm and level, parallel to the line of motion, with no crabbing. The breed shows a marked tendency to move in a circle rather than a straight line.

TEMPERAMENT: Correct temperament is essential to the working character of the Belgian Malinois. The breed is confident, exhibiting neither shyness nor aggressiveness in new situations. The dog may be reserved with strangers but is affectionate with his own people. He is naturally protective of his owner's person and property without being overly aggressive. The Belgian Malinois possesses a strong desire to work, and is quick and responsive to commands from his owner. Faulty temperament is strongly penalised.

FAULTS: The degree to which a dog is penalized should depend upon the extent to which the dog deviates from the Standard and the extent to which the particular fault would actually affect the working ability of the dog.

DISQUALIFICATIONS: Males less than 58.5 cms (23 inches) or more than 68.5 cms (27 inches), and females less than 53.25 cms (21 inches) or more than 63 cms (25 inches). Ears hanging as on a hound, or semi-pricked ears. An undershot bite, in which 2 or more of the upper incisors lose contact with two or more of the lower incisors. A cropped or stump tail.

Approved July 10, 1990. Effective August 29, 1990. Reproduced by kind permission of the American Kennel Club.

FÉDÉRATION CYNOLOGIQUE INTERNATIONALE (FCI) STANDARD

FCI Classification: Group 1 sheepdogs and cattle dogs (except Swiss Cattle dogs).

GENERAL APPEARANCE: A balanced dog of medium proportions, harmoniously proportioned, intelligent, rustic, accustomed to open-air life, built to resist the bad weather of the seasons and the atmospheric variations so frequent to the Belgian climate.

By the harmony of his shape and the proud carriage of his head, the Belgian Shepherd Dog must give the impression of that robust elegance which has become the heritage of the selected representatives of a working breed. In addition to his inborn aptitude for guarding flocks, he has the precious qualities to be the best guard dog for the property. When necessary he is, without hesitation, a tenacious and ardent defender of his master. He is vigilant and attentive, his look is alert and enquiring, denoting his intelligence.

HEAD: The head is well chiselled, long without exaggeration, dry. The skull and the muzzle are of sensible equal length, with, at most, a very slight advantage for the muzzle, which gives an impression of perfect finish to the whole.

Multi Ch. Max Van Kriekebos.

NOSE: Black, well-open nostrils.

MUZZLE: Of medium length, tapering gradually towards the nose. The bridge of the nose is straight, in profile parallel to the imaginary line extending from the skull. Mouth well split.

LIPS: Of thin tissue, closing tightly, strongly pigmented, not showing the red of the mucous membranes.

CHEEKS: Dry, quite flat, although muscled.

DENTITION: Strong, white, regular teeth, firmly set in well-developed jaws. Scissor bite: i.e. the incisors of the upper jaw fitting closely over those of the lower jaw, extending slightly beyond them without losing contact with them. Super-position of the incisors is tolerated: in fact it is this bite, named pincer bite, which is preferred by drivers of sheep and cattle.

STOP: Moderate, but marked.

SUPERCILIARY RIDGES: Not prominent, muzzle well chiselled below the eyes.

SKULL: Of medium width, in proportion to the length of the head, with forehead rather flat than rounded, with median line little pronounced. Seen in profile, its extension is parallel to the bridge of the nose.

EYES: Of medium size, not prominent nor sunken, slightly almond shaped, of brownish colour, preferably dark, black-rimmed eyelids. Direct look, lively, intelligent and inquisitive expression.

EARS: Of definite triangular appearance, stiff and erect, set high, proportioned in length, the lobe edges well rounded at the base.

NECK: Reachy, slightly elongated, well muscled, without dewlap, broadening gradually towards the shoulders. Nape: Very slightly arched.

FOREQUARTERS: Solid bone structure all over, muscles dry and strong. Shoulders: The shoulder blades are long, sloping and flat, sufficiently angulated with the humerus to give the elbows easy play. Upper arms: Should move in a direction strictly parallel to the longitudinal axis of the body. Forearms: Long and well muscled. Front pasterns: Strong and short. Pastern joints clean without traces of rickets. Feet: Rather round. The toes arched and well closed. The pads thick and elastic. Nails dark and strong.

BODY: The body is powerful without heaviness. Length from point of shoulder to point of buttocks approximately equal to the height at the withers in the dog. May be slightly longer in the bitch. Forechest: Seen from the front, not very broad, without being narrow. Chest: Not very broad, but deep and well let down, as in all animals of great endurance. The rib cage is constructed of ribs arched in their upper parts. Withers:

Pronounced. Topline (Back and loin): Straight, broad and powerfully muscled. Belly: Moderately developed, neither drooping nor tucked up, continuing the underline of the chest in a harmonious curve. Croup: Very slightly sloping, broad without excess.

HINDQUARTERS: Powerful, without heaviness, moving in the same planes as the forequarters. In stance perpendicular to the ground. Upper thighs: Broad and strongly muscled. The stifle nearly perpendicular to the pelvis. Lower thighs: Long, broad, muscled and sufficiently bent at the hocks without excess. Hocks well let down, broad and muscled. Seen from behind, they should be perfectly parallel. Rear pasterns: Solid and short. Dewclaws not desirable. Feet: Slightly oval. Toes arched and well closed. Pads thick and elastic. Nails dark and strong.

TAIL: The tail is well set on, strong at the base and of medium length. At rest, the dog carries it hanging down, the tip bent slightly backwards at the level of the hock. On the move he lifts it, accentuating the curve towards the tip, but at no time forming a hook or deviation.

COAT: The fact that in the Belgian Shepherd Dogs the coat differs in length and direction, and varies in appearance, means these aspects have been adopted as the criterion to distinguish the different varieties. In all varieties the coat must always be abundant, close and of good texture, forming with the woolly undercoat an excellent protective covering.

MASK: The mask must extend to include the upper and lower lips, the corner of the mouth and the eyelids in a single black area.

COLOURS:
• Tervueren: The fawn colour with black overlay (fauve-charbonne) being the most natural, remains the preferred one. The fawn should be warm, neither light nor washed-out. Any dog whose colour does not

correspond to the desired intensity cannot be awarded the qualification Excellent, and even less receive a proposal for CAC, CACIB or the 'reserves'.

- Malinois: Only the fawn colour with black overlay (fauve-charbonne) with black mask.
- Groenendael: Only solid black.
- Laekenois: The fawn colour (fauve) with traces of black overlay (charbonne), mainly on the muzzle and the tail. In all varieties a little white is tolerated on the forechest and on the toes.

SKIN: Elastic. but well tight over the whole body. External mucous membranes strongly pigmented.

SIZE: The desired height at the withers is, on average, 62 cms (24.5 inches) for dogs, 58 cms (22.75 inches) for bitches. Tolerance: Minus 2 cms (0.75 inches), plus 4 cms (1.5 inches).

GAIT: The movement is brisk and free, covering a maximum of ground. Always on the move, the Belgian Shepherd Dog seems tireless. Because of his exuberant temperament, he has a marked tendency to move in circles rather than in a straight line.

FAULTS: Any departure from the foregoing points should be considered a fault and the seriousness with which the fault should be regarded should be in exact proportion to its degree.

- Character: Aggressive or timid.
- Nose, lips, eyelids: Traces of depigmentation.
- Dentition: Slight superior prognathism (Overshot bite).
- Eyes: Light.
- Shoulders: Too straight.
- Hindquarters: Weak, straight hocks.
- Feet: Open.
- Tail: Carried too high, forming a hook. Deviating from the central line of the body.
- Coat: Absence of undercoat.
- Colour: Grey, tints not warm enough or washed-out. Reversed mask.

DISQUALIFYING FAULTS
- Dentition: Pronounced overshot or undershot bite. Lack of certain premolars. The absence of one small premolar, P1, situated just behind the canines, should not be penalised. However, the absence of two P1s, or of one other premolar, whatever its rank, requires a lower grading. Finally, the absence of three premolars, whatever their rank, or of two molars, implicates disqualification.
- Ears: Drooping or having been manipulated.
- Tail: Absent or shortened, from birth or through docking.
- Colour: White patches elsewhere than on forechest and toes. Absence of mask in the Tervueren and Malinois.
- Character: Dogs which are unapproachable and exaggeratedly aggressive, and also the hyper-nervous and cowardly subjects must be disqualified. The judge should take a calm and bold character into consideration.

MEASUREMENTS: The normal, average proportions in a Belgian Shepherd male, measuring 62 cms (24.5 inches) at the withers are: Height at the withers 62 cms (24.5 inches); Length of body (from point of shoulder to point of buttock) 62 cms (24.5 inches); Length of back (from the withers to the crest of the pelvis) 41 cms (16 inches); Circumference of the chest just behind the elbows, minimum 75 cms (29.5 inches); Depth of chest 31 cms (12.25 inches); From ground to chest 31 cms (12.25 inches); Length of head 25 cms (9.75 inches); Length of muzzle 12.5 to 13 cms (5 to 5.1 inches).

VARIETIES:
Long coat: Short on the head, the outer surface of the ears, and the lower part of the legs, except on the back edge of the forearm, which is covered from the elbow to the pastern joint with long hair called fringes. Long and smooth hair on the rest of the body, longer and more abundant around the neck and on the forechest where it forms a ruff

(collarette) and an apron (jabot). The ear opening is protected by dense hair. The hair from the base of the ear is raised and frames the head. The buttocks are covered with very long and abundant hair forming the 'culottes' or 'breeches'. The tail is furnished with long and abundant hair forming a plume.

Note: In the long-haired variety we name: Groenendael: The solid black. Tervueren: The fawn colour with black overlay (fauve-charbonne) being the most natural, remains the preferred one. The fawn should be warm, neither light nor washed-out. Any dog whose colour does not correspond to the desired intensity, cannot be awarded the qualification Excellent and, even less, a proposal for CAC, CACIB or the 'reserves'. As far as the mask is concerned, it is defined by a strict minimum of eight visible matching points of pigmentation (phaneres): the two ears, the two upper eyelids, the two upper and the two lower lips, which must be black. Long hair other than fawn with black overlay: see Coat and Faults.

Faults: Coat woolly, curly or wavy; coat insufficiently long. In the Groenendael: reddish reflections in the coat, grey culottes. In the Tervueren: grey, not warm enough or washed-out tints; absence of black overlay (charbonne) or its uneven distribution in patches; insufficient mask or reversed mask. An excess of black overlay on the body is not desirable.

Short coat: Very short on the head, outer surface of the ears and on the lower parts of the legs. Short on the rest of the body, more abundant on the tail and around the neck, where it forms a ruff which starts at the base of the ears and stretches to the throat. In addition, the buttocks are feathered with longer hair. The tail is well furnished with hair, spicaté (epiée).

Note: In the short coated variety we name: Malinois: Short coated, fawn with black overlay with black mask. The same eight visible matching points of pigmentation as applicable for the Tervueren are required. Any short coat other than fawn with black overlay is not recognised.

Faults: Semi-long coat, where it should be short, harsh hair among the short coat, wavy coat. Total absence of black overlay, or its uneven distribution in patches. Insufficient mask or reversed mask. An excess of black overlay on the body is not desirable.

Harsh coat: What characterises this variety is, above all, the wiry appearance and dryness of the coat, which is also tousled. The length is noticeably the same all over the body, about 6 cms (2.25 inches). Neither the hair around the eyes, nor that on the muzzle should be so developed as to give the head the appearance of a Barbet or a Briard. However, furnishings on the muzzle are obligatory. The tail must not form a plume.

Note: In the harsh coated variety we name: Laekenois: The wiry-coated fawn, with traces of black overlay, mainly on the muzzle and on the tail.

Faults: Coat too long, silky, curly, wavy or short; the coat full of fine hairs scattered in tufts among the wiry hair. Hair too long around the eyes and on the chin. Bushy tail.

INTERVARIETY BREEDING
Mixed (intervariety) mating is forbidden, except in particular cases, when derogations are accorded by the competent national breeding commissions (Text agreed upon in Paris, 1974).

NOTE: Male animals should have two apparently normal testicles fully descended into the scrotum.

Date of publication of the valid original Standard 16/10/89.

INTERPRETATION AND COMPARISON OF THE STANDARDS
Ask several different Championship show judges to explain and to illustrate any Breed Standard, and no person will give you the same answer. The interpretation is subjective rather than objective; each person has different ideas of what the

written word means. The following guide is a personal interpretation, as I see it from a judge's viewpoint.

GENERAL APPEARANCE

The key words are 'well proportioned' and 'alert'. The Belgian Shepherd should be a balanced, co-ordinated dog, without any form of exaggeration. He should be of medium bone, not heavy like a Bernese Mountain dog, nor light like a Border Collie. The judge should feel for bone, because, in some heavily coated dogs, or dogs that have cast their coats, appearance can be deceptive. Bitches should be finer boned than dogs. The dog should appear alert and interested in what is happening in his surroundings.

CHARACTERISTICS

The UK Standard mentions 'graceful strength'. The dog should convey an impression of great elegance and yet look robust. Looking proud, and carrying his head high, the Belgian should look at you with an alert, inquisitive expression. He is a 'natural' dog and should be exhibited as such. The silhouette of a Belgian shows a square dog, with a beautiful line from the top of the head through a slightly arched neck, a straight topline, and a softly rounded croup.

TEMPERAMENT

The Belgian is a lively, exuberant dog, always 'on the go', and difficult to tire. He should not be timid, nervous, or aggressive, but should instead be calm and confident. He may be wary with strangers, towards whom he may appear reserved, but he should not be nervous in any way. At times, he may become carried away with his own enthusiasm and have to be calmed down. He has been likened to a good champagne – bubbling,

sparkling and effervescent! All the Standards reflect this, with the AKC describing the Belgian Sheepdog (Groenendael) and the Belgian Tervuren as "observant and vigilant with strangers, but not apprehensive. He must be approachable, standing his ground and showing confidence to meet overtures."

A similar description applies to the Belgian Malinois: "The breed is confident, exhibiting neither shyness nor aggressiveness in new situations. The dog may be reserved with strangers."

The UK stands alone in describing the Belgian as "wary". Over the years, temperament has improved greatly in the UK, but nervous dogs, with suspect temperaments, are still excused as 'wary' by too many judges and exhibitors. I will forgive this trait in a youngster, but I will penalise it in a mature dog.

HEAD AND SKULL

The head is the main feature by which owners recognise their dogs. Some breeds, such as Boxers, are described as 'head breeds'. Their Breed Standard goes to great lengths to describe how the head should be. However, a Belgian Shepherd should be, first and foremost, a working dog – he must be sound in mind and construction – therefore, he is not a head breed. The Belgian's head is long, flat, and wedge-shaped. The cheeks are flat, with no excess flesh, and the muzzle tapers to the nose, which should be black.

The skull and the muzzle should be of equal length, with the muzzle being slightly longer, perhaps. When looking at the head from the side, there should be a 'step up' from the line of the muzzle to the forehead. This is known as the 'stop'. When viewed from the side, the forehead should be parallel to an imaginary line extending from the muzzle. The forehead

HEAD AND SKULL

Correct head.

Incorrect: Rounded skull, loose lips.

Incorrect: Too deep.

Incorrect: Too fine, insufficient stop.

THE EYES

Correct: almond-shaped.

Incorrect: Slightly rounded.

is flat, and the skull should be of medium width, not heavy or unbalanced. The muzzle is finely chiselled under the eyes, and the eyebrows are not prominent. The face should be covered with short, fine hair.

Head type differs in the US, with many dogs being considered two heavy or broad in head and skull for most European specialists. This is reflected in the Standards, with the AKC requiring "width approximately the same as, but not wider than the length" and the FCI stating "of medium width, in proportion to the length of head".

EYES

The eyes should be of medium size, slightly almond shaped, set obliquely, and preferably dark brown. If they are a lighter brown, or a yellow colour, they look dreadful (especially in a Groenendael), giving the dog a hard expression. The correct expression should be a direct, enquiring, unwavering look, which melts even the hardest heart.

EARS

These should be of medium length. They should not be as large as a German Shepherd's. The Belgian's ears should be triangular, of "moderate length", and should be set on the top of the head. They should be erect and stiff, not crumpled in any way.

A Belgian Shepherd communicates with his ears. On greeting you, if you are a friend, the ears are pulled back, and the mouth usually splits into a broad grin. If you are not known to the dog, the ears

Correct: well-set, triangular.

Incorrect: tall, high-set.

Incorrect: Small, wide-set.

remain erect, until you have been assessed and your status has been decided. Hair on the outside of the ears is short, with longer hair protecting the opening and the sides of the ear.

The Standards differ regarding ears. The FCI states "proportioned in length." The UK Standard and the AKC Standards for Belgian Sheepdog and Malinois are similar. The AKC Tervuren differs with "height equal to width at base". It is common to see dogs with ears that are too big or too wide at the base of the ear. All AKC Belgian Shepherd Standards agree that "the base of the ear does not come below the centre of the eye".

MOUTH

The mouth should be well split, with thin, dark-pigmented lips. Some dogs lose lip pigment as they mature, and this is considered a fault. The AKC Standard requires "no pink showing on the outside when the mouth is closed", whereas the FCI Standard requires lips to be "strongly pigmented, not showing the red of the mucous membranes".

The Belgian should have 42 strong, white teeth, which are firmly set into the jaws. On the European continent, missing teeth are severely penalised, with dogs being disqualified. A scissor bite is preferable, i.e. the incisors of the top jaw fit snugly over the incisors of the bottom jaw, not dissimilar to a pair of scissors. A level, or pincer, bite, where the jaws meet edge-to-edge, is tolerated and will not be penalised. Interestingly, the original herdsmen pioneers of the breed preferred the level bite.

The AKC Standards differ for mouths. Both the Malinois and Tervuren Standards state "An undershot bite, in which two or more of the upper incisors lose contact with two or more of the lower incisors, is

DENTITION

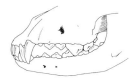 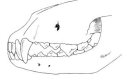 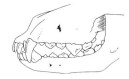 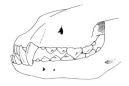

Correct: Scissor bite.   *Permissible: Level bite.*   *Incorrect: Overshot.*   *Incorrect: Undershot.*

a disqualification". This is not mentioned in the AKC Belgian Sheepdog (Groenendael) Standard.

NECK
This should be slightly elongated, broadening towards the shoulders and slightly arched. Dogs with short necks are called "stuffy". Again, a hands-on approach is essential, as a profuse coat can make an otherwise-elegant dog appear stuffy.

FOREQUARTERS
The withers should be distinct. The shoulder blades should be long and flat, with wiry, powerful muscles. The shoulder should be normally angled. If it is too steep, the neck may appear stuffy and the chest too shallow. Legs, when viewed from the front, should be parallel and

FOREQUARTERS

Correct: Well-arched neck, good head carriage.

Correct.

Incorrect: Wide, out at elbow.

Incorrect: Short and stuffy.

Incorrect: Narrow.

Incorrect: Weak pasterns, splayed feet.

Correct stance and conformation.

Incorrect: Flat topline, low underline.

Incorrect: Long, heavy coat, soft topline.

Incorrect: Strongly built, heavy-boned.

Incorrect: Fine-boned, long limbed.

Incorrect: Hunched, timid.

well-muscled, with the feet pointing to the front. Dewclaws are permitted on the front legs. The chest in an animal built for endurance should not be broad, but it must be deep. You should be able to place a minimum of four fingers between the front legs of the dog.

BODY
The body should be powerful and yet still remain elegant. When viewed from the side, the body should appear square – the distance between the point of shoulder to the point of buttocks should be approximately equal to the dog's height at the withers. In bitches, the body may be slightly longer. The ribs should be slightly sprung, but not slab-sided or barrelled. The topline should be straight, with the rump sloping very slightly. The belly should not be well developed, so that it follows the line of the chest in a graceful curve. The deepest point of the rib cage should reach slightly above the elbows.

HINDQUARTERS
Like the forequarters, the hindquarters should be well muscled and powerful. The angulation of the hindquarters should not be excessive. Viewed from behind, the legs should be parallel. Dewclaws should have been removed.

FEET
The feet should be tight, with the toes arched, not slack. The front feet should be round, while the hind feet should be slightly oval. The claws should be dark. A dog that is well exercised will have tight feet, corresponding muscle, and short nails.

TAIL
This should be strong at its base and of medium length. The tip of the tail should

HINDQUARTERS

TAIL CARRIAGE

Correct.

Incorrect: Too high.

Correct.   Incorrect: Cow-hocked.

Incorrect: Too low.   Incorrect: Gay tail.

reach to the top of the hock. The tail should be straight with no kinks in it; kinks are easy to discover, feeling like a knobble on the tail bone. The tail should not deviate to either side, nor should it curl over the dog's back.

Standing at rest, the tail should hang down, with its tip bent slightly backwards at hock level. On the move, the tail should be raised level with the topline, accentuating the curve towards the tip. The tip of the tail may be carried slightly higher than the topline, especially in a class of all-male dogs, where each is trying to show off his masculinity.

MOVEMENT
The UK Standard states "brisk, free and even", which is not very explicit. A dog is often quoted as having "good movement", with many judges believing they know what this means. Every breed has its own movement, and the Belgian is no different. Generally, he should move straight in front, without toeing in or

flicking out his feet; neither should he use his front legs in a hackney fashion. If he is slack in the elbows (i.e. the elbow joints do not lie parallel to the body), he may move wide in front, which looks ungainly. Rear movement should also be straight, with no cow- or barrelled hocks. At slow speeds, a Belgian steps out in a double track, moving to a single track when the pace quickens. He should be light on his feet, covering maximum ground, as an efficient gait means maximum progress.

COAT
There are three separate coat types. The Groenendael and the Tervueren should have a waterproof coat, which is long, straight and abundant, neither silky nor wiry. For both varieties, the hair is long and abundant, being almost ruff-like around the neck, particularly in males. There are fringes of long hair down the back of the forelegs, and long, abundant hair is present on the hindquarters and tail. Males have a longer coat than females.

MOVEMENT (PROFILE)

Correct: Brisk, free, even gait.

MOVEMENT (FRONT)

Correct.

Incorrect: Too wide.

Incorrect: Restricted.

Incorrect: Toeing in.

Incorrect: Crossing.

Incorrect: Hackney action.

Incorrect: Loose elbows, weak pasterns.

Incorrect: Pacing.

The Laekenois coat is harsh and wiry, but not curly.

Like most female mammals, a bitch's appearance is dominated by her hormones. It is common for a bitch to have a heat, followed by a significant moult approximately four months later. There is little point entering a bitch in competition when she has had a moult (known as being 'out of coat'). It will take several months before she returns to being fully coated. Most judges will not penalise a bitch severely for being out of coat, but, all things being equal, a bitch in full coat would win.

Occasionally, some Groenendaels are seen with a reddish tinge running through the coat. Some breeders put this down to climatic conditions (i.e. dogs lying in the sun), and the AKC Standard states that dogs should not be disqualified for this. However, the FCI is not so generous, stating that reddish reflections in the coat, and grey culottes, are a fault.

The Laekenois has an unusual coat, which needs to be felt by any prospective judge. It is harsh, wiry, and dry, and yet not curly. The length of coat should be about 6 cms (2.25 inches) on all parts of the body. There should be hair around the eyes but it should not obscure the eyes – you should be able to see the dog's expression clearly. The muzzle hair should not make the head appear square or heavy. The tail should not be plumed.

The Malinois' hair is very short on the back of his head, on the exterior of his ears, and on the lower parts of his legs. It is generally short all over the dog's body, but it becomes thicker on the tail and around the neck, where it resembles a ridge or collarette. The hindquarters are fringed with longer hair, and the tail is thick and bushy. The tail coat is thick and dense, with a good firm texture and a woolly undercoat.

COLOUR
The Belgian's coat colour is related directly to his coat type. The Groenendael is black, or black with some white. Groenendaels with white hair should have small-to-moderate patches or strips of white on the chest, between the pads of the feet, or on

Chivas Regal v't Belgisch Schoon: A limited patch of white hair is permissable in the Groenendael.

the tips of the hind toes only. Many people are confused when they look at Groenendaels, taking them to be of a great age when they are, in fact, quite young. The reason for this deceptive appearance is due to the Groenendael's propensity to develop 'frosting', which is a grey or white muzzle, at any age. Not all have it when they reach veteran classes at seven years of age, while others look as if they should be

there from the age of four. The Groenendael should not have any grey culottes (large patches of grey hair in the breeches), and a curly or wavy coat is also penalised.

The Tervueren and the Malinois come in all shades of grey through to deep mahogany, with a black overlay and mask. The mask should not extend above the line of the eyes, and the ears should be mostly black. The coat is characteristically double-pigmented, where the tip of each light-coloured hair is blackened. On mature males, this blackening is especially pronounced on the shoulders, the back, and the rib sections. The tail should have a darker or black tip. A small-to-moderate white patch or strip is permitted on the chest, between the pads of the feet, and on the tips of the hind toes. Like the Groenendael, frosting is permitted on the muzzle. Beyond the age of 18 months, a washed-out colour, or a colour that is too black, is undesirable.

Tervueren and Malinois should have a distinct black 'mask', which has a strict minimum of eight visible matching points of pigmentation, the two ears, two upper eyelids, and two upper, and two lower, lips. The AKC Standards for Malinois and Tervuren state "black mask" but give no guidelines as to where it should start or stop. The FCI Standard gives the above eight points, while the UK Standard states "black mask on face not extending above line of eyes".

The Laekenois should be a reddish-fawn colour, with black shading, principally on the muzzle and tail.

6 *THE SHOW RING*

Many Belgian owners express an interest in showing their dogs, but few have the time, or the inclination, to turn it into a reality. For those that enter the world of showing, the lure of winning, or the adrenaline rush of a big win, can be addictive. Many people become so hooked that winning becomes the be-all and end-all of what should be a wonderful hobby. Every dog owner, like any proud parent, thinks that their dog is exceptional, and many a bemused breeder has been told that the pet owner's dog at home is far better than the one that they saw on television competing at Crufts!

In putting your dog up for competition you are asking the judges' opinion, not only of the dog, but of your own handling ability and presentation skills – or lack of them – an opinion which, in some cases, you may not want to hear. However, if you have a genuine interest in the development and appearance of Belgians, if you enjoy competition, and if you are prepared to take criticism of the parts of your dog that you may be unable to change – construction, for example – showing may be for you. A few competition wins, as well as days out in the company of like-minded people, can make this a very enjoyable hobby.

GETTING STARTED

Seek advice from your breeder, or, if he is inexperienced, the owner of the stud dog. No breeder or stud dog owner wants to see an inferior dog, carrying their affix or breeding, competing in the show ring, so their advice should be constructive. If the breeder lives a prohibitive distance away, ask him to recommend someone near you

UK Ch. Ailort Black Adder: You must be confident that you have a dog that is worthy of being exhibited in the ring.
Photo: David Dalton.

who is experienced and compassionate enough to give you an honest, but not brutal, appraisal. Read the Breed Standards carefully, and compare them to your dog. If your dog has disqualifying faults, such as an undershot mouth, or missing testicles, do not waste your time and money – these are major faults and the dog will never be considered for the top awards.

No dog is perfect. The saying 'one man's meat is another man's poison' has never been more accurate when describing the judging of dogs. What may be described as 'lacking substance' by one judge may be considered typical by another. A dog should appreciated for his virtues, not dismissed for his faults.

You will need to learn how to present your dog in the most attractive manner. Ringcraft classes, which are not dissimilar to the basic-training classes you may have attended with your puppy, will teach you the basics of show training.

However, apart from the benefits of socialisation, these classes are only as good as the instructor. Unless the instructor is a breed specialist in Belgian Shepherd Dogs, it is unlikely that he will be familiar with the finer points of the breed, so do not get excited by the opinion he has of your dog. Ringcraft classes should help you to make your choice of show lead, teach you and your dog the basic performance tips, and guide you towards your first show. The rest is down to experience.

SHOW PREPARATION

Do not bath your Belgian in the week prior to the show. This strips the natural oils from the coat, making it soft and fly-away. Instead, give your Belgian a thorough brush-out 48 hours before the show is due to start. Cast a critical eye over your dog and decide if he is in good enough condition to compete.

Organise a show bag – a small hold-all is ideal. You will need entry passes, grooming equipment, polythene bags for picking up dog excrement and grooming waste, a feeding dish and water bowl, and a bottle of water for the dog, because some dogs do not like the taste of unfamiliar water, especially if they are used to soft water. For yourself, you will need a ring clip, the show schedule, a waterproof jacket, and a thermos flask or refreshments. It is also useful, if you live in an inclement climate such as the UK, to keep a pair of wellington boots in the car – most venues turn to liquid mud after downpours of rain.

Entry passes are posted to exhibitors at general Championship shows. Passes usually arrive 10 days before the show. A slip of paper containing the order in which the breeds will be judged, plus known roadworks, etc., is usually included as well. Read this carefully and plan your journey accordingly. On the day of the show, allow yourself plenty of travelling time – there are often weekend roadworks. At general Championship shows, dogs are always judged before bitches, and always in schedule order.

Plan to arrive at the show at least one hour before you are due in the show ring. This will give you and your dog time to settle. Your exhibit number must be prominently displayed when you are in the ring, so the purchase of a special clip for this is a must. Only pre-entered dogs are allowed at these shows, so your entry pass will be checked at the gate. An exhibitor rummaging in his bag to find his pass can cause queues to build up. Have your pass ready for arrival at the gate. You will also need it, for security reasons, to leave the show.

TREATS

Although Belgians are a natural breed, most exhibitors use treats to attract the dog's attention in the ring, making him look alert with his ears pricked up. The most used treat is liver, which even the most laid-back, bored dog usually finds interesting. Many exhibitors have their own recipes, but I find it most successful to boil and then bake the liver, so it is dried and hard. That way, it can be put cleanly into a pocket or bait bag. Remember, if you follow this advice, to empty your pockets – numerous jacket pockets have been eaten by overenthusiastic Belgians, desperate for that last crumb of liver.

HANDLER PRESENTATION

There is no point in spending a great deal of time preparing and presenting your dog if you do not make the same effort with yourself. Watch any judging in progress at a Championship show, and you will spot the prepared handler easily. He will be wearing an outfit that complements the dog, but does not draw away attention from him. For example, if you are showing a Groenendael, do not wear black clothing, as the dog will 'disappear' against you. Light colours set off the Groenendael beautifully, but an overenthusiastic Belgian can have other ideas, leaving you covered with an unattractive safari pattern of paw prints. Make sure you are well prepared. Have an outfit in a suit carrier in the car, so that you can change before entering the show ring. After showing your dog, you can change back again, so that your good clothes are not ruined.

Whatever your choice of outfit, it must be practical. Women should avoid gaping cleavages, and fussy, floaty scarves, which can be off-putting for a nervous dog.

Skirts are suitable only if the hem is not so wide that it hinders the judge's observations when the dog moves around the ring. Shoes must be practical – high heels and platform shoes are impossible on soft grass. Likewise, make sure you have a smart, warm coat. If the show is held in an outdoor venue, and the weather is not favourable, you may have to show your dog in your coat.

RING PREPARATION

On the day of the show, you will need between 20 minutes and half an hour to groom each dog you are exhibiting. Start by brushing all the hair on the dog's body in the wrong direction. Then brush out the rear trousers and tail using the slicker brush. Brush the chest and front from the bottom upwards, towards the chin. Most exhibitors use a water spray on the coat once it has been brushed the wrong way, then the water is massaged into the coat. This sets the coat, making it look fuller. When the coat is almost dry, a final shake from the dog should make every hair fall into place. Never use a comb on the dog's undercoat, unless he is moulting, as this removes too much hair. Belgian Shepherds require no trimming prior to exhibition, except to tidy up the hocks into a smooth line. Lift the dog's back leg, brush the hock hair upward and outward, and trim upwards, so that the outline is not spoilt.

Some trade stands at the shows may sell preparations that 'enhance' the coat. Be wary of buying these, however. It is against UK Kennel Club regulations to use any substance that alters the natural colour, texture, or body of the coat. The UK Kennel Club takes this so seriously that random coat samples are taken from winners to be tested for any banned substance. There are severe penalties for those who are caught.

AWAITING YOUR TURN

Watch some of the previous classes being judged and mentally prepare yourself. Study the level of the ring. Does it slope in one direction? Are there any hollows or dips that may affect the level of your dog's topline if you unsuspectingly stand in one? Observe how the judge organises the ring. On what side are the exhibitors lining up? How is the judge asking the exhibitors to move the dogs? Some judges request a triangle, so they can see the movement both coming and going, observing the dog's topline as he moves across the ring. Others may ask you to move in a straight line. Some judges request that exhibitors line up in the ring in numerical order, others are happy for you to find your own place. At Championship shows your ring numbers are usually on the benches – check if there are two numbers, otherwise collect them in the ring, from the steward.

IN THE RING

Once you enter the show ring, the judge will normally walk past the line of dogs, possibly reassuring the dogs with a light pat. This has two benefits; firstly it gives the judge an idea of the quality of dogs in the class, and secondly it gives the dogs a chance to look at the judge. Some judges may ask for all the dogs to move around the ring together, either once or twice. Again, this is useful for settling the dogs. Do not allow your dog to run up the back of the dog in front. If you are moving much faster than the dog in front, use the corners of the ring to extend your circle. Conversely, if your dog is moving more slowly than the rest, restrict your circle.

Each dog will be examined individually. Stand the dog, making sure that his legs are parallel, and that he is standing straight and square. Practise placing your

The judge will generally start at the front of the dog, assessing the head and skull, and the dentition.

dog's legs if he tends to stand with them out of alignment. To place a foreleg, take hold of the leg near the elbow, so that the dog's weight adjusts with the leg. Adjust the hindlegs by moving them from the hock. Do not stand directly in front of your dog, but slightly to one side, so that the judge can see the dog's front and expression. If you need to gain your dog's attention, use a treat as bait. From years of unintentional practice, my dogs automatically go into a show stand if anyone places a hand in a jacket pocket – in the hope that food might be forthcoming.

THE JUDGE'S VIEW

The judge will view the dog from the front, the side, and the rear, before moving in to 'go over' the dog. Other than to ask the dog's age, and some judges will not do even this, there is no need to make conversation. Do not try to influence the judge by making comments like "Another CC would be nice", which is foolish.

The judge will examine the dog, initially checking for a good mouth, with the required bite, and then checking the shape of the head, the width of the skull, and the colour of eyes, etc., before moving on to the neck, the lay of shoulders, and the body, ending with a testicle check of male dogs. At this point, the judge may step back to take another view of your dog before asking you to move him, so keep your dog's attention. Listen carefully to the judge's requests – there is nothing as annoying as an exhibitor doing the opposite of what a judge has asked.

CORRECT MOVEMENT

When the judge asks you to move your dog, you should try to move in a straight line. Fix your eyes on the point of the ring you are heading towards, so that, hopefully, you will move in a straight line. I remember the well-known all-rounder, Tom Horner, sarcastically commenting that obviously none of the ladies in one class had studied geometry, as none knew what a triangle looked like.

Keep one eye on the dog when you are moving. Are you moving at the right speed? If not, slow down. If your dog starts off moving badly, do not feel ashamed to go back to the start, apologise to the judge, and start again. You only have a few minutes to make an impression on the judge, so it is worth getting it right. On your final move, get ready to bring your dog to a smart stand in front of the judge, before being dismissed to the end of the line.

If you are in a large class, encourage your dog to relax while the other dogs are being examined. Keep a mental note of which dog was first judged, so that you know when to have your dog ready for the final decision by the judge. While the last dog is being examined by the judge,

Ch. Tri Sorts Bold Retainer: A wonderful example of a Belgian Shepherd on the move.

position your dog in a show stand, making sure that you are not crowded or being hemmed in by other exhibitors. Make sure your dog is standing square and looking attentive. The judge will then make a final assessment of the exhibits. Occasionally, they may ask some exhibitors to move their dogs again, before placing the dogs either first to fifth or first to fourth. Once the prize cards have been handed out, unless you have won first or second in the class, you may leave the ring. Congratulate the winner, praise your own dog and leave the ring.

THE JUDGE'S VERDICT

The judge will write a brief critique on the dogs that attained the first and second places. The critique should explain the dogs' virtues and why they won that class. These critiques are usually published in the dog papers, or, if it is a breed show, in the club newsletter. If your dog is entered in subsequent classes under the same judge, you are considered a 'seen dog' and may be directed to the other side of the ring. The procedure is the same, but the steward may ask you to line up according to the awards you have previously won. Dogs that have won a previous class will stand first, followed in order by second place winners, etc. The judge will not handle your dog again but may come back for a second look, checking for qualities such as shoulder placement, etc.

It is common practice to stand your dog while the judge makes his initial assessment, then to relax your dog while the class is being judged. When the judge has examined every exhibit in the class, you will be told to join the line of dogs, while the judge makes his final assessment. Should you be fortunate to win your class, and not to be beaten in any subsequent class, you will be eligible to 'challenge' for Best of Sex. At Championship shows, Challenge Certificates are awarded for both Best of Sex and Reserve Best of Sex (known as CCs and RCCs respectively).

If you attain second place in your class, do not become despondent – you could still be awarded the RCC if the winner of your class is given the CC. At Open All-Breed shows, where you have only a few mixed-sex classes, you will compete for Best of Breed (known as BOB). The next stage is for Best of Breed winners to compete for Best in Group, and then, if they win that honour, for Best in Show. At the conclusion of judging, do not corner the judge and ask their opinion of your dog – your placing should be self-explanatory.

THE GOOD LOSER
As your experience grows, you will discover some so-called 'experts', who will always voice their opinion as to which dog will win. These 'experts' will have an opinion (usually derogatory) against the judge or other exhibitors, unless they have won – in which case, the judge did a good

UK Ch. Out Of The Gloom: This dog was found wandering as a stray and was eventually traced. With his new owner Helen Fletcher, he went on to win 21 CCs and numerous Group placings.

job! The usual comment is that the judging was 'facey', which means that only top names won the classes. However, these 'facey' people have been in the breed for numerous years, and only show very good dogs, which is why they often win! They are often very good handlers and can present their dog to advantage, something that is learnt only with experience.

There are, of course, some judges who are incompetent, who appear to be unable to see when a dog is severely lame, who make a habit of letting their best friends win, or who generally make some very strange decisions.

However, if you are really dissatisfied, you have the option not to exhibit under them again. Whatever your feelings, keep them to yourself, and make sure that your displeasure on leaving the ring cardless does not show on your face, as other exhibitors will take great delight in reporting that you are a bad loser.

7 THE WORKING BELGIAN SHEPHERD

Working Belgian Shepherds can be divided into two groups, those that 'work for a living' (e.g. service dogs), and those that accompany their owners in dog sports (e.g. Agility, Obedience or Working Trials). The Belgian Shepherd has been well established as a forces dog in both America and Europe, but, in the UK, the breed has been less well taken up by the armed services and police. Belgians have been bred in the UK for more than 30 years, but it is only within the last decade that the breed has been taken seriously by Her Majesty's Forces. Elsewhere, the versatility of the Belgian knows no bounds, with the breed being utilised as search and rescue dogs, assistance dogs, herding dogs, and bomb disposal dogs, as well as taking top awards in almost every form of competition, be it Working Trials, Agility, Flyball, Obedience or jumping competitions.

THE POPULAR MALINOIS
The Malinois is by far the most popular international choice of Belgian Shepherd, being used extensively across the continent, the US and by several police forces in the UK. The working Malinois tends to be more 'highly-strung' than the other varieties of Belgian, but his high energy level gives him a tremendous drive and enthusiasm. The harnessing of this energy, strength, and agility, has resulted in an outstanding working dog, as can be shown by the number of police and military organisations throughout the world that now use Malinois as field service dogs.

In the US, the Malinois is a commonly seen breed, working alongside police officers in a variety of roles, such as explosives dogs that are trained to sniff out incendiary devices, and drug dogs and Customs and Excise dogs that are trained

Rusty from Montgomery Police Department, US, handled by Sharon Sparks Burke.

85

Members of the South Pasadena Police Department with their general-patrol dog.

to find illegal substances or contraband. The police general-patrol dog is trained for a variety of roles, from accosting dangerous suspects, to tracking either criminals or vulnerable missing persons, and even tackling armed suspects. In France, the anti-terrorist squad use Malinois working in pairs to disarm any armed suspects.

NARCOTICS DOGS
In the US, Sharon Burke works with her Malinois partner Rusty, a Belgian trained in both patrol and narcotics work. Together, they work four 10-hour shifts with three days off, and they spend a day retraining every three weeks. When Rusty is not working he is part of Sharon's household, living and sharing her home with her other dogs. In the last eight years, Rusty has been responsible for more than 150 arrests and has recovered more than $1,000,000 worth of drugs. Such are Rusty's skills that he has found 40 lbs (18 kgs) of marijuana – wrapped in plastic, and packed in rose petals inside a locked trunk that had been covered by a

blanket and locked into a cupboard. He has also captured suspects hiding in a wooded area after an unsuccessful car theft, during which the thieves had shot and killed the owner of the car and wounded his companion. On his retirement Rusty will continue to live with Sharon, and the bond of trust and love that has been built between them will continue.

POLICE DOGS
In the UK, the police have been slow to recognise the working capability of the Belgian Shepherd, preferring the heavier-boned German Shepherd. This is slowly changing, and several forces in the south of England are now successfully working Malinois. Thames Valley Police were the first police force in the UK to train a Malinois. Sabrefield Time Traveler, or Jack

PC Stuart Brace from Thames Valley Police with Jack (Sabrefield Time Traveler.

UK Ministry of Defence Police Dog, Sabrefield Quire Master, wearing his camera.

Sabrefield Quire Master displaying his agility skills.

as he is better known, was introduced to his handler, and, after a basic course lasting several weeks at the force's training centre, went on his first patrol. Within minutes of starting work, Jack and his handler, PC Stuart Brace, were informed of a robbery that had just taken place, in which a woman's handbag had been snatched. The youth involved had made his way from the crime scene on foot. Within four minutes, Jack apprehended the alleged thief, who was immediately arrested. The success of Jack, and other Malinois like him, has led to many other police forces changing from a German Shepherd-only policy to one including the Belgian.

Another Malinois, Sabrefield Quire Master, works for the Ministry of Defence Police. He shot to national fame when he took part in the Royal Tournament, which is held annually at Earls Court in London. During his demonstration, he wore a video camera strapped to his head while he completed an Agility course. The images were then transmitted to a large

screen for the audience to see a dog's eye view of proceedings. The video camera, developed by Cambridge Police, allows the dog to work independently, with the handler able to watch a monitor and to control the dog as necessary. This has significant potential for use in dangerous conditions or for gaining entry to areas not easily accessible to the handler.

SEARCH AND RESCUE BELGIANS
In Europe, all varieties of Belgian are used as search and rescue dogs, being preferred to the German Shepherd Dog and the Border Collie. One dog can swiftly cover an area that would take humans several hours to search. Detection rates are also increased dramatically. The warm, waterproof coat of the Belgian, combined with his strength and stamina, make him ideal for search and rescue work. Furthermore, the dog locates people using scent detection, which means he is able to work at night equally as well as during the day. Search dogs are able to locate bodies in up to 3 metres (10 feet) of snow.

Royal Air Force Groenendael, Ailort Corporate Image.

out of helicopters in hazardous conditions. The training is hard on both dog and handler, with only 25 per cent of dogs making the grade. Training is done on a reward basis, using hide and seek games with gradually increased time periods between 'finds'. Equally important is the 'negative find' or no result, as this shows the handler the strength of the dog's motivation. The ideal dog will continue to search even without success, because, to him, to find is sufficient reward, and he will keep on looking. Other dogs, which search to please their handler, may produce false finds, hoping for the reward. Dogs can also be trained for 'catastrophe' work, such as avalanches or earthquakes.

MOUNTAIN RESCUE
In Scotland, Belgians have been used for

Both dogs and bitches can be trained for search and rescue work. However, dogs are preferred, due to the hormonal changes that occur in bitches. Dogs should be at least one year old before training starts, to allow them to develop both physically and mentally. They must have basic obedience skills, be sociable with people and dogs, and be totally trustworthy with livestock, as deer and sheep abound in most mountainous regions.

The Belgian must be of sound temperament and be highly adaptable – the dog may need to be winched in and

Viroflay Anitra, the first UK Groenendael to be Search and Rescue qualified. She is pictured as she passed her tests in 1969.

some years as search and rescue dogs. The first one was Viroflay Anitra, bred by Jack and Doreen Bushby, and used by Glencoe Mountain Rescue, first qualifying in 1969. More recently, the Royal Air Force Mountain Rescue have successfully worked a Groenendael, Ailort Corporate Image, or Gun as he is also known. Gun has now passed all his exams and is available on a permanent call-out basis with his handler Dave Wilcox. Other Belgians are used by SARDA (Search and Rescue Dog Association), but these dogs are owned by volunteer civilian mountain rescuers.

MILITARY DUTY DOGS

In Sweden, dogs can compete to gain their tracking and search and rescue title of TJH. The test consists of several parts, for which training can take months or even years to complete. Once a pass has been gained, the handlers can be contracted to the Army on a call-out basis. Their duties include patrolling an area to seek out intruders, or following the tracks of missing or vulnerable persons. This work should be differentiated from search and rescue work. Working dogs with their TJH qualification must refrain from barking, as this would let the 'enemies' be warned. Therefore, 'noisy' dogs are not suited to this work.

Dogs that successfully pass the TJH course receive a certificate or CC for 'duty' dogs. In Sweden and other European countries, many dogs are now trained using a special leather collar called a Bringsel Alert, which consists of a rolled-up piece of cloth, or leather, which is fastened to the collar. When the dog finds a person, he will either return to the handler with the bringsel in his mouth, or bark to attract the handler's attention to the fact that something has been found.

Fakaisers Nowak d'Nuit, the first Belgian to be accepted into the Marine Corps in Sweden.

Swedish Working Dog, Our Turf K.A.

Therior's Red Baron: the first Tervueren to gain his herding trial championship.

MARINE CORPS
In Sweden, a Groenendael, Fakaisers Nowak d'Nuit, was the first Belgian Shepherd to pass the test to become certified to work with the Swedish Marines. The dog is loaned to the Marine Corps to act as a watchdog for several weeks a year. There are currently 22 privately owned dogs that have passed this test. The dog's skills include being able to indicate the scent of people hiding on an island when being taken round the island by boat. The dog must also be able to follow long tracks and to detect movement at distances of 200 metres (220 yards). To be accepted for this training, a dog must be highly sociable, and capable of working with different handlers on every assignment. He must not react to any form of noise, and he must not be gun-shy, as the soldiers, both in training and on active duty, may do some shooting. Not only has Fakaisers Nowak d'Nuit obtained his working qualifications, but he has also gained his Swedish and Finland show titles.

HERDING
Although the Belgian was originally used as a herding dog, there are few Belgians that still remain working sheep. However, some European breed shows and American Specialties hold herding competitions specifically for the breed, where novice dogs and handlers can also try their hand at this aspect of working a Belgian. In the US, the American Belgian Tervuren Club established the herding certificate in an attempt to encourage and to continue the herding instincts of the Belgian.

In 1986, the American Australian Shepherd Club of America started issuing herding titles to breeds other than their own, followed in 1990 by the American Kennel Club's own version of a herding competition and the issue of the AKC herding title. To date, few Belgians have won the title of American Kennel Club Herding Trial Champion. Those that have are, according to breed:
• Tervueren: Ch. and Herding Ch. Therior's Red Baron, H Ch. Snowflower Diamond Tiara, and H Ch. Snowflower California Girl.

Peggy Richter and her top herding Groenendael Nyel.

• Groenendael: H Ch. Rigelde Breeze, and Ch. and H Ch. Bonntyme Diamond Solitaire.

FILM STARS

Few Belgian enthusiasts can have failed to spot their favourite breed working as a stunt dog on television. In the 1980s, *The Company of Wolves*, a Red Riding Hood-based horror movie, was filmed in Britain, with Tervueren taking the part of wolves. They were sprayed grey with vegetable dye. The lead dog in this film was Wings – Kyan Without Wings of Minka. Her skills were impressive, and included jumping through a glass window. She appeared in numerous productions, including *Precious Bane*, *All Creatures Great and Small*, and *Oliver Twist*.

A talented Agility dog, she appeared at the Agility finals in Olympia three times, as well as winning her Working Trials

The multi-talented Wellard (Minack Edgemont Chancer).

awards: Companion Dog Excellent, (CDEX), Working Dog Excellent (WDEX) and Police Dog Excellent (PDEX).

Her half-sister, Kyan Vision of Minka, joined her in *The Company of Wolves* and *All Creatures Great and Small*. More recently, Minka Independence has taken the lead roles in *A Touch of Frost* and *Peak Practice* as well as the popular *Gladiators*.

Another famous TV dog, from the same kennel, is Wellard, starring in the popular UK TV soap *Eastenders*. Supposedly a mongrel dog, she is actually a Tervueren bitch, Minack Edgemont Chancer. She has also appeared in *999*, *101 Dalmatians* and *102 Dalmatians*. Chancer is not only a top Agility dog but she has further proven her worth as a brood bitch, with her children and grandchildren now doing well in Working Trials, Agility and Obedience.

Kyan Vision Of Minka with Christopher Timothy, who was her co-star in 'All Creatures Great And Small'.

Mary Ray and Ch. Minack Red Aral winning the Obedience CC at Crufts.

WORKING FOR FUN

On the 'fun' working side in the UK, Belgians have excelled in Obedience, Working Trials, Flyball and Agility. There have been several Tervueren Obedience Champions – all bitches – the most famous being Mary Ray's Ch. Minack Red Aral, winner of an incredible 19 Obedience Challenge Certificates, including Crufts. There is only one Groenendael Obedience Champion in the UK and that is Sarah Delaney's Obedience Champion Vanistica Gideon's Moon. With several youngsters working their way up the Obedience ladder, the list will soon be extended.

In Eire, Rosemary Daly's Groenendael Ir. Ch. and Obedience Ch. Stargazer at Leircote is one of the few dogs to hold joint titles in both breed and Obedience.

FLYBALL

Flyball is an up-and-coming sport in Europe. The dog goes away from his handler, jumping over a set of hurdles. At the end is a machine, which has a pedal the dog must depress. This releases a ball. The dog must catch the ball, and return, over the hurdles, to his handler. Once the dog has completed this, another dog is released, to run the course in the same way. The event is timed, with the fastest relay team winning. In the UK, two Belgian teams have done extremely well, winning major competitions; a Groenendael team run by Anne Challis called The Jets, and an all-Malinois team bred by the Sabrefield kennel. The sport has also become very popular in both Europe and the US, with many Belgians competing at the top level.

AGILITY AND JUMPING

Agility has surged in popularity in the UK and Europe, with up to 1,000 dogs being entered in some classes. Although the Border Collie breed tends to dominate this sport, several Belgians have made their mark. Working at the advanced level in the UK, there are currently two Tervueren Agility dogs: Talamo Pandemonium, owned by Phil Hicks, and Dream Crystal of Delark, owned by Bruce Newman.

Agility dogs are not allowed to compete until they are 18 months old and fully developed. Classes are divided into starter, novice and senior. A course is set up by the judge and will consist of jumps, A-frames, dog walks, etc. Contact points are clearly marked on the equipment and the dogs are faulted if they miss these. The UK Kennel Club is currently looking at ways to award Agility Championship status, with titles being awarded to the winners of senior Agility.

Jumping competitions are also gaining popularity. They differ from Agility in that there are no contact points, and they are merely a speed competition.

Highly-trained Agility competitors, based in Hungary.

Up and over: Agility is a sport enjoyed by dogs and owners alike.

Ch. HR Legacy's Mountain Sprite UDT, Schh3, FH, AD, OA: All-round top working dog, owned by Denise Fenzi, with titles in tracking, Agility, endurance, and Schutzhund – as well as his breed title.

CHARACTER ASSESSMENT

Over the last two decades, the position of the dog in society has changed beyond all recognition. No longer is the dog automatically regarded as 'man's best friend'. The surge in the anti-dog lobby in the UK and Europe, and the 1991 British Dangerous Dogs Act, has produced media coverage that has vilified the dog owner. The importance of breeding dogs with sound temperaments has never been greater, and many owners now put their dogs through a character assessment.

The late Terry McHaffie began performing character assessments in the UK in 1981. He discovered that, as a breed, the Belgian Shepherd is more sensitive than the German Shepherd, but this is no excuse for poor temperament. Character assessments have proven to be popular, and there are now several accredited examiners throughout the UK.

Character assessments are a series of exercises, which are not designed to assess the owner's ability as a handler or trainer, but to observe how the dog behaves in everyday settings – is he friendly, reserved, or confident? The exercises consist of a friendly approach, an unusual approach, reaction to traffic, an unusual obstacle, a noise test, reaction to being left alone, and reaction to a crowd and to other animals. The examiners grade the dogs according to their recovery rate, i.e. on the noise test they would not be marked down if they were startled but then immediately recovered. Many owners are still reluctant to put their dogs in for this, believing that the examiners are trying to trick the dogs, but this is far from the case. The whole experience is great fun, and can be very enlightening.

ASSISTANCE DOGS

Belgian Shepherds are becoming increasingly used as assistance dogs, although their numbers are still small in comparison to the many Golden Retrievers and Labradors that have been successfully used for some years. Although

The first group of Assistance Dogs in Hungary.

An Assistance Dog at work, bringing the wheelchair to his owner.

Belgians have been used in the US as assistance dogs for many years, they have only recently been recognised globally for their versatility.

In 1999, an assistance dog training programme was established in Hungary, with Tervueren as the main breed. Disabled people in wheelchairs may be seen as vulnerable by the criminal element, and, sadly, many are robbed. Taking this into consideration, the Belgian Shepherd seems an obvious choice – his trainability and his impressive looks should dissuade any potential attacker.

Assisstance dogs are chosen as puppies, and are sent to live with puppy walkers, who house-train them and teach them basic obedience until they are 12 to 18 months old. At this age, specialised training begins, which can take from 12 to 18 months. All training is based on play, with the dogs learning a variety of tasks, including assisting with the removal of socks and shoes, pulling down zipper fastenings, lifting items from shelves, and even rolling their owner into the recovery position.

HEARING DOGS

The ideal Hearing Dog has a positive, fearless reaction to sounds, and yet still reacts to some stimuli. He must have a low, or non-existent, level of aggression and fearfulness, and yet have an easily triggered, friendly and excited reaction to people and to places. Although, in the US, most varieties of Belgian Shepherd are used as Hearing Dogs, these are trained and selected by their own owners rather than by any organisation.

The Malinois usually has the sort of temperament that reacts strongly to stimuli and has a low threshold for triggering reactions. This can be both beneficial and detrimental for Hearing

Dog work. The beneficial aspect is that these dogs react to sounds with a fascinated, investigative reaction, not a fearful one. Selection for Schutzhund and ring sport, in which the dog must work confidently during gunfire, has apparently resulted in working-bred Malinois showing far less fear of sounds than the other varieties of Belgian Shepherd. This positive reaction to sound makes it easy to train a dog in sound alerting, using praise, treats and games, so that he becomes used to household sounds which are normal, and those which are not. Once this happens, sound alerting becomes the high point of the dog's day and he is eager to interrupt his normal daily activities, even waking up from a deep sleep to alert his owner to sounds. The dogs are taught to nudge their human with their nose, or to touch them with a paw, combined with running back and forth to lead the human partner to the sound.

The Malinois' reaction to sound can prove detrimental if there is any fearfulness or aggression in the dog's temperament. How he reacts to stimuli that trigger the negative side of his character may mean he is unsuitable to work in any place to which the public have access, as well as being a challenge to manage in pet situations by all but experienced dog trainers.

Any assistance dog must be able to react appropriately in public situations that are more difficult, and last far longer, than the most rigorous temperament tests. A test would never include putting the dog under stress for several hours, or having a stranger stepping hard on the dog's tail, or a toddler screaming at, and grabbing for, the dog and refusing to let go, or continuous loud noises, such as fireworks or brass bands. Yet these are some of the things that all types of assistance dogs need to have a cheerful, stress-free approach to.

SERVICE DOGS

American service dog users have greater access rights than their British counterparts. The Americans With Disabilities Act allows all service animals – not just guide dogs – the right to accompany their owners everywhere, including restaurants, stores, medical facilities, supermarkets, and public transportation, including aeroplanes.

Disabled people acquire their service dogs in several ways. They can obtain a trained dog from a training programme, although there are frequently very long waiting lists involved with this route – years in some cases. The disabled person is also often required to pay hundreds, if not thousands, of dollars for the dog.

Alternatively, the disabled person can hire a trainer to train a dog, or they can train their own dog. There is no requirement for certification for a service dog in the US, and, in fact, it is illegal to ask for any. The only questions that someone can legally ask is "Are you disabled?" and "Is that a service dog?". They cannot ask questions about the person's disability, nor can they ask for any proof that the person is disabled or that the dog is a service dog.

Laurie Graichen, of Sky High Belgian Shepherd Dogs in South Carolina, chose to train her own service dogs. She wanted a dog with the temperament to be a competition and performance dog (e.g. in Obedience, Agility and Herding). Such dogs are often too difficult to train for the average pet owner, and would, therefore, have been rejected from most service dog programmes. She also required a dog with breed type and structure suitable to show in the conformation ring. Laurie considers that Belgians, as a whole, tend to notice more than other, 'traditional' service dog breeds, and their handler/trainer has to realise this and plan for how to deal with it.

Laurie has two young Belgian Shepherds, both of the Tervueren variety. The oldest is two-year-old Dillon, whose registered name is Am. Ch. Arlequin Debonair of Hyline, Am. NA, HIC CGC and Tdi. His titles indicate an AKC conformation Championship, AKC Novice-standard Agility title, the herding-instinct certificate (he should have his pre-trial AKC herding title soon) and a Canine Good Citizen and Therapy Dog International. The latter certifies him to visit nursing homes and hospitals as a pet therapy dog. Her younger male is the 15-month-old Bravo, formally known as Klaar Right on the Money, HIC. He is learning Obedience, Herding and Agility. Interestingly, both dogs have British ties – Dillon's paternal grandsire is Corsini Aragon, and Bravo's paternal granddam is Ombre de la Quiviere, leased by Amanda McLaren to produce the Corsini 'G' litter.

Although she starts basic obedience and 'public manners' training as soon as she gets a dog, Laurie did not start real service dog training with Dillon until he was 18 months old, as he still had that teenage Belgian mind, and the attention span of a gnat. To overcome these Belgian characteristics, Laurie uses positive reinforcement and clicker training – she finds it is the most effective way to train a Belgian as a working partner. She also finds it a great tool to overcome some of the strange behavioural phases that Belgian puppies go through.

Her dogs are mobility dogs, trained to assist her up and down the stairs, to help her to get up from being seated, and to pick up or retrieve things that she drops or cannot reach. Laurie says that "life with a Service Dog is not a life for the weak-willed or shy person – if you start out that way, you will not stay that way for long! A dog is an instant people magnet, and a dog in a place where dogs are not normally allowed draws all kinds of attention, from people who want to pet the dog, people who bombard you with questions, and people who want to know how dare you bring a dog in here? Sad to say, even though the Americans with Disabilities Act was passed 10 years ago, American Service Dog users (especially those with 'invisible' disabilities – that is, those who are not in wheelchairs, or do not use crutches or canes) are still being challenged as to our right to be accompanied everywhere by our dogs.

"You will also find that there is an astonishingly large percentage of the population who apparently cannot read. They will walk up to Dillon and start petting him, with their hand only inches from his 'Please Don't Pet Me, I'm Working' patch. When using a Belgian as a Service Dog, you also have to be prepared for the question 'He's a Collie-cross, right?' Or 'I have a German Shepherd too' and even 'Is he part wolf?' There is also a portion of the population who seem to be terrified of dogs, and will scream and leap away as soon as they see a Belgian – and they wonder why they have been bitten by other dogs!"

SLED DOGS
Some people compete in sprint sled dog racing over distances of 4 to 50 miles and some do skijoring (where a dog pulls a person on cross-country skis for a set distance, or uses rollerblades or wheeled 'rigs' in non-show areas). There are also long-distance endurance races, which range from 100 miles to 500 miles.

Rob Greger and his team in training.

Rob Greger from Montana regularly takes part in these races. He races Groenendaels along with a team of Alaskan Huskies – a non-registered breed – a combination created specially for sled dog racing. Training starts at around nine months of age, working on short distances and with no weights, and is gradually built up. The herding instinct in Belgians naturally makes them move in circles; it can be difficult to overcome this instinct. However, Rob maintains: "Once you take the time to explain what you want them to do, they do it with all their heart."

The Race to the Sky, which is over 350 miles, is considered to be one of the most difficult races in the US, up dangerous, steep terrain. It is deemed significantly more challenging than the famous Iditarod, which, although it is much longer, is held mainly on flat terrain. Rob Greger's team has up to four Groenendaels, Ch. Kaori's Eagle Venture, Ch. Starwind's Aura de la Onyx, Ch. Starwind's Alexis in Ebony, Ch. Anduril's Lady Eowyn CD (whose three progeny out of Zachary are currently in training

with the team), Starwind's Zachary CD, and Tervueren littermates Ch. Starwind's Feather and Starwind's Koing North. The team participated in the Race to the Sky in Montana in 1995, achieving a creditable seventh place. In 1996, they were placed second. In the 500-mile Minnesota Beargrease in 1998 they were placed eleventh. Considering that the team covers 200 miles in less than 48 hours, it makes one appreciate the versatility of the Belgian Shepherd to excel in something they do not have an inherent instinct for. Even if you own just one or two dogs, winter sledding and skijoring can be a great sport for you and your Belgian to enjoy together.

WORKING TRIALS

In Working Trials, ring sport, KNPV and Schutzhund, the general aim is to produce as good a working dog as possible, and Belgian Shepherds of all varieties excel at this. The responsibility of the handler is to produce an animal that is stable and confident, but most important of all, disciplined. The dog should be a trusted companion, and, because of the type of training and varied experiences he is regularly exposed to, he should achieve

UK Ch. Alcyon Comet CDEX. UDEX, WD, owned by Mo Glenton. He was the first breed Champion to hold working titles. Photo: Dalton.

discipline and stability, but still be fun to live with.

In British Working Trials, any dog must be a minimum of 18 months old before he is eligible to compete. There are Open Trials where the dog can gain Certificate of Merit, and Championship Trials, where qualifying certificates can be gained, including Companion stake, Utility Dog stake, Working and Tracking Dog stakes, and Patrol Dog stake.

RING SPORT AND SCHUTZHUND
Ring sport, and to some extent, Schutzhund, tend to be held in more restricted venues, such as sports stadiums or purpose-built fields that have their own clubhouse and special facilities.

RING SPORT
Ring sport is a worldwide style of training, which originated in Europe, mainly in France, Belgium and Holland. Compared to Schutzhund, the work of the dog in ring sport tends to be less

formalised. As in Working Trials, the dog is independent, and with the bite work, he is permitted to hold the helper anywhere, as the helper is wearing a full bodysuit. Unlike Working Trials and Schutzhund, there is no tracking.

In ring sport, the dog can heel on the left or right, he can recall in any position near the handler (front, side, between the legs, sit down, etc.) and he can escort the helper in any position. The emphasis is on getting the job done correctly, rather than on how this is accomplished. Although the control seems flexible, the marking and rules are strict, especially at level III.

When the dog is competing, apart from the heel on lead exercise, the dog has no lead or collar on at any time. Food rewards cannot be used, nor can any physical corrections or excessive praise. A round of ring sport can last from 20 minutes for a novice dog, to an hour for level-III dogs.

As in Working Trials, the ring sport dog

US Groenendael Megaspirits Action Reaction pictured during Schutzhund training.

must show an excellent level of control, independence, and bravery. The control exercises involve heeling on lead, heeling off lead with a muzzle, sit or down stays, food refusal, a high jump (one metre/six feet), a palisade (up to two to three metres/six to ten feet), a long jump (four to five metres/thirteen to sixteen feet), positions, seen and unseen retrieves, and a sendaway.

The patrol work exercises involve a face attack (test of courage), a fleeing attack (chase), defence of the handler, facing an attack with a gun, a search hold and bark with an escort, a stopped attack, and the guarding of an object. In this fascinating exercise the dog is told to guard an object. The handler then moves out of sight. The helper, or decoy, tries three times to steal the object. The dog must guard the object by biting the helper if he gets too near, but release him before he is lured too far away from the object he is guarding. The order of these exercises is drawn at the start of the competition, and, therefore, appear at random.

SCHUTZHUND

Schutzhund emerged at the same time as ring sport and the Dutch KNPV. Schutzhund was originally developed as a temperament and breed-suitability test for the German Shepherd Dog. It has developed over many years into an international sport, and it is now worked by dogs of many different breeds. Tracking, Obedience and protection work are the three areas tested in a Schutzhund trial, requiring the dog to have courage, endurance, and a willingness to work.

In Schutzhund, there is a formal order of events, and, like Working Trials, nosework is an important part of the test. As in all of these sports, the levels of achievement are graded. In Schutzhund, the dogs begin with a general companion dog level of work (known as BH), and then move on to Shutzhund levels I to III. On achieving level III, many dogs compete repetitively to attain the highest score they can. The aim is to compete in the national finals. There is also an advanced tracking title.

8 BREEDING A LITTER

Most people who consider breeding a litter of puppies have an image of cute puppies (requiring little input from the human owner) snuggling into their contented mother. Making lots of money from the sale of these puppies, having dogs that they bred taking top honours in the show ring (which, in their opinion, will make them doyens of the breed and respected by other exhibitors); these are all parts of the dream. If only it were so easy...

UK Ch. Valson Skol with his daughters Valson Mirage and Valson Curaco. The aim of every breeder is to produce typical specimens that are sound in mind and body.
Photo: David Dalton.

BREEDER RESPONSIBILITIES

To start with, you, as the breeder, are responsible for these puppies for the rest of their lives, not just for the eight weeks they reside with you. A puppy has to be of merchandisable quality – breeders can be sued at any time in the dog's life if it can be proved that the necessary steps were not taken to health-check the breeding stock and to check for hereditary illnesses. You must be in a position to retrieve and to rehome your dogs if required. I had three puppies back within a year from my first litter, all through no fault of the dogs. Although breeders' circumstances can change, and you may not always be in a position to take back one of your dogs, it is not acceptable to expect the burden to fall on Belgian Shepherd Rescue.

BREEDING EXPENSES

Many people assume that dog breeding is exceedingly profitable, and, indeed, some people make a living from it. However, if you put in the necessary time and effort, you will make very little profit indeed.

Hip-scoring and eye-testing your bitch is expensive. The cost of a stud fee can be equated to the price of one puppy. There are also veterinary fees, registration fees, the cost of feeding both mother and puppies, and other ancillary expenses (e.g. new fleecy blankets for the puppies, the whelping box, and printed kennel stationery). The cost of rearing a litter can be equated to the purchase price of four puppies. With an average litter size of six, little room is left for profit, and any profits made will not reflect the hours of care that you have put in.

TIME COMMITMENTS

Do you work? Can you take at least four weeks leave to be there for the bitch? If not, can you afford to pay someone to be available so the bitch is not left alone? You will need somewhere quiet in the house for the whelping, where the bitch can be left undisturbed, feeling secure. I use a spare bedroom, but I have had to replace the carpet, where the bitch tried to dig in a corner and make her own nest, and then, after the birth, stained the carpet when she had diarrhoea during the night.

As the puppies get older, friends and prospective purchasers will want to visit the puppies. Although I try to encourage people to visit – it is excellent for socialisation – it is exhausting. It is also embarrassing to have your house stinking of disinfectant, while you are left feeling permanently dishevelled as you take on the role of canine lavatory attendant wearing your oldest, tattiest clothes.

When, eventually, the puppies are sold, you will find that you can rarely sit down to a meal in the evenings without the telephone ringing with a proud owner telling you how wonderful Teddy is and how he barked for the first time tonight. Any responsible breeder should encourage owners to keep in touch. Indeed, if they do not keep in touch with me, I keep in touch with them. However, you will find that new owners call when you are sitting down to eat – a microwave is essential!

UK Ch. Ir. Ch. Leircote Freyja Of Ailort: The bitch must be tested clear of all inherited conditions. Photo: Jan Ralph.

BITCH QUALITY

Any bitch used for breeding should be hip-scored, and have received a score not above the breed average (currently 12). She should also have passed the eye tests for juvenile cataract and should have a first-class temperament. Ideally, she should have been character-assessed, and either passed or gained an excellent. She should also have had some success in the show or working rings, and be a minimum age of two years.

Research the bitch's family, especially for epilepsy. If possible, speak to other exhibitors who own her siblings; find out if they have experienced any health problems. Your breeder should be the first point of call, and will, hopefully, tell you all they know. Some Belgian Shepherd lines have a problem with epilepsy, and sadly, some breeders and owners have a 'head in the sand' attitude that does not assist anyone.

If you are contemplating breeding to gain another puppy like your bitch, go back to the breeder and purchase another dog from the same line. Compared to breeding a litter, this will work out far cheaper, with less heartache.

The aim of any breeder should be to produce puppies that have the characteristics typical of the breed, are of sound construction, health, and temperament, and that are of superior quality to your bitch – the purpose is to improve the breed.

BREEDING CHOICES

Your choice of stud dog will reflect the type of breeding practice that you want to follow. There are three main types.

LINE BREEDING

This is when two related dogs are mated (e.g. grandfather to granddaughter, or cousins). It is commonly used among breeds that have an outstanding and influential dog. Line breeding doubles up the number of shared genes, so that the resulting puppies should be more uniform in appearance. However, although good qualities can be strengthened, so can the negatives. Line breeders must have extensive knowledge of the virtues and failings of each animal bred from, as well as the several generations of dogs in each dog's pedigree. When line breeding is successfully carried out, over several generations, it stamps type into the line, making the dogs instantly recognisable.

OUTCROSSING

This is when two unrelated dogs are mated. General improvements, and breed charateristics that are absent, can be introduced using outcrossing. However, it is far easier to introduce faults than virtues. Often, puppies produced from an outcross can have more variation in type. However, Belgian Shepherds originate from a small gene pool, and, although comparison of a three-generation pedigree may show no commonalities, further investigation may reveal some surprising common ancestors.

INBREEDING

This is when two closely related dogs are mated (e.g. mother and son, or brother to sister). It can be used to produce and to develop a strong breed type, but, like line breeding, it can also bring out unwanted characteristics that may have been previously unknown. This form of breeding is rarely used in Belgian Shepherds and should only be undertaken with great care.

STUD DOGS

Although any entire male dog can be used

UK Ch. Domburg Sweet Talking Guy: A good stud dog stamps his mark on puppies from different bitches.
Photo: Linda Collins.

at stud, a good stud dog is one that stamps his finer qualities on a number of puppies from different bitches. If your bitch is slightly long in the loin, do not choose an ultra-short stud dog expecting all the puppies to balance somewhere in between. The likelihood is that some puppies will carry the bitch's faults, some will carry the stud dog's faults, and only one or two will display the ideal balance.

Choosing a stud dog should be based on research. You will need to know about the stud's background, to understand what his father's shortcomings were. There is a tendency for many new breeders to use the latest import. However, you have only the owner's word on his pedigree. Old-timers in breeding say that, if you really like a dog, use his father, as it is already proven that he can produce quality puppies.

Make sure the stud dog has been health-tested, and that he is of excellent temperament. Ideally, he should have been used already at stud, and you should have seen his progeny from more than one bitch. Do not be misled by some breeders who do not hip-score and eye-test, insisting that their stock is 'healthy'. The only way that a dog can be assessed is by veterinary examination, which, especially when X-raying for hip dysplasia, is costly. If breeders do not have sufficient interest in the health of the breed to carry out these basic checks, they do not deserve to be part of their future.

STUD FEES
Much confusion and bitterness can arise from disagreement over what the stud fee covers. You are paying for the dog's service, and, even if the bitch does not become pregnant, you are not entitled to your money back. Common practice is that you are entitled to a further mating, with the same bitch, when she is next in season. However, if no puppies are forthcoming on this attempt, you have lost your money.

Some stud dog owners may ask for a puppy in lieu of the stud fee. This should be agreed, prior to mating, in writing. Is the stud dog owner entitled to pick of the litter, or his pick of dogs or bitches? What if there are no live puppies, or only one puppy? The only safeguard is to have a written contract.

STUD DOG OWNER
Once you have decided on your choice of stud dog, contact the owner well in advance and ask if the dog is available at

stud. Expect to be asked for details about your bitch's pedigree and her health-check results, whether you have any bookings for the potential puppies, and whether you intend to keep any yourself. The stud dog owner may want to view the bitch prior to making a decision, to see if the bitch will suit their dog.

Some stud dog owners may insist that your bitch has a vaginal swab to ensure that she is free of sexually transmitted infections. There are numerous bacterial infections that can be found high up in the vagina and uterus. Most of these come from the streptococcus family. One of the most common, Beta haemolytic streptococci, can impair fertility. Most bitches, when they urinate, squat very low to the ground and this is when the bacteria can be transmitted, so even maiden bitches can be carriers. A course of antibiotics will clear up the infection. Your vet will then take a further swab, and, if this is clear, issue a certificate confirming a clean bill of health.

On most occasions, the bitch will travel to the dog to be mated, simply because some dogs perform only in familiar surroundings.

BITCH IN SEASON
Most bitches come into season at either six- or nine-month intervals. Often, bitches may appear 'off-colour', becoming jumpy and acting out of character. Some may begin scent-marking for a few days before oestrus.

The season begins with the vulva swelling considerably, and a bloody discharge appearing. Some bitches keep themselves very clean and it can be difficult to confirm oestrus. Dab a piece of white tissue on the vulva when the bitch wakes up; if a coloured discharge shows, count this as day one. A bitch's season

lasts for approximately three weeks.

Having lived with bitches for many years, I found no major problems when they came into season, and, even living in a town, never had any unwanted attention from other dogs. Most bitches keep themselves incredibly clean, with very little blood 'spotting' around the house. Although we take our bitches for their normal exercise, we avoid areas where we are likely to meet other dogs, or we keep them on leads in public parks. There are preparations on the market which mask the smell of the oestrus with varying success.

MALE REACTIONS
If you have an entire male dog and several bitches, prepare yourself for sleepless nights. Even if your dog has not been used at stud, the effect of a bitch on heat in the same house is electric. He will lose his appetite, he will be generally distracted, and, during the time the bitch is mateable, he will howl constantly.

Male dogs also have a tendency to 'mark' their territory, and you may find your dog attempting to scent mark throughout the house, including into visitors' shoes and bags, etc. This may become worse during the period the bitch is in season, as he becomes more protective of his property and 'his bitches'! I once decided to try a change of tactic, with our resident male going to live with friends for the week that his sister was 'standing'. That plan had to be changed when he escaped by scrambling over a two-metre fence, crossed two main roads, and ran home, to howl outside the back door.

BITCH RECEPTIVENESS
For the first 10 days of the season, the scent from the bitch will attract strange

dogs, but the bitch will be exceedingly hostile to them should they come near her. The exception is a male that she lives with and is familiar with – some bitches will stand for these dogs from the first day of oestrus. Usually, on day 11, the discharge turns straw-coloured and the bitch's behaviour changes. She will become flirtatious with any dog, raising her tail and showing off her private parts to almost anyone, human or canine.

If you also own a male dog, it is quite normal for him not to be 'interested' in the bitch for the first few days of her oestrus. However, this can change very quickly, and it is not recommended to leave them alone together, even for a few minutes.

When your bitch first comes into season you should notify the owner of the stud dog. Most people, keen not to miss the receptive period, travel to the stud dog as soon as the bitch begins holding her tail to one side or standing to mount. This is common behaviour with a familiar bitch, but it can soon change when she is presented with a strange dog who wishes to take 'liberties'. If you have used one of the many products on the market aimed at disguising the smell of the on-heat bitch, do not use them for one week prior to mating.

There are many scientific preparations, available through your vet, which can eliminate the guesswork of timing. One of these is swabbing, where a swab is taken from the bitch's vulva and transferred to a slide. A dye is added and the mixture viewed through a microscope. Swabs are then taken daily, and the changes in cell shapes are easily detectable, giving a clear indication of the time of ovulation.

MATING

A common misconception is that mating is a simple procedure of shutting two dogs in a room together and hoping for the best. Although this may work, it is fraught with danger, mainly for the stud dog. The bitch, in a panic, may fiercely defend herself from what she sees as unwanted attention from a strange dog. If a mating does take place and the bitch attempts to sit down while they are 'tied', the dog can be seriously injured, with the prostate gland above the penis becoming bruised and inflamed. The dog can be put off mating for life, with his lasting memory being of searing pain.

If the dog has not been used at stud before, it is essential that someone experienced is present for the mating. Experience has shown that some 'pet' dogs will not mate if their owners are present! A little detective work usually shows that such a dog has been continually chastised for sexual misdemeanours in his youth, when he may have mounted children or furnishings, etc.

A minimum of two people should be present, and both dogs should be wearing strong collars (not choke chains). You will need to have a muzzle (a length of bandage will suffice, or, if you are desperate, a stocking) and a lubricant (e.g. petroleum jelly). Plan ahead and know where the mating is to take place. If you are using a room inside, it needs to be large, with adequate ventilation, and with a non-slip floor. If the mating is to take place outside, it must be somewhere relatively secluded, where there are no other dogs or an audience.

Introduce the dogs in an open area, so the bitch will not feel intimidated. Keep the male on a long lead and allow the bitch some freedom to explore her surroundings. Ideally, she should approach the dog and invite him to play, by pawing him and then twisting away, before bouncing back to tempt him again. The person holding on to the dog should be watching his reactions closely. If he is an experienced stud dog he will be aware of what is expected of him and will know if the bitch is ready. If the dog shows a distinct lack of interest, the bitch is probably not ready and mating may be more successful the following day.

A mating can take up a considerable part of a day, and, if the owners have travelled far, it may be convenient for them either to leave the bitch to stay with the stud dog owners, or to stay overnight themselves. Time taken off work, petrol costs, and the stud fee can all eat into any small profit that the breeder hopes to make.

PROBLEMS
The demeanour of the bitch determines how things will proceed. Ideally, she will allow the male to lick her vulva and will then arch her tail to one side, inviting further inspection. However, some bitches take an obvious dislike to some dogs, and, even when they are ready to be mated, keep them at bay. The same lady may then take a shine to another male and find him quite agreeable – especially if he is of a different breed or of doubtful parentage! In some cases, a bitch will play hard-to-get in the presence of her doting owners, but, when they leave, she may adopt the morals of a lady of the night!

Some bitches refuse to be mated, which can be remedied by muzzling the bitch and holding or supporting her while she is mated. Some owners find this abhorrent, so discuss the issue if you feel strongly about it.

Other bitches may grumble constantly at the male, although their tail is lifted to one side exposing their vulva and giving

differing signals. Sometimes, size can be a problem, if the bitch is tall and the dog is of medium size or vice versa. This can be remedied by finding a convenient slope and standing a tall bitch downhill, or a large dog uphill.

Even if a bitch is responding favourably, I find it safer to muzzle her. Dog reflexes are very fast, and, especially with a maiden bitch, it is not unknown for her to whip round and bite one of the helpers! Wrap the bandage securely around the muzzle, crossing under the chin, and tying behind the ears. The bitch's owner should kneel beside her, holding her by the collar, with an assistant ready to kneel at the side of the bitch to support her or to help direct the male.

PROCEDURE
Bring the male into position at the rear end of the bitch. An inexperienced dog may, in excitement, try to move around the bitch and may need nudging back to the right end. If the dog is a novice, the bitch may be lubricated with petroleum jelly at this point. Do not do this earlier in the proceedings as it may disguise the scent of the bitch, which the dog may find off-putting.

When the dog mounts the bitch, the person kneeling at the side of the bitch can put their hand underneath her, palm upwards, under her tummy until slight pressure can be applied. This will make the bitch's vulva tilt upwards and open slightly. It will make entry for the dog easier.

If this is a bitch's first mating, it is understandable that she may experience some discomfort, and, at the critical time, she may try to pull away, or whip round and snap at the dog. After rapid thrusting, the dog will ejaculate. The glands at the base of the dog's penis swell and a 'tie' occurs, when the bitch's internal muscles grip the glands. The dog then becomes very relaxed and will rest all of his weight on the bitch's back. Some dogs try to turn around by lifting a back leg over the bitch's tail end. You can assist him with this, or slide him over to one side so they are standing shoulder to shoulder. Again, at this time, I find maiden dogs and bitches may panic as they find themselves held tied and vulnerable. The 'tie' can last for up to 40 minutes and the dog will not be released until the bitch relaxes her muscles. Trying to force them apart – which can happen with a misalliance mating and a panicky owner – is futile, and the old wives' tale of throwing a bucket of water over them is a waste of energy.

It is quite common for the inexperienced dog to become so excited that he ejaculates prior to penetration. If this happens, take him away and allow him half an hour to calm down.

POST MATING
When the tie is over, both dogs will immediately wash themselves, and it is a good opportunity for the handlers to check for any sign of injury or bleeding. Remove the dog quietly, before he starts to show interest again. It is quite normal for the dog's penis not to return immediately to its sheath, which may concern the novice owner. The bitch should be given the opportunity to clean herself and then be given a drink of water. It is normal practice for a bitch to be mated twice, perhaps on arrival and then the next morning, prior to departure. The stud dog owner should give you a copy of the dog's pedigree (if you have not got one already) and sign the registration form confirming that the mating has taken place.

ACCIDENTAL MATING
Sadly, even with the best of intentions, accidental matings can occur. I have had a bitch wriggle through a ground-floor window, only open a few inches, to reach a male in the garden outside, and I have had a male destroy an inner door in an attempt to get to a bitch. Family ties are not recognised in the canine family; thus a stud dog will mate his daughter or sister and vice versa.

If an accidental mating happens, do not panic. As previously stated, if a dog and bitch are tied, nothing can be done to speed up this process. However, vets can administer a 'morning-after pill' or a misalliance injection. Although brands may differ, the injection can usually be given up to 48 hours after the mating. This prolongs the bitch's season, so extra care has to be taken. These injections can cause long-term infertility problems if you intend to mate your bitch at a later date, and are better avoided if possible. The best solution is not to allow your bitch to be 'caught' in the first place.

PREGNANCY
As soon as the owners and the bitch have returned home, they will start watching her closely in the hope that their time (and money) has not been wasted, and that the bitch is in whelp. Several times I have met bitches whose owners are convinced they are expecting, only to find a smug, overweight bitch who is anything but pregnant. There are few hormone changes in the early days of pregnancy, so blood or urine tests are not appropriate.

With my own bitches I can usually tell at about the three-week stage, as I find the hair growing over the loins starts sticking out slightly as the bitch's girth increases. This will be coupled with a change in her nipples, as they become pink and slightly prominent. Your vet may be able to feel the puppies between three to four weeks. Pregnancy can be confirmed by an ultrasound scan, which causes no harm to the bitch or the unborn puppies. Agricultural colleges may also offer this facility.

Ultrasound can be conducted successfully after 28 days into the pregnancy. Do not accept the ultrasound operator's diagnosis about the number of puppies. Some may be hidden, out of view, under the rib cage. On one occasion we could see 7 foetuses and the bitch produced 12 puppies! The next time we saw 10 foetuses and she had 10 puppies.

BITCH CARE

Treat your bitch as normal until she is six weeks pregnant. Pregnancy is, after all, only a condition, not an illness. After six weeks, increase the amount and frequency of food. It is normal for a bitch's stomach to be constricted because of the puppies, and she will be unable to eat her normal quantity of food. Start to feed her smaller meals at more frequent intervals. Watch her weight closely, as an extra layer of fat will not assist her during the whelping.

Be aware of the quality and composition of food that you are feeding her. You need to increase the protein level to around 30 per cent, and remember, if you are feeding a 'complete' food, do not give supplements, which can do more harm than good. Allow your bitch to set her own pace during exercise. If you have other dogs, you may find that, within a couple of weeks of being mated, she will ignore the rough and tumble of playtime and settle into a matronly trot when out for a walk.

WHELPING PREPARATIONS

All of my dogs are house dogs, and they would be disturbed if they suddenly found themselves alone, outside in a kennel. I also find it more comfortable to spend a night whelping in the house, within easy reach of a telephone and a kettle. Experience has shown that we spend far more time with litters who spend their first few weeks in the house, where we can wander through at any time of the day or night, rather than having to put on waterproofs to make the dash from house to garage in inclement weather.

The whelping area needs to be away from the bustle of the house, where other dogs cannot gain access. I find a spare bedroom is ideal. You will need a whelping box that is large enough for the bitch to lie stretched out across the shorter side. Inside the box you need a puppy rail, which is a pole about four inches (10 cms) wide, and the same height off the ground, which runs around the inside of the box. This is then a safe area for the puppies, as it prevents the bitch squashing them should she lie against the side of the box. If you only intend to use the box for one litter, it is possible to cut costs and to make it from plywood or a similar material.

Do not paint the wood, as the paint may contain toxins that could harm the puppies when they start teething and chewing the edges of the box. I prefer to use marine ply, which, although expensive, is durable and easy to clean. If you have no handyman available, these boxes can be purchased – look for adverts in the dog papers.

BEDDING

Consider what sort of bedding to use. Some kennels use hay or straw, but these can damage the puppies' eyes, and may contain mites. Other breeders use newspaper, which is economical, but

A Groenendael bitch pictured six days before whelping.

offers no purchase for scrabbling feet and can stain the puppies with newsprint. I find it easiest to use newspaper at the bottom of the whelping box, covered by a synthetic fleece known as Vetbed™. Although this is expensive to purchase, it washes beautifully and lasts for years. It is easier to purchase two pieces, one of which can be washed while the other is in use. This fleece is excellent, as it retains heat, and all moisture passes through it onto the absorbent newspapers below. I start collecting newspapers for weeks before the whelping, and I find that broadsheets are easiest to use. I accept newspaper donations from non-dog friends only, so that there is no risk of cross-contamination.

You will also need to organise an additional source of heat for the puppies. It is important that the temperature in the vicinity of the puppies is maintained at 75 to 80 degrees Fahrenheit (24 to 27 degrees Celsius). The easiest method is to suspend a pig lamp at a height of approximately one metre (three feet) over the box and positioned over one end. If the puppies are warm enough, they will move away from the source of heat to the opposite end of the box.

WHELPING

Your bitch should whelp between 61 and 65 days after mating. It is common for bitches carrying large litters to whelp prematurely, and I have had experience of them whelping up to a week early, with no ill effects. Approximately two weeks prior to the whelping, you will notice that the hair on the bitch's abdomen falls out, leaving a bare tummy. At this point, if not earlier, accustom your bitch to being in the room in which you intend her to whelp, and show her the whelping box. With one week to go, your bitch will start looking for a suitable nest, and you can guarantee that your carefully prepared whelping box will be the last place on her mind. Favourite places include under garden sheds, under oil tanks, and even inside my bed!

A few days prior to whelping, the puppies descend into the abdomen, giving the bitch a distinctive pear-shaped appearance. A bitch's temperature is normally 101.5 degrees Fahrenheit (38.5 degrees Celsius), and, prior to whelping, it will lower to about 99.5 degrees Fahrenheit (37.5 degrees Celsius). Some people swear that this is one of the best guides; however, I have found it to be inaccurate.

ONSET OF LABOUR

The first signs of the bitch beginning labour are severe panting and attempts to dig up her bed. Panting and digging may last for several hours, with there being at least one false alarm. Some bitches will refuse a meal, while others scoff their

The onset of labour is usually marked by heavy panting and restlessness.

food, only to vomit later in the proceedings. If this happens, the bitch may attempt to bury the food, with the intention of returning to it later on.

When labour begins in earnest, you will be left in no doubt. The bitch will be exceedingly restless and unable to be pacified. She may ask to go outside. Let her go, but accompany her. Take a torch if it is dark, as the bitch will be looking for a dark, safe place to 'hide' her puppies away from human interference, and, often, she may give birth to the first puppy when she squats to urinate.

Once the bitch begins straining, the first puppy may be born within a few minutes, or after some considerable time. If straining goes on for more than half an hour, contact your vet. Some bitches lie down to strain, others may prefer to stand up and 'bear down'. Whichever your bitch prefers, resist the temptation to interfere. Remember that, if the bitch had her own

way, she would be in a dark, isolated place without human help.

GIVING BIRTH
When the bitch begins straining, her 'waters' will break and a small amount of fluid will be passed. The bitch will clean this up. When the first puppy passes through the cervix, the contractions increase and the bitch will arch her back and lift her tail. A large swelling will appear under the anus, followed by a blue-black sac appearing through the vulva opening. After some more contractions, the puppy is born. Most puppies are born head first, which is easier for the bitch, but do not be concerned if the puppies arrive tail first.

The puppy's survival depends on the sac containing him being broken, to allow oxygen to enter; his link to his mother's oxygen supply will have been severed during the birth. Sometimes, the puppy may be half way out of the vulva but trapped by the umbilical cord, and the rest of the sac, which has not yet been pushed out. If this happens, tear open the sac covering his head and clear the pup's mouth of mucus, to enable him to breathe. The novice bitch can appear panicky and scared one minute, and calm and capable the next – cleaning the puppy, tearing away the sac, and chewing on the umbilical cord. However, unless your bitch appears confident, assist her and tear the umbilical cord. Never use scissors, but fray and tear the cord about two inches away from the puppy. Once you can see the sac and puppy appearing through the vulva, the puppy should be born fairly quickly. However, if you can see the puppy, and the bitch appears to be having trouble passing him, you should assist, as the puppy has no oxygen supply and may die.

PROBLEMS

If, at any time during the whelping, you are unsure of what to do, contact your vet immediately. He will explain what to do, or he may ask you to bring your bitch to the surgery. Do not expect the vet to come to you – if a Caesarean is required, valuable time can be lost and the vet will have all the equipment he needs at the surgery.

If the puppy is not breathing well, pick him up and rub him roughly with a dry towel. Do not worry about hurting the puppy – vigorous rubbing is required to stimulate the circulation and the breathing. It is quite normal at this point for the bitch to ignore the puppy and to concentrate on eating the afterbirth and cleaning the detritus.

INTER-BIRTH

Normally a bitch will rest between puppies; which can be anything from ten minutes to two hours. Use this period to ensure that the puppy has had a drink from the bitch – the stimulation of a puppy feeding will in turn stimulate more contractions. I also find it useful to keep a pen and paper handy, to note the times of delivery, the sex of the puppy, and any distinguishing marks. I do not weigh puppies at this point, preferring to wait until the bitch has finished.

Keep the heat lamp switched on during the delivery because it helps to dry the puppies. I have a small cardboard box nearby, lined with towels, and I put the new arrivals into this when another delivery is imminent, placing the box within the whelping box. Some bitches are incredibly clumsy and can tread on the newborn puppies when all their attention is drawn to the latest arrival. You will also find that, as each puppy is born, the bitch will pass a considerable quantity of fluid, which can soak the earlier arrivals.

Between puppies, offer the bitch a drink of water or milk, but not solids in case she requires an operation as the result of problems. Never put a bowl of water into the whelping box with the bitch, as a puppy could fall into it and drown. I learnt this the hard way when working in kennels as a teenager. A bitch had been given a bucket of water, the idea being that it was too high for any puppy to climb into. However, the following morning, we found the biggest puppy, aged about four weeks, drowned in the bucket. We could only assume that in play he had climbed on to his mother and fallen into the bucket when she stood up.

The bitch will eat all the placentas, which give her nourishment. If she is resting between puppies, offer her the opportunity to go outside and relieve herself. Again, accompany her at all times.

TIDYING UP

Whelping is a messy business, and you will require a lot of newspaper to mop up the liquid. When the bitch has finished, replace the newspapers again and top with a clean, synthetic fleece or Vetbed™. The bitch will find it most comfortable to lie on her side with the puppies lined up against her teats.

When all are comfortable, consider weighing them. I have found that newborn Belgians can differ considerably, with larger puppies weighing between 1 lb 2 oz and 1 lb 4 oz (500-600 grams), and smaller ones weighing considerably less. Although the smaller ones have given great concern at the time, they have not been impaired in any way and have developed into full-size dogs.

Some breeders have their bitches examined by the vet as a matter of course. The vets can administer a pituitary

Two days after whelping, the puppies and the bitch are comfortable and contented.

hormone injection, which causes uterine contraction. This can be beneficial, as it ensures that no placentas have been left inside her. However, it can cause abdominal pain, and some breeders feel that their bitch has been through enough already.

THE FIRST FEW DAYS
In the first few days after birth, the puppies lie against the bitch constantly, waking only to suckle, often falling asleep at the nipple. The lower nipples, near to the back legs, carry the most milk and you will find the strongest puppies taking up residence at this place.

Some bitches are exceedingly 'house-proud', washing their puppies constantly, and nibbling away at the remains of the umbilical cord until it shrivels and drops off. During the cleaning process the bitch's tongue will stimulate the puppy to urinate or defecate. This is eaten by the bitch – do not let her lick your face afterwards!

Do not be alarmed by the rough treatment the bitch may appear to give to her new family. Typically, the bitch will be licking her pup's bottom while he is

attached to a nipple. She will shove the bottom into the air while the puppy's neck bends at an unnatural angle. The puppy does not release his hold of the nipple and ends up swivelling around upside down while he is cleaned, apparently unconcerned.

It is normal for the bitch to continue to have a dark discharge for several days, and some may continue to pass blood. As long as the discharge is not smelly, antibiotics

It is a good idea to keep a regular check on each puppy's weight.

are not required. It is also quite normal for the bitch to have loose motions for a day or two, which will be almost black in colour as a result of eating placentas.

Puppies lose weight in their first few days, but they should have doubled their birth weight by the end of the first week. The lactating demands on the bitch increase considerably in the first few weeks. She will need to eat at least four times her normal calorific content. If she has a problem with milk production, it is possible to begin weaning the puppies at two weeks old.

There are several things that can go wrong at this stage. The most serious is eclampsia, which is caused by a decrease in calcium in the bitch. Although this can occur just after whelping, it usually happens within the first few days, when the bitch's own supply of calcium is passed to the puppies. The initial symptom is nervous, restless panting, which progresses to trembling. If treatment is not given within a few hours, the bitch will die. Treatment is given in the form of injections of calcium, and produces a rapid turnaround.

REMOVING DEWCLAWS
Check the puppies carefully for dewclaws. Dewclaws on the rear legs will need to be removed as a matter of course, and many breeders, myself included, ask the vet to remove the front dewclaws as well. This procedure is carried out when the puppies are about three to four days old. The dewclaws are situated on the front legs, on the pastern on the inside of the leg. They catch on clothing and bedding, etc., and can easily become damaged, bleeding profusely.

If dewclaws are removed in an adult dog, the operation requires a general anaesthetic along with stitches, and

dressings, etc. In young puppies, however, no anaesthetic is required. Your vet can remove the dewclaws using a pair of curved scissors, and any resulting bleeding can be stemmed easily, using a silver nitrate pencil.

Even the most docile of bitches may become fiercely protective of her puppies. Ensure that other house dogs are not able to get into the room, as she will defend her puppies against intruders, even dogs that she would normally live with. If the vet is coming to the house to examine the puppies, take the bitch away from the puppies and distract her for the few minutes taken by the examination or dewclaw removal. With this in mind, do not let anyone view the puppies at this early stage, other than household residents or immediate family, whom the bitch knows and trusts.

PUPPY REARING
The puppies' eyes and ears begin to open between 12 and 14 days after birth. The pups become mobile, on wobbly legs,

The puppies are two weeks old and still taking all their nourishment from their mother.

often crawling or half-dragging themselves along the floor of the whelping box.

Both the bitch and the puppies should be wormed at 21 days after birth. There are many preparations on the market and your vet can advise. Thereafter, the puppies should be wormed every two weeks, until they go to their new homes at eight weeks. Keep a note of the worming preparation you have used, and pass on this information to the new owners.

WEANING

By 21 days, the puppies should have been offered their first solid food. It is easiest to rear them on 'complete' foods, rather than time-consuming scraped-beef or scrambled-egg preparations. Most manufacturers cater for puppies, starting with a porridge-type food, and building up with small pellets designed for small mouths.

Most starter foods are mixed with warm water, to form a gruel. Even with a large litter, you need only mix up a saucerful to begin with. Take each puppy individually, and offer him your finger after first dipping it in the gruel. The puppy will attempt to suck your finger before mouthing the food. Next, put the puppy

on the floor beside the saucer and again offer your finger, trailing your finger in the food. The puppy quickly gets the correct idea, but he normally ends up sliding into the food or walking through it. The end result is that very little of the food is eaten by the puppy; most is worn by both of you. Have the bitch sitting nearby; she will be dying for a chance to clean up both the saucer and the puppies.

Initially, give the puppies one solid meal, adding another on the second day, etc. Eventually, the puppies should have four to five feeds a day. Always feed the puppies manually, before allowing them to feed from the bitch, otherwise they will not be hungry. It is useful to keep a bowl of warm water and a cloth available to wipe them when they have finished eating. To watch a litter sit, roll, and slide through a tray of food, covering themselves, is great fun. They will then try to clean it from each other afterwards – if the dam does not beat them to it.

It is important at this stage to keep the food sloppy and lump-free, until the puppies develop teeth that can cope with harder material. It is not necessary to feed the puppies milk, as they will be receiving far better-quality milk from their mother.

A big change is seen by five weeks of age.

As they grow, I make the food less sloppy, and give them something to work their teeth on.

Once the puppies are eating solid food, the bitch becomes less inclined to clean them. During this time, I have found a common trait with my bitches when they are separated from their pups. When the puppies are about five weeks old, and the bitch's own food has been reduced slightly, the bitch may suddenly becomes frantic, whining at the door and demanding to see her puppies. On letting her through to see them, she immediately starts scoffing their food. The puppies are also delighted to see mum and will leave the food and start suckling from her. She stays there just long enough to finish their food before whirling round and demanding exit from these hungry mouths that are now devouring her nipples with teeth like needles.

SOCIALISATION
Puppies should be handled as much as possible by a wide selection of the public, including children. Whenever we have puppies, all our dog-oriented friends are invited to visit. However, this is very demanding, and can become too exhausting.

From birth, I keep a radio tuned to a pop channel in the same room as the puppies, to accustom them to strange noises. I also try to have the pups in the house for several hours each day, where they become used to normal household noises, such as the vacuum cleaner, the dishwasher, and the washing machine.

Although a puppy may be physically ready to go to a new home at six weeks, most breeders will wait until the pups are at least eight weeks old. If you are intending keeping a puppy yourself, and you are in the fortunate position of being able to make a choice, you will want to

At seven weeks, the puppies are completely weaned, but they can still learn a lot from their mother.

make the final decision as late as possible.

Between six and eight weeks, the puppies learn a great deal from their mother and each other. They will have learnt to play and will be familiar with the canine body language of 'come and play' or 'go away, I'm tired'. They will also be aware of the dominant puppy in the litter and how to submit to him. Their mother will play with them, encouraging them, but, when they become overexcited or bite too hard, she will chastise the puppy, grabbing him on the neck and growling loudly. Although she is unlikely to hurt them physically, mentally she is dominating them and teaching them to submit. Studies have shown puppies that leave the litter at six weeks, even if there are dogs in their new home, miss out on this important training and may have trouble mixing with other dogs when they become older.

By eight weeks, the puppies should be totally relaxed and confident with strangers. Do not, however, give in to the puppies when handling them. If they squirm to be released for no apparent reason, hold on until you are ready to put them down. Roll the puppies onto their backs and tickle their tummies. Initially

115

they will squirm and fight to be put upright, as this is a submissive position that the dominant dog may be uncomfortable with, but it avoids dominance problems later in the pup's life (see Chapter Four).

REGISTERING THE LITTER

Before rehoming the puppies, you need to register them with your national kennel club. A pedigree must accompany each puppy, along with a diet sheet and general directions for new owners to follow. The puppies will be named with your kennel name or affix first, and then the name of your choice. Some breeders work their way through the alphabet, with the first litter being 'a' then 'b', etc. Other people go on themes, such as mythical gods, pop songs, or the sire's name (e.g. some dogs sired by the UK Tervueren record-holder, Ch. Valivue Bon Chance, have the name Chance incorporated in their kennel name). The choice is unlimited, but remember that, if the dog is being campaigned in any aspect of showing, Obedience, etc., and he is successful, the name you have chosen will be with him for life, and your quaint choice may make you cringe in later years. Most registrations take approximately four weeks to be processed. Most delays are the fault of the breeder, who has completed the form incorrectly.

Insurance is a must when selling puppies, as accidents can happen and the cost of vet fees are ever-spiralling. It can only take someone to trip over the puppy in his new home for a small leg to break and the cost of the veterinary treatment to be more than double the purchase price of the puppy.

There are numerous insurance companies that will supply you with a book of cover notes. The breeder pays the first month's premium, and, thereafter, the company contacts the new owners with an invitation to continue the cover for the next 12 months. In European countries and the US, insurance is handled differently, with few commercial companies offering vet insurance. It is always possible to insure your dogs for third party risks through your contents insurance, but this may not cover dogs used for breeding or showing.

FINDING PROSPECTIVE OWNERS

Finding suitable owners and selling puppies can be very difficult. There is limited time for breeders to meet prospective owners and to make a decision. Appearances can be deceptive, and some seemingly ideal people can be totally unsuitable. If the would-be purchasers live outside your area, find someone involved in the breed, who lives near the prospective owners, to do a home check to make sure they do not live on the tenth floor of a tower block.

Although many people may be tempted to purchase a Belgian, many can be ruled out immediately. I will not sell to people who live alone and work full-time. It is not fair on any puppy to be left for nine hours a day. The rest of my list is mainly personal, but one thing I have learnt is to go with instinct – it is usually right.

Ideally, you should have at least five potential bookings before the bitch becomes pregnant. However, you may need help to sell any remaining puppies. The stud dog owner may be in a position to assist – most experienced breeders will 'network' and assist each other with sales. Do not rely on this approach, however. Stud dog owners may also have litters due and be inclined to keep any enquiries for themselves.

Most breed clubs have a puppy register where, for a small fee, members can advertise their puppies. In the UK, the

Kennel Club offers a similar scheme where, for a token amount paid with the puppy registrations, all enquirers for the breed are sent a current list of breeders with puppies available. Advertising can be a gamble, with no guarantees, and I usually find that most prospective owners from this route have no knowledge of the breed.

FLYING THE NEST

The day dawns when the puppies are ready to go to their new homes. This is a sad day for the breeder, as your life has revolved around these puppies for the last few months. You know their individual characters, feel protective about them, and worry that their new owners will not be able to give them the tender loving care that you have given them. However, if you have made the proper enquiries about the new owners, you have done everything possible to ensure the puppies are going to loving new homes.

Prior to rehoming, you should ask your vet to examine the puppies. This safeguards you against any nasty surprises when the new owner does likewise. For a small fee, your vet may issue you with a certificate stating that the puppy has been examined and is healthy.

Along with the formalities of paperwork, I give the new owners a supply of food to last them at least a week (plus a local stockist, if practical), a piece of the synthetic fleece that they have been reared on that will have the familiar smell of their mother, an application form to join the breed club, and the reassurance that I am always on the other end of the telephone if they need advice.

When the last puppy has gone, other than the one I am keeping, I always give a huge sigh of relief, and promise never to put myself through that again!

In no time, it is time for the puppies to leave the nest and start out on their new lives.

9 GENETIC INHERITANCE

Dogs are made up of millions of cells, each of which contains a nucleus. In the nucleus are thread-like objects, visible under electron microscopes, which are called chromosomes. All dogs, regardless of breed, should have 78 chromosomes, just as all humans have 46 and all cats have 38. It is, however, more correct to talk of 39 pairs in the dog, because each chromosome is found twice, one member of each pair coming from each parent.

On any homologous (matching) pair, there are specific sets of genes that are always located at specific places (loci) on that chromosome. Genes are an integral part of the chromosome. They are made up of DNA (deoxyribonucleic acid), which is composed of sugar, phosphate and nitrogen bases called purines and pyramidines. The former comprise adenine (A) and guanine (G), and the latter thymine (T) and cytosine (C). The order of these proteins in the chromosome distinguishes one gene from another. Therefore, a particular genetic feature may have the order DDAGC and an alternative to that gene may have the order DDATC.

GENE BEHAVIOUR
During normal growth, which geneticists call mitosis, cells multiply in such a way that they remain identical but increase in number. When it comes to reproduction, germ cells (ova and sperm) have only one member of each chromosome pair. If sperm contained 78 chromosomes, and ova the same, when fertilisation occurred, cells would contain 156 chromosomes, not

The Groenendael. Photo: Ritta Tjorneryd.

the required 78. Therefore, during the formation of ova and sperm, there is a reduction division, called meiosis, in which the germ cell acquires only one member of each chromosome pair, and, consequently, has only 39 chromosomes. When ovum and sperm meet to create a fertilised embryo, the 39 chromosomes in the sperm and ovum seek out their matching pair, to form 39 pairs.

Each dog will have only two of any gene, because the dog has only two homologous chromosomes. The genes can act in a dominant, recessive, or co-dominant way. The alternative versions of genes are known as alleles. Genes are usually designated by a letter (e.g. A or B), or a letter and an affix (e.g. a^t), and they are represented by upper- or lower-case letters. Alleles are normally represented by upper-case letters if they are dominant, and lower-case letters if they are recessive.

A dominant gene will act even if it is present only in a single dose (i.e. on only one of the chromosome pair). For example, a dog carrying the allele B will give rise to black pigment regardless of the partner allele. In contrast, the alternative to B is termed b and is recessive. This allele gives rise to brown pigment, but it will only work if it is present in duplicate (bb), i.e. on both matching chromosomes.

In this example, there are three versions: BB giving rise to black, Bb also giving rise to black, and bb giving rise to brown. Although BB and Bb are genetically different (different genotypes), they are identical in appearance (phenotype). The BB animal will pass B to all its offspring, all of which will produce black pigment, but the Bb dog will give half his progeny a B gene and the other half a b. Consequently, if two Bb dogs are mated, they can give rise to black and to brown (bb) offspring, as shown below.

MATING: Bb x Bb
Gametes: B b B b

		Sire's genes	
		B	**b**
Dam's genes	**B**	BB (black)	Bb (black)
	b	Bb (black)	bb (brown)

In this mating there is a ratio of 3:1 black to brown: one homozygous (pure-breeding) black; two heterozygous (not pure-bred) black; and one homozygous brown. Many defects are recessive and can appear in litters resulting from two seemingly normal parents that carried the defect without the breeder's knowledge.

Although the term 'black' is used, an animal carrying BB or Bb may not necessarily be black in coat colour, because the overall colour depends on the other genes carried by that dog. However, a BB or Bb dog will carry black pigment, and consequently he will have a black nose, pads, and lips, etc. For example, a Dobermann carrying BB or Bb, but with the combination at another locus of dd, will have the black pigment converted to blue. For the BB or Bb dog to be black, he must also carry DD or Dd. Similarly, a Labrador carrying BB or Bb will only be black if he is also EE or Ee. If he is ee, he will be yellow, but with black pigment on the lips and pads. Breeders need to realise that defects and virtues are not always dependent on one gene alone, but on what is found elsewhere in the genetic make-up of the dog.

119

SEX INHERITANCE

Females have one large pair of matching chromosomes. In males, there is one large and one small chromosome. These are known as the sex chromosomes, and the terms XX for females, and XY for males, are used to describe them. Anything carried on the Y chromosome will pass directly from father to son and cannot be seen in females. In contrast, anything on the X chromosome can pass to either sex, but, if a dog has a defective recessive gene on the X chromosome, it will be obvious even though it appears on only one of the sex chromosomes. This is because the Y chromosome does not carry anything to counteract the X. In females, a defective recessive gene on one X will not work unless the other X also carries it.

The Y chromosome carries very little, but the X chromosome may carry many traits, such as haemophilia A and muscular dystrophy, both of which are recessive. If we designate haemophilia as h, and normal as H, there are five kinds of genotype:
- Female $X^H X^H$: Normal
- Female $X^H X^h$: Carrier
- Female $X^h X^h$: Haemophiliac
- Male $X^H Y$: Normal
- Male $X^h Y$: Haemophiliac.

In general terms, haemophiliac males are born when a normal male mates a carrier female, but for a haemophiliac female to arise, a male haemophiliac must mate with a female carrier. The odds against this are very high, and affected females are rarely seen.

Traits inherited like this are called sex-linked traits because they are linked to the sex chromosomes. In contrast, a sex-limited trait may be autosomal (i.e. carried on the chromosomes that are not X or Y), but will only appear in one sex even though both sexes carry it. For example,

milk production is only seen in bitches, but males carry genes that affect the level of production. Similarly, cryptorchidism (failure of the testicles to descend) is only seen in males, but predisposition towards it can be carried by females.

Sex-controlled traits appear in both sexes, but they are more common in one sex. Examples include spina bifida, hip dysplasia, and elbow dysplasia. The first two of these is more common in females, and the last is more common in males.

POLYGENIC TRAITS

Although much attention is paid to simple inherited traits, affecting features like coat colour, most of the important traits in dogs are polygenic (i.e. caused by several genes, and, possibly, by environmental factors). Most breeders aim to produce Belgian Shepherds with specific conformational and behavioural features, and these are almost always polygenically inherited.

Canine genetics has not been particularly well studied, with most research focused on the German Shepherd. The main conclusion is that most conformational traits have a moderate or high heritability; the proportion of the parents' conformational characteristics (relative to the population from which they come) that are passed on to the progeny is moderate to high. Traits like wither height were 65 per cent heritable, and body length was 44 per cent heritable. Although these figures apply to the German Shepherd, they suggest that selection for conformational traits might be effective. In contrast, reproductive traits (e.g. litter size) are of low heritability, and selection for these traits will be less successful.

BELGIAN COAT COLOURS

Tervueren coat colour is caused by the

The Tervueren. Photo: Ritta Tjoreneryd.

dominant yellow allele found in the agouti series. This allele gives rise to sable coloration: a yellow or golden coat overlaid with black guard hairs and with a black facial muzzle. The allele is termed 'A^y', and sable Tervueren must carry at least one A^y allele.

Solid black, also found in the agouti series, is dominant to sable. It is designated by the symbol A or A^s. Groenendaels carry at least one As allele, with there being three possible combinations of the A^s and A^y alleles:

- A^{s}A^s: Groenendael producing only black offspring regardless of mate.
- A^{s}A^y: Groenendael producing black or sable depending on mate.
- A^{y}A^y: Tervueren/Malinois/Laekenois producing only sable unless mated to one of the above two genotypes.

A mating between two Groendendaels of type A^{s}A^y could give rise to a proportion of Tervueren phenotypes – a phenomenon known to occur. Mating A^{s}A^y to A^{s}A^y would, on average, produce 25 per cent Groendael (A^{s}A^s), 50 per cent Groendael (A^{s}A^y), and 25 per cent A^{y}A^y, or, in other words, a ratio of three Groenendael types to one Tervueren. These ratios apply at population level, not to any specific litter. Groenendaels of type A^{s}A^s and A^{s}A^y would be distinguishable only by their breeding record, and not by their phenotypic appearance.

RECESSIVE COLOURS

There are recessive black genes in the Belgian Shepherd. However, they are normally coupled with tan points, such as those often seen on the Dobermann and the Rottweiler. This pattern is caused by the 'at' allele, which is part of the agouti series and is recessive to A^y and A^y.

If we accept the presence of a recessive black-and-tan allele in addition to the three genotypes already discussed, there are further genetic combinations making up the coat colour of the Belgian Shepherd:

- A^{s}a^y: Black
- A^{y}a^t: Sable
- a^{t}a^t: Black and tan.

A Belgian Shepherd can carry only two of the three alleles. Looking at all six genotypes, there are numerous combinations possible. If, for example, Ayat was mated to Ayat, the average litter would comprise: 25 per cent black and tan (atat), giving rise to the theory that Tervuerens can produce Groenendaels. In reality, this would not appear to be the case since two sables cannot give rise to a genuine black. In view of origins, one might expect that the recessive black of the German Shepherd is present in the Belgian

Shepherd, but Robinson found no evidence for this.

A so-called grey Tervueren is known, thought to be attributable to the ch allele at another locus, which, when present in duplicate, will dilute sable to a pale cream or grey colour. The ch allele does not act on black pigment.

The Belgian Shepherd carries many other colour genes, but will be homozygous for only one version. The merle gene M found in many sheepdog breeds is not present in the Belgian, but its alternative, non-merle m is, with the result that all Belgian Shepherds are genetically mm. They are also believed to be non-ticked (tt) and have black, not brown, pigment (i.e. BB not bb or Bb).

TERVUEREN PIGMENT LOSS
In the US, Tervueren have been reported

The Malinois. Photo: Ritta Tjorneryd.

with pigment loss around the face and mouth. A university study of the phenomenon found that the condition varied in severity according to age, being first seen in young adulthood (around two years or slightly less). Analysis of the pedigrees of affected dogs suggested a genetic cause, but the mode of inheritance, if any, was not determined. Stress may be a factor in inducing the condition.

COAT TYPE
Long coat hair (l) is recessive, while short coat hair (L) is dominant. The Tervueren and Groenendael, both long-coated varieties, have the ll genotype, breeding true for a long coat. The Malinois is short-coated, most being LL, although some may be Ll. In Malinois and Groenendael/Tervueren crosses, most progeny would be Ll and short-coated. If the Malinois was Ll in genotype, the progeny would be divided into Ll (short) and ll (long).

The wire-haired Laekenois is thought to be dominant to other coat types. Matings between Laekenois and Belgians with other coat types tend to produce more pups with wire hair than with long hair.

HIP DYSPLASIA (HD)
The hip joint comprises a ball (femoral head) and a socket (acetabulum). Dysplasia refers to a faulty fit of the joint, usually by too shallow an acetabulum. Most developed countries have set up schemes to assess HD, all of which are based on radiography of the hip from 12 months of age, although the OFA system in the US works on a 24-month minimal age. In most countries, hips are graded into one of several categories, usually from 4-7. For example, in Norway grades are 0, 1, 2 or 3 with lower numbers being better. In the UK, a 3-grading scheme was set up in

1965, but this was replaced in 1978 by a scoring scheme. In this, eight features of the hip are scored on a scale of 0-6, and one feature is scored 0-5. A dog can score from 0 to 53 per hip, or from 0 to 106 for both hips combined, with lower numbers indicative of the healthier hip.

Tervueren appear slightly less affected than Groenendael, and the number of Laekenois and Malinois included in the study are too few to be meaningful. A total of 16 per cent of those assessed did not have variety specified, making it difficult to assess predisposition for each variety. Generally, the Belgian Shepherd takes 62nd place (1st is worst) among the 75 breeds with 40 or more animals scored. Over 50 per cent of the breed score 10 or better,

which is an excellent score, and only about 3 per cent score 30 or more, which is the level at which problems might be seen. The overall standard in the breed is acceptable, but there is no room for complacency.

Hip Dysplasia is an inherited, polygenic trait controlled by many genes. It has a heritability of 25 to 40 per cent, depending on the breed. Belgian Shepherd breeders in Britain, Australia or New Zealand should hip-score (or grade in other countries) all breeding stock and as many others as possible. No sensible breeder should breed from unscored/ungraded animals, and an upper limit should be set, beyond which animals are not used for breeding. As fewer dogs

HIP SCORES FOR BELGIAN SHEPHERDS (UK SCHEME)

VARIETY	No.OF DOGS RADIO-GRAPHED	BEST SCORES	WORST SCORES	MEAN SCORE	% SCORING LESS THAN 11	% SCORING MORE THAN 30
Groen-endael	276	0	104	11.7	63.4	5.1
Laekenois	2	2	13	7.5	50	0
Malinois	44	0	60	10.52	59.1	2.3
Tervueren	602	0	93	10.55	46.7	2.3
Not specified	180	2	98	12.36	55.6	5
Total:	1104	0	104	11.3	52.7	3.4

(@ May 2000)

The Laekenois.

than bitches are used for breeding, stricter rules should apply to dogs, which should score less than 15. An upper limit of 20 may be more appropriate for bitches. These levels are arbitrary, and will depend upon the merit of the dog – a dog should not be used for breeding simply because he has good (low) hips. Individual breeders

will set higher standards than others, and, in some countries, breed clubs will establish breeding limits.

EPILEPSY

Epilepsy in the Belgian Shepherd was first reported in the 1960s in the Netherlands. Scientist Van der Velden began his investigation following an apparent upsurge in reported cases. His results showed that there was a higher incidence (84.6 per cent) of epilepsy in progeny from two affected parents, than there was from litters with one affected parent (66.6 per cent), and that was higher than the incidence (4.3 per cent) in litters where neither parent was known to have suffered an epileptic attack. Although the numbers used in the study were small, the results of the study gave a strong indication that epilepsy was caused by an inherited trait.

Epilepsy can be inherited or acquired. Poison, brain tumours, brain damage, nutritional failings, and even severe teething, can cause the onset of epilepsy. However, primary or idiopathic epilepsy is inherited. In the US, Dr Tom Famula has been working on the subject and established the polygenic nature of the defect, but he has also suggested that a major gene may be implicated. Epilepsy is a serious problem among Belgians, and more needs to be done to combat it.

10 *HEALTH CARE*

Belgian Shepherds are generally healthy, although, like any breed, they are susceptible to some diseases. Responsible breeders will carry out every test possible to ensure that their breeding stock is sound, but no guarantees can be given. To date, there are testing schemes available for eye problems, and hip and elbow dysplasia.

It is important to be able to assess when veterinary attention is needed, or when an ailment can be treated at home. Dogs are natural scavengers, which can result in bouts of sickness or diarrhoea, and, if the dog has no obvious pain or distress, a diet of boiled water for 24 hours, followed by feeding small amounts the next day, is usually all that is needed. Many Belgians go through life with barely a visit to the vet other than for inoculations.

ADDISON'S DISEASE
This is a problem caused by the malfunction of the adrenal gland, which is attached to the kidneys and produces hormones. If the adrenal gland is underactive, muscular weakness, heart irregularities, thirst, and mild kidney problems may occur. Addison's can be confirmed by a series of blood tests that measure cortisol levels and eliminate other possibilities. Treatment requires a lifelong steroid replacement, with varying degrees of success. This is not thought to be a hereditary problem, but it may have genetic tendencies.

ADMINISTERING MEDICATION
Administering medication can be problematical, with some dogs refusing tablets hidden in the tastiest of foods, while others are adept at hiding tablets in their mouths, then spitting them out when your back is turned. Hiding the tablet in a teaspoonful of paté or butter can work well with dogs such as these.

For the 'picky' dog, suspicious of anything, it is usually easier to offer an undoctored tasty morsel first, followed by another, identical treat, this time containing the tablet, and ending again with an undoctored treat. This is easier if you have several dogs that compete for food and do not want to miss out on a tasty morsel.

ANAESTHESIA
For many years, Belgian Shepherd breeders have informed puppy purchasers that the breed has problems with anaesthetics, with many dogs dying under the procedure. In the past, traditional anaesthetics were barbiturate-based, and, during the recovery period, were broken

125

UK Ch. Taloma Luna. Int. Norway, Swedish sand Danish Ch. Tropisk Maggie.
The Belgian is a hardy breed, and generally suffers few health problems.

down in the body fat before being eliminated from the system. As the majority of Belgians have little body fat in comparison with many other breeds, this meant that the dog took longer to regain consciousness, and, in some cases, died. Today's anaesthetics are more sophisticated, and, while any anaesthetic procedure carries an element of risk, the degree of risk is drastically reduced from 20 years ago. However, if your dog suffers from epilepsy, inform your vet prior to any anaesthetic being given, as certain types of pre-medication should not be given to epileptic dogs.

AUTO-IMMUNE DISEASE
The immune system produces antibodies to fight infection. Auto-immune occurs when the system turns rogue and attacks its own tissue. There are numerous forms of auto-immune disease, covering a whole range of conditions, and none are contagious. Some of the most common are pemphigus and pemphigoid, which affect the skin and mucous membranes, or haemolytic anaemia, which affects the blood.

Auto-immune disease is diagnosed by blood tests, or, in the case of skin complaints, by skin biopsies. Treatment consists of massive doses of steroids, which tend to have side effects and may shorten the dog's life expectancy.

DILATED CARDIOMYOPATHY
This is a disease of the heart muscle, which becomes stretched and flabby, and does not pump efficiently. The blood circulation decreases, causing an intolerance of exercise in affected dogs. Irregular heart rhythms may also be detected. The progression of the disease eventually leads to heart failure, where pressure in the heart causes fluid to accumulate in the lungs. The symptoms may not be apparent until the disease has progressed considerably. In other cases, the dog may show no symptoms but drop dead without warning, usually during exercise. Unless post-mortem examinations are carried out by heart specialists or universities, it could be easily missed. Although cardiomyopathy can be treated by drugs and careful management, the disease is a killer.

There is not a great deal of research undertaken in connection with Belgian Shepherds and this disease. However, there have been an uncomfortable number of unexplained sudden deaths in the

126

breed, which, in some cases, have affected several dogs from the same litter, and the conclusion from the veterinary profession has been that cardiomyopathy is the most likely cause. Affected stock should be removed from breeding programmes.

EPILEPSY

Some forms of epilepsy are inherited, and usually manifest between 18 months and 3 years of age. Fits can be caused by many problems, the most common being hypoglycaemic fits, which happen when the glucose level in the blood falls to a low level. It is rare in a family pet, but more common in working dogs that expend large amounts of energy.

Epileptic fits can be split into two categories, petit mal and grand mal. Owners may not notice their dog having a petit mal fit, which may last only a few seconds, during which the dog appears to lose concentration and to 'switch off'.

The extreme is the grand mal, when a dog has a full-blown fit. He will fall over, paddle his legs as if running, salivate, and lose control of both bladder and bowels while his muscles stiffen. Usually, this lasts for a few seconds only. During the fit the dog is unaware of his surroundings or what is happening to him. He should not be restrained as this may induce panic. Instead, other dogs should be removed from the area, and steps taken to ensure the fitting dog cannot harm himself (e.g. blocking access to nearby steps).

Most epileptic fits happen during the night or after periods of rest. On recovery, the dog is often sick, through shock, and he may appear disorientated. Even if the dog comes round from a fit and appears to be well, he should still be taken to the vet to be examined, as a precaution. However, there are usually no clinical abnormalities.

If you have a dog that begins seizuring, keep a diary and record when the fits occur. If the fits are occasional, with weeks or months separating them, you may not want to consider medication. Anti-convulsant drugs can be prescribed, but once the dog has begun treatment, he will remain on it for the rest of his life. These drugs can, in the long term, cause liver damage, so this medication should not be prescribed unless the dog's quality of life is affected by the fits.

Contact your breeder and the stud dog owner when it becomes apparent that your dog is having epileptic fits. The knowledge can be invaluable and change breeding programmes.

EUTHANASIA

There comes a time in most dog owners' lives when a decision has to be taken regarding their dog's quality of life. This can be the result of disease or injury, or system failure due to old age. In an ideal world, the decision could be made for us, and many an owner has gone to bed hoping that the decision will be taken out of their hands and the dog will pass away naturally in his sleep. However, the cruel reality is that it is unfair to let your dog suffer, and euthanasia may be the kindest course of action in some situations.

Some dogs detest or fear the vet and his premises. If possible, arrange for the vet to come to the house, as this causes less stress to the dog. If it is impractical for the vet to come to your house, arrange an appointment at the surgery and inform them of your intention. This will help to ensure that you are not kept waiting and that you are given some privacy. If possible, take someone with you who can drive your car, as you will not be in a frame of mind to drive. Do not take the coward's way out and enlist someone else to take the dog to the surgery. You have had a long journey together and it is only fair that you see it through to the end. I insist on holding my dogs (rather than have the veterinary nurse do it) so they go to sleep in my arms, comforted by my familiar touch, smell and voice.

Euthanasia is performed with a single injection, and it happens extremely quickly and peacefully. Your vet can dispose of the body for you, or arrange for a cremation service. Alternatively, you can take the body home for burial in your own ground.

EXTERNAL PARASITES

FLEAS
Many owners are shocked when they find that their dog's 'minor' skin infection is an allergic reaction to flea bites, which they were not aware were living on their dog and in their home. Fleas are not easy to detect, as they spend most of their lives off the dog. Modern housing, with its central heating, fitted carpets, and double glazing, provides the flea with an ideal environment in which to survive and to multiply. For every flea you find on your dog, there may be up to 100 hidden in your carpet.

Part the coat and examine your dog's skin. Flea faeces looks like specks of dark-coloured dust. If you dampen a piece of cotton wool (cotton) and gather some of these particles on it, you will see the speck of dust dissolving slightly into a orange-red smudge, confirming that it is flea dirt. The actual fleas are dark-brown insects, without wings, which move at great speed through the dog's coat and feed by sucking blood, hopping on and off their host with ease.

FLEA CONTROL
There are several methods of controlling fleas, ranging from herbal remedies to chemical sprays. Flea powders can be ineffective, as it is difficult to distribute them evenly throughout the dog's coat and bedding, and most of it blows away. Flea sprays purchased from the pet shop or supermarket can solve the local problem, but will have no long-term effect and will need reapplication on a regular basis. Flea collars should be used as a preventative measure only, as the collar will be unable to kill all the fleas on an infested dog, and the chemicals released from the collar are not particularly effective at the dog's tail end. In shorter-coated breeds, flea collars can cause an allergic reaction with close contact to the skin, but this should not be a problem with the Belgian Shepherd.

Recently, a flea treatment has been released that is added to your dog's food. The chemical enters the bloodstream, and, when a flea bites the dog, the blood ingested has the effect of sterilising the flea, breaking the flea's reproductive cycle. However, this treatment is expensive, and it does not work immediately, requiring an additional spray to be used initially.

Another treatment available through your vet is a chemical solution applied to the back of your dog's neck. The chemical is absorbed into the body and distributed all over the skin. When the fleas next bite the dog, they are poisoned and die. This is an effective treatment, but it is expensive. Remember, if you have cats living in the same household, they will need to be treated at the same time.

Fleas are unable to live exclusively on human blood, but they will make an occasional meal of you. The classic signs are bites on your ankles and lower legs. Like dogs, some people can have a allergic reaction to the bites. Do remember that as well as treating your household pets, you will also need to treat your home, otherwise reinfection rapidly occurs.

TICKS

These are found predominantly in areas populated with sheep or deer. They are found in dense vegetation, usually heather or bracken, attaching themselves to any passing animal. Usually, ticks attach themselves to the front of the dog, as this is the area with which they first come into contact.

Ticks cause itching, and, in some cases, severe skin irritations. They can also cause Lyme disease, which, although rare, is a very debilitating illness.

Ticks look like small spiders crawling on your dog, varying in size from a few millimetres, when they first make contact with the dog, to about one centimetre (0.4 inches) when they are engorged with blood.

Ticks bury their mouths into the skin of their host, feeding for between 5 to 14 days, depending on their age and size, before dropping off, drum-tight with blood. Removal of ticks is difficult because, if they are pulled out, it is easy to leave the head still attached to the dog. This can fester and cause an abscess.

TICK REMOVAL

Do not try to burn off ticks as it is distressing to the dog, which can be easily burnt. It is simpler and more effective to dab the ticks with flea spray, after which they will die and drop off easily.

To remove ticks manually, hold the tick, as near to its head as possible, and slowly twist it anticlockwise. If in doubt, consult your vet. Keep a close watch on the area where the tick has been. The dog will find this area irritating and there may be localised scratching. If the tick is positioned in an awkward area (e.g. on the eyelid, or the inside of the ear), it is easier to leave them to develop for a day or two, when the increase in size makes them easier to handle.

MANGE MITES

Common mites are Demodex and Sarcoptes mites, both of which cause skin irritations.

Demodectic mange is a serious condition caused by mites living in the dog's hair follicles. The mites are passed from mother to puppy and normally cause no harm to the dog. However, if the dog's immune system is weakened by stress or illness, the mites thrive, causing itchiness and mange. Demodectic mange can take the form of dry, bald, or scaly patches, or a weeping type, which may have secondary bacterial infection.

Sarcoptic mange is caused by another mite that inflicts more discomfort than Demodex mites. Again, it causes spots and bald patches. The patches can become infected with an eczema-type infection. Sarcoptic mange can be passed to humans, and is usually seen as small, red pimples at the ankles and wrists.

ERADICATING MITES

Demodectic mange is treated with specialised baths. Infestation is commonly seen in young puppies, but they respond well to treatment. However, if adult or veteran dogs are infected, medicated baths may be required for up to eight weeks before any improvement is seen.

Sarcoptic mange requires treatment with a special shampoo, available only from your vet. All animals that are in contact with the infected animal should be treated at the same time, to prevent recurrences.

HEATSTROKE

The Belgian Shepherd has a thick coat given to retaining heat. In particular, the Groenendael, having a black coat, easily retains heat. In the UK heatstroke is relatively uncommon, but, at the height of summer, it is sensible to avoid exercising your dog during the hottest part of the day, and you should never leave your dog unattended in a car, even if it does not seem that warm. The interior of a car heats up like an oven, and, even at a dog show, it is not unusual to hear tannoy messages being broadcast regarding dogs in cars in warm weather. Heatstroke causes problems with breathing, with the inhalation and expulsion of air sounding tortured and laboured. Hosing down a dog, or immersion in a tank or child's padding pool, may provide some relief prior to the attendance of a vet.

HIP DYSPLASIA

This is a hereditary condition (see page 122) in which the ball-and-socket hip joint is malformed, leading to the development of arthritis. The ball part of the joint, the femoral head, is held in the pelvic socket by ligaments.

Severely affected dogs can undergo surgery on the pectineus muscle, which may give some relief. Some badly affected dogs can live a normal life and even take top honours in the show ring. It would be unwise, however, to breed from these dogs.

In the UK, there is a widely used scheme, run by the British Veterinary Association and the Kennel Club, which assesses the amount of dysplasia in the hips using a scoring system (see page

123). Obtaining a hip score requires your dog to be put under anaesthetic or into deep sedation, while his hips are manipulated and recorded by X-ray. The X-rays are then examined by experts, and a score given.

The BVA system is also used in Australia and New Zealand. The US and Canada have a different system, based on the Orthopedic Foundation for Animals (OFA). An OFA number is given to dogs with hips considered to be within the normal range for the breed. The hips are graded into seven different grades, ranging from excellent to severe. Only the first three are eligible for an OFA number. Dogs must be more than two years of age to be graded.

In parts of Europe and Scandinavia, the grading is different and unique in each country.

INTERNAL PARASITES

Unless your dog is wormed regularly, either roundworms or tapeworms are usually present. Most people will be familiar with the worm-infested dog, pot-bellied with protruding ribs and a dull coat. However, dogs do not have to be exhibiting these signs to be hosts to worms. The adult dog can ingest worms from raw meat, or from directly eating the worm eggs. It is vital for both your dog's health, and the health of your family and other small children, that your dog is properly wormed and that you do not let him defecate in public places without cleaning up.

TAPEWORM

These worms cause a loss of body condition, with the dog constantly scavenging. The dog becomes infected by eating infected fleas or lice. Segments of the worms break off and can be seen in the dog's faeces or around the anus. When first passed, they are cream-coloured and flat in shape, but they soon dry up and look like grains of rice. Often, the worms irritate the skin around the anus, causing the dog to drag his bottom along the ground ('scooting') to alleviate the itching. The worm segments that are passed in the faeces contain tapeworm eggs, which are then eaten by flea larvae. If the dog then swallows the flea, the cycle continues, so it is important, if you suspect that your dog has tapeworm, to also check for fleas.

WORMING
Tablets are available from your vet, who should first weigh the dog to calculate an exact dosage. Dogs in hot countries can also suffer from heartworm infestation, which can cause coughing and a loss of energy. Again your vet can give you advice on prevention and control.

JUVENILE CATARACT
The correct term for this condition is Posterior Polar Subcapsular Cataracts. It is a condition that affects all varieties of Belgian Shepherd, and it cannot be seen with the naked eye. Cataracts are an opacity in the lens of the eye, appearing in one or both eyes. The cataract is usually triangular in shape, although this can vary.

Cataracts are usually classified by the age at which they appear in the dog; hence the common name, juvenile cataract. They can develop at any time, but they usually occur in dogs aged 18 to 24 months. This disease is not usually progressive and should not affect the dog's ability to take part in any sport, or his lifestyle generally. There is no scientific data available on how the condition is inherited, but affected dogs should not be bred from.

'KENNEL COUGH'
This is a form of infectious bronchitis that causes a dry, persistent cough that sounds much like the dog has a fish bone stuck in his throat. The dog may also cough up a small amount of mucus. The cough can be controlled by antibiotics. If the dog is exercised excessively when suffering from kennel cough, permanent damage to the lungs can result. It is a viral, airborne infection and can spread rapidly where there are numerous dogs. Most kennels demand that owners wishing to board their dogs have routine vaccinations up to date, plus the kennel cough vaccination. The vaccine is sprayed into the nostrils and gives protection for five months.

MONORCHIDISM/CHRYPTORCHIDISM
These terms describe the condition of retained testicles; one testicle retained in the case of monorchidism, and both retained in cryptorchidism. Both conditions may have serious repercussions for the dog's long-term health. By the time a male puppy is eight weeks old, both testicles should be descended into the scrotum. Although it is possible for them to descend at any time, if they are not down when the dog reaches six months old, there is cause for concern. Either one or both testicles can be retained within the groin or abdomen area. Because of the raised temperature within the body, the undescended testicles will be infertile. A dog with one descended testicle is still fertile, but he should not be bred from as the condition is hereditary. Once a dog reaches maturity, any retained testicles should be surgically removed, as there is a serious risk of them becoming cancerous.

OESTRUS
Your bitch will come into heat, or season,

from nine months of age onwards. Some bitches have been known to be as late as two years of age. The seasons are usually at six- or eight-monthly intervals, and it is worth taking a note of these, either if you intend to mate your bitch, or if you are planning a holiday and kennelling the bitch, as this information can be invaluable to the kennel owner.

Like some female athletes, bitches who are exceedingly active and carry little body weight may have irregular seasons. This is not a cause for concern, but should be mentioned to your vet when he performs his annual health check.

OSTEOCHONDRITIS DISSECANS (OCD)

This is a chronic cause of lameness in larger breeds, and is first noticed when the dog is six to nine months old. It is usually seen in the shoulder, elbow, and other weight-bearing joints, developing when the dog is going through a fast growth period.

It is caused when there is interference with the blood supply to the cartilage. A flap of cartilage develops and the bone underneath is poorly calcified. Research has shown that dogs fed on an unbalanced diet may be more prone to developing OCD, although predisposition must also be present.

An operation is usually required to have the offending cartilage removed, followed by rest. The affected joint may develop arthritis later on.

PHANTOM PREGNANCY

Unneutered bitches may develop a phantom or false pregnancy. This can be mild, with the bitch looking for a nest and tearing up her bed, or serious, with a manic, milk-producing bitch that is so proud of her imaginary puppies she will not want to go for a walk in case they miss her! Her toys may become her 'babies', and rolled-up pairs of socks will disappear to become substitute babies.

It is easiest to distract the bitch, keeping her busy with an interesting routine, rather than pandering to her whims. It is easier to have a bitch spayed if she has regular false pregnancies. This overwhelming maternal instinct is no guarantee that, at the appropriate time, the bitch will make a fantastic mother – if anything, the reverse can be true.

VACCINATIONS

Puppies' inoculations are an essential part of rearing. However, although owners may remember the first booster, thereafter many forget, remembering only when they attempt to book their dog into boarding kennels or dog training clubs.

Vaccination provides protection against:

* Distemper: A fatal virus that attacks the nervous system, causing inflammation of the brain or the spinal cord, resulting in fits and coughing.
* Hepatitis: Jaundice accompanied by diarrhoea, vomiting, abdominal pain, and intense thirst, which may lead to death in some cases. There may also be damage to the cornea, with the eye turning a shade of blue.
* Leptospirosis: Another type of jaundice that is fatal if not treated. It can be passed to humans and can attack the liver and kidneys.
* Parvovirus: Causes extreme vomiting and diarrhoea, which will contain blood. If treated at the onset, it is possible to save a puppy with intravenous fluids and antibiotics. Parvovirus is a major killer of dogs and can wipe out whole litters.

11 *INFLUENTIAL SIRES AND DAMS IN THE UK*

The study of pedigrees is fascinating, and it quickly becomes apparent that certain dogs and bitches have made a significant contribution to the breed. Dog showing and breeding has changed drastically since the Second World War. Prior to this, it was common for breeders to own large kennels with 30 to 50 dogs. Today's more successful breeders own only a few dogs and produce litters rarely. With space and time at a premium, litters are planned with great consideration, as the breeder realises that the next litter may not be for four or five years.

Although modern breeders may not have the awe-inspiring list of Champions produced by the old-fashioned larger kennels, their contribution to the breed is often greater. In the current economic climate, more people are returning to work, and, with the small financial rewards breeding brings, the part-time breeder is more prevalent. It is also to the dogs' advantage – Belgian Shepherds are not natural kennel dogs; they enjoy nothing more than the pleasure of human company, and the smaller breeder, who keeps his dogs in the home, is fulfilling this need for human contact.

Included below are a small number of dogs of each variety that have made a significant contribution to the breed in the UK.

GROENENDAEL

CH. QUENTIN DE LA BARAQUE DE PLANCHES

Sire Ch. Quentin de la Baraque de Planches was born in quarantine in 1967, the progeny of American Champion Polar Star de la Baraque de Planches and Peggy de la Baraque de Planches, bred by Leon Bottemanne. The importation had been

UK Ch. Quentin de la Baraque de Planches: The first UK breed Champion.

organised by Arlette Stomers. Quentin, and his sister Quamille, were purchased by Ann O'Shea of the Zellik Kennels. Quentin was a large dog, with a profuse coat, and he was a natural 'smiler'. He was of a more continental breed type than was current in the UK at that time, being a heavier, less elegant dog. He quickly gained his title when CCs became available, and was the first Groenendael in the UK to do so, going on to win an incredible 20 CCs – quite an achievement given that Groenendaels had only six sets of CCs per year. He sired many Champions and his offspring can be traced to the present day.

CH. AUST. CH. EZAU DU PAYS DES FLANDRES

This dog was a descendent of Quentin, imported by Graeme Carroll and Barbara

UK Ch. Woodlyn Penny Black, sired by Aust Ch. Ezau du Pays des Flandres. She went on to produce five UK Champions.

Simpson from Belgium in 1984, when he was four years old. He was bred by Madame Camus and sired by James de Clos de Raze and Zazoe van de Rechterhove. He was shown successfully on the Continent, winning the CACIB at Antwerp in 1983 before being imported to the UK.

He gained his title within a month of leaving quarantine and was used at stud only six times, once with a Tervueren bitch, and five times with various Groenendael bitches. From these few matings he produced, in dogs, Ch. Woodlyn Pagan, Ch. Woodlyn Prize Guy, Ch. Questenberg Quadrille, Ch. Mystrica Earnshaw and Ch. Passat of Questenberg at Janallan. In bitches, he produced Ch. Woodlyn Penny Black, Ch. Zellik Cleopatra, Ch. Woodlyn Pandora, Ch. Alycon Thira, Ch. Zellik Corinna of Chimay, and Ch. Mystrica Isobella. In 1984, Ezau went to Australia to live with Graeme, quickly gaining his title there.

VAINQUEUR IXION DE LOUP NOIR AT VALSON

Scott, as this dog was more affectionately known, was imported by Val Thompson from the US, where he was bred by Melanie Babich and Mary Linda Adams. He came through quarantine as a puppy, causing his new owner some concern as his second testicle did not descend until he was eight months old. Sadly, as a youngster, an injury to his front leg left him with arthritis in the knuckle joint and finished what would have been a promising show career. His influence on the breed cannot be overestimated and he continually stamped his wicked, humorous expression on his progeny.

In dogs, he produced Ch. Valson Washington Bear, Ch. Vanistica in Style, Ch. Valson Oregano and Ch. Vaze Atom

Ant at Valson. In bitches, he sired Ch. Vanisticas Galaxy Pursuit, Ch. Tanje Midnight Serenade, Ch. Delark Calvados of Lochnorris and Ch. Somnar Aeneas. He is behind some of the top-winning Groenendaels of all time, including his daughters, Ch. Vanisticas Galaxy Pursuit (11 CCs) and Ch. Tanje Midnight Serenade (15 CCS), and his grandchildren, Ch. Out of the Gloom (21 CCs and the Groenendael record holder), Ch. Zodiac of Questenberg at Jalus (40 CCs), and his great-granddaughter, Ch. Leicote Freyja of Ailort (14 CCs).

DAN. NOR. AND UK CH. GOOITZEN VT BELGISCH SCHOON
'Blackie' was born in 1986 in Holland, and imported in 1987 to the UK by

Danish, Norwegian and UK Ch. Gooitzen vt Belgisch Schoon. Photo: Dalton.

Barbara Simpson (Leircote) and Graeme Carroll. Bred by the Barbes in Holland, Blackie was sired by Belgian Ch. Engel du Domaine Ponti out of Elga of Lady Mary.

Blackie was to spend only a short period in the UK before travelling on to Graeme in Australia. However, Carol Winfrow, of the Delark Kennels, realised his potential and persuaded Barbara and Graeme to sell him. He quickly gained his title, and went on to sire some quality offspring: Ch. Delark Moonbeam at Munark, Ch. Kehala Sugar Candy, Ch. Foryd Gerhys Pyp and Delark Mercury (2 CCs), Frostye Foam Follower (1 CC), and the import from Norway, Fakaisers Jason le Delark at Foryd.

In 1992, Blackie was exported to Norway for Dag and Bente Harlem to enhance their breeding programme, proving his worth very quickly. He was soon awarded his Norwegian title and began to make his mark as a prepotent sire. Even after his death in 1997, Blackie's descendants continue to improve the breed in their respective countries.

CH. GYDO VT BELGISCH SCHOON AT EBONTIDE
Bred by Bertus and Angela Barbe in Holland, and imported to the UK by Roger and Janice Clifford in 1993, Ch. Gydo vt Belgisch Schoon at Ebontide was a year old when he arrived in the UK. He won his first CC within a month of leaving quarantine, quickly gaining his title; with his extrovert character winning him many friends.

Mated to Ch. Foryd Palesa, he produced the successful Foryd J litters, with Ch. Foryd Jai and Ch. Foryd Joyau Noir de la Nuit gaining their titles. Other Gydo progeny on their way to stardom are Xelbi Foreign Agent, Xelbi Distinctly Dutch, Xelbi Dutch Debutante, Ch. Ebontide

UK Ch. Gydo v't Belgisch Schoon At Ebontide.

Infatuation, Ebontide Impace and Ch. Delark Ace of Spades.

With Gydo being the youngest of the dogs profiled, it should be understood that many of his progeny are not yet mature, but they are continuing to make a great impression on the Groenendael Belgians in the UK.

ROXANE DE LA BARAQUE DE PLANCHES

Roxane was imported in 1970, by Jack and Doreen Bushby from the Bottemannes Kennel in Belgium. She was imported as a means of improving stock in England, and had to serve a nine-month quarantine as there were two cases of rabies that year, with the result that all quarantine periods were extended.

Although Roxane achieved some success in the show ring, she did not enjoy it,

and, as a result of her apparent unhappiness, it was decided to stop showing her and let her enjoy her life. She was mated to Ch. Quentin de la Baraque de Planches and produced Ch. Viroflay Frambois and Viroflay Fabian. Her next litter, mated to Ch. and Am. Ch. Laralee's Traveler, produced Ch. Viroflay Honest Abe, Ch. Viroflay Wichita and Swedish Ch. Viroflay Yankee Doodle, and her descendants have continued to do well for their owners.

CH. TANJE LONG HAIRED LADY

Bred by mother and daughter Jenny and Janet Biddlecombe, Ch. Tanje Long Haired Lady was born in 1979, out of Viroflay Fabian and Tanje Capella. When she was mated in 1983, to the import

UK Ch. Tanje Long Haired Lady.
Photo: Caroline Harvey.

Vainqueur Ixion de Loup Noir at Valson, she produced Ch. Tanje Midnight Serenade, known as Flicka, also, in my opinion, is one of the best Groenendael bitches ever seen in the UK. Flicka was a tremendous character, winning an impressive 15 CCs. She was top Belgian Shepherd Dog in 1986, and was top Brood Bitch in 1991 and 1993.

CH. VANISTICA BLUE MINK
Born in 1979, from Ch. Seahart Shipmate and Ch. Nirvana Amazing Grace at Vanistica, Ch. Vanistica Blue Mink was bred by Paul and Lorna England, and became the foundation bitch in a long line of bitch Champions. Mated to Vainqueur Ixion de Loup Noir at Valson, she produced Ch. Vanisticas Galaxy Pursuit, who went on to win 11 CCs and 10

UK Ch. Vanisticas Galaxy Pursuit. Photo: Dalton.

UK Ch. Vanistica Blue Mink. Photo: Dalton.

reserve CCs in the short time that she was shown. The rest of the time was spent trying to get her in whelp, as she did not ovulate when she threw her tail. Mated to the import Ch. Kadok de la Maison de Bois of Alycon, she produced Ch. Vanistica Moondust.

Galaxy Pursuit's most famous litter was to the Tervueren Ch. Bergerac Love Kills, which produced Ch. Vanistica Georgio, Ch. Vanistica Knowing, and Ir. Ch. Vanistica Obsession. Ch. Vanistica Moondust quickly gained her title, winning her first Challenge Certificate as a puppy. She was not shown often, but she produced many great dogs, including

Ch. and Ir. Ch. Vanistica Parisien Moon, Ch. Vanistica Simply the Best at Woodbriar, Ch. Vanistica Cornish Affair, and the breed's first Obedience Champion, Ch. Vanistica Gideons Moon.

TERVUEREN

CH. BANDOL DE LA POUROFFE AT SNOWBOURN
Bandol was imported from Belgium in 1977. At this time in the UK there were more American than Continental imports, the general opinion being that American dogs had superior construction to those from the Continent. Bandol proved this assumption wrong. With his rich, red colouring, and his excellent movement and construction, he had many admirers. As a stud dog he has been one of the biggest influences, appearing in the pedigrees of the top Tervueren throughout the UK, and undoubtedly influencing the concept of the modern Tervueren. He was the first Tervueren male Champion.

CH. NORREVANG BACCHUS OF BELAMBA
Born out of French Ch. Sam de la Douce Plaine ex Jerome Nille, Ch. Norrevang Bacchus was imported from Denmark by Marcelle King in 1985. He went on to become Britain's first grey Tervueren Champion. He had a remarkable temperament, being gentle with no nervous tendencies and showing no aggression – traits he passed to his offspring. He was so laid-back that it was difficult to get the best out of him in the show ring.

   He sired the top-winning UK Tervueren Ch. Vallivue Bon Chance (a dog that won the Group at Crufts and 42 CCs), the breed record holder in South Africa, SA

UK Ch. Norrevang Bacchus of Belamba: The first UK grey Champion.

Ch. Vallivue Appolyan, and the Ir. Ch. Belamba Harvey Wallbanger. Such was his success that his name appears in the pedigrees of 37 British Champions. His semen was exported to Australia, where he has Champion progeny, giving him Champion progeny in four continents.

CH. LANCE VAN DE HOGE LAER AT CORSINI
Lance was born in 1997, at the well-known van der Hoge Laer Kennel, in the home of Jean Louis Vandebemden. Lance was sired by the legendary National and International Ch. Grimm van de Hoge Laer, out of Ijes van de Hoge Laer. Lance was imported into Britain at the age of 11 months by Karen Ellis and Amanda McLaren, living with Karen. He soon gained his title and was a prolific stud dog. He passed his excellent type to his

138

Ch. Lance van de Hoge At Corsini.

UK Ch. Domburg Let 'em Talk: Sired by Ch. Lance van der Hoge At Corsini. Photo: John Daniels.

UK Ch. Delark Yasmine of Kehala: Top Puppy 1993.

offspring, which can still be seen several generations down the line.

His Champion offspring include the Groenendael bitches Ch. Tanje Starlight Sensation, and Ch. Tanje Starlight Silhouette of Xelbi, from his only Groenendael litter. In Tervueren, he sired Ch. Topsette Tycoon, Ch. Timberhall Rampant Riley, Ch. Bergerac Intermezzo of Zantal, and Ch. Zandros Forest Fairie, culminating in several stud dog awards. His grandchildren have continued in style, Ch. Domburg Sweet Talking Guy, Ch. Crisvale Touch of Frost at Zanusky, Ch. Domburg Let 'em Talk, Ch. Delark Yasmine of Kehala and Ch. Banderlog Bewitched.

CH. OPIUM VAN DE HOGE LAER AT CORSINI

Born in 1990 at the famous van de Hoge Laer Kennel in Belgium, Ch. Opium was sired by Ares de la Clairiere aux Louves ex Cartouche de Perigord Vert. He was imported by Amanda McLaren and Karen Ellis, and sailed through quarantine. An elegant, slow-maturing dog with a beautiful breed type, Opium gained his title in 1993, and he was Top Stud Dog for five years.

Opium's Champion progeny include Ch. Corsini Deal an Ace, Ch. Corsini Distinction, Ch. Niavana Rembrandt, Ch. Domburg Melodie D'Amour with Monamour, Ch. Domburg Jeu D'Amour, Ch. Domburg Parfait Amour, Ch. Domburg Reve D'Amour, and Ch. Niavana Rive Gauche.

CH. DELARK BABYCHAM

Born in 1984, Ch. Delark Babycham was produced by Fanfare Of The Two At Niavana, and Gruline Bess, the foundation bitch of the Delark Kennels. Known as Briar, she was for her breeder, Carol

Ch. Opium van de Hoge Laer at Corsini. Photo: Amanda McLaren

UK Ch. Bergerac Love Kills: He sired Ch. France de la Douce Plaine of Belamba's third litter. Photo: J. Ralph

Winfrow, a once-in-a-lifetime dog, exuding a character and temperament that were obvious both in and out of the show ring. She qualified for Crufts at her first Championship show, and, at the tender age of nine months, she was awarded the highest honour of the Challenge Certificate and then Best of Breed.

Babycham proved her worth as a brood bitch in her first litter to the imported Groenendael Ch. Gooitzen vt Belgisch Schoon, producing Ch. Delark Moonbeam at Munark, Delark Mercury (2 CCs, 4 RCCs), and Delark Mirage at Leircote, a dog exported to France after a successful puppy career. A French Tervueren, Ch. Cashmire de la Clairiere aux Louves, was chosen for her next litter. This liaison resulted in the quarantine-born Delark 'P' litter, from which there were three British Champions, Ch. Delark Pliquette, Ch. Delark Private Dancer, Ch. Delark Picotee at Tobara, and the Norwegian Ch. Delark Paco Rabanne. Briar was also mated to the French Champion Emir de Condivicnum. This litter produced the youngest Champion in the breed, Ch. Delark Velvet Touch, crowned at just 12 months old.

CH. FRANCE DE LA DOUCE PLAINE OF BELAMBA

Ch. France de la Douce Plaine of Belamba was imported from France as a puppy, along with her brother, Ch. Ferry. Both pups were born of the well-known Fr. Ch. Sam de la Douce Plaine. France quickly became a successful show dog, winning her title at 16 months, and going on to win 12 CCs.

She had three litters. The first, to Ch. Domburg Sweet Talking Guy, produced three British Champions in Ch. Belamba Mardi Gras At Tervanty, Ch. Belamba Monopoly At Nightstorm, and Ch. Belamba Mostly French. Two of the litter were exported to America and became Am. Ch. Belamba Bonheur Madrigal and Am. Ch. Belamba Seaflower Montage. Her second litter was to the UK record-holding Ch. Valivue Bon Chance, which produced Ch. Belamba Ooray Enry, a UK Group winner. Her third litter was to Ch. Bergerac Love Kills, and produced Am. Ch. Belamba Bonheur Protocol, Am. Ch. Belamba Paramour, and Aust. Ch. Belamba Par Avion. In 1997, Ch. France was the 8th top brood bitch in all breeds in the UK.

Her lines are continuing with her grandchildren: Ch. Nightstorm's Fotocopy, Am. Ch. Domburg French Lieutenant, Am. Ch. Domburg French Flair, and Am. Ch. Domburg French Silk, and UK CC winners Belamba Red CoCo and Domburg Daydreamer At Tiffany.

CH. LEYLA VAN HET WOUWENHOF AT CORSINI

Imported from Belgium by Amanda McLaren and Karen Ellis, Leyla arrived in the UK in 1998, as a seven-and-a-half-week-old puppy. Bred by M. Van Bauwelgiers, she was out of Tomrick Du Sat Des Bois and Isaura van het Wouwenhof. She gained her title in 1989, and made breed history by becoming

UK Ch. Leyla van het Wouwenhof At Corsini. Photo: Amanda McLaren.

what was then the youngest-ever Tervueren bitch Champion. She went on to produce two litters and proved to be an influential brood bitch.

Her first litter, to Ch. Bergerac Love Kills, produced the grey, Ch. Corsini Bitter Sweet, the breed record-holder in bitches, winner of 13 CCs. In 1992, Bitter Sweet became Best of Breed at both the Belgian Shepherd Breed Club Championship shows. A stunning grey, her glamour appealed to a wide variety of judges. Her brother, Corsini Breakaway, was exported to the Mahogany kennel in Sweden, where he also became the record-holder for the highest number of CCs won by a Tervueren.

Leyla's next litter, to the import Ch. Opium van de Hoge Laer at Corsini, gave the Corsini D litter. Ch. Corsini Distinction won eight CCs, including three times Best in Show at the Breed Club Championship show. Her brother, Ch. Corsini Deal An Ace, was also a Breed Club Best in Show winner.

Continuing the line are Distinction's daughters, with the M litter, Ch. Moulin Rouge (two CCs), Ch. Millennium (two CCs), Ch. Mayfair and Manhattan (four Reserve CCs). Her latest litter, to the import Magnum de la Clairiere Aux Louves, has produced the Corsini Q litter, which, although very young, look set to continue the winning trend.

GOVETON SUNBEAM

Sunbeam was born in 1979, for breeders Mr and Mrs Sedgman, out of Ch. Bandol de la Pouroffe at Snowbourn and Shepherdess. She was fairly successful in the show ring, winning two CCs. Mated to Fanfare Of The Two at Niavana, she produced the Snowbourn 'D' litter, of which three went on to win their titles – Daybreak, Dominique, and Dazzler. Ch.

Snowbourn Dazzler, mated to Snowbourn Lady, produced Ch. Janeth Amiable Adelaide, Ch. Woodlyn Aristocrat, and Ch. Janeth Advancer of Hollinswell. Janeth Advancer went on to win five Groups.

Dazzler was also mated to the Groenendael import, Folie du Pays du Flandres, and his name can still be found in the pedigrees of top-winning Groenendael. Sunbeam's next litter, to her father Ch. Bandol, gave Ch. Snowbourn Enchantress of Vallivue, another Group winner. Enchantress, in turn, produced the most famous UK record-holder, Ch. Vallivue Bon Chance.

CH. SNOWBOURN DOMINIQUE AT BERGERAC

Snowbourn was born in 1982, for breeders Eric and Mary Brownbill, out of Fanfare Of The Two At Niavana, and Goveton Sunbeam (a Ch. Bandol

UK Ch. Snowburn Dominique At Bergerac.

daughter). As a puppy, she qualified for the Spillers' Pup of the Year competition, beating 240 other puppies. She won four CCs, including Best of Breed at Crufts in 1986, and Reserve in the Working Group at Paignton in 1982. She had one litter only, to the grey Ch. Norrevang Bacchus of Belamba, the Bergerac 'Love' litter: Ch. Bergerac Love Kills, Bergerac Love on the Rocks, Bergerac Love for Sale, and Bergerac Easy to Love. Her two daughters each produced two Champions: Ch. Bergerac Intermezzo of Zantal, Ch. Bergerac Blue Knight, Ch. Niavana Rembrandt, and Ch. Niavana Rive Gauche.

CH. BERGERAC SWEET TALK DASH

Bred by Ken and Cathy Croad in 1988, Sweet Talk Dash was out of Ch. Bergerac Love Kills, and La Mouche of Questenberg at Bergerac. Purchased by Linda Collins, she had a very successful puppy career and went on to win seven CCs. Her first litter, to Niavana On Fire, produced the 'Talk' litter: Ch. Domburg Sweet Talking Guy, Ch. Domburg Lets Talk at Shalaka, Ch. Domburg Let 'em Talk, and Ch. Domburg Careless Talk at Nightstorm. Her second litter, to Ch. Bergerac Blue Knight, produced the top-winning Tervueren of 1998 and 1999, Ch. Domburg Dressed to Impress at Talamo (17 CCs). Her final litter, to Ch. Opium van der Hoge Laer, produced the 'Love' litter: Ch. Domburg Melodie D'Amour with Monamour, Ch. Domburg Jeu D'Amour, Ch. Domburg Parfait Amour, and, the only bitch in the litter, Ch. Domburg Reve D'Amour.

XARINA VON SVITTO OF QUESTENBERG

One of the most remarkable brood bitches ever seen in the UK, Xarina had a major influence, not only on the Tervueren variety, but also on the Groenendael and Malinois varieties. She was bred in Switzerland by Auf der Mauer, in June 1980, out of Ch. Zultan Of The Two and Mahdia des Trois Fleuves. She was imported to the UK by Karen Watson.

Xarina's first litter was to the well-known Ch. Bandol de la Pouroffe at Snowbourn, producing Ch. Questenberg Masai and the CC-winning Mazurka. She was then transferred to Vic and Lynne Salt and was mated to the Groenendael Ch. Ezau du Pays des Flandres. Five of this litter became Champions: Ch. Woodlyn Pagan, Ch. Woodlyn Prize Guy, Ch. Woodlyn Penny Black, Ch. Woodlyn Pandora, Ch. Passat of Questenberg at Janallan, and the CC-winning Polka of Questenberg.

Her final litter was to the quarantine-born Ch. Leircote Brecht, which produced Ch. Woodlyn Black Velvet, and Ch. Woodlyn Bewitched. Her grandchildren continued the family tradition, in Ch. Woodlyn Gifted N Black, Ch. Woodlyn Gaiety Girl At Hollinswell, Ch. Woodlyn Grandmaster, Ch. Woodlyn Entertainer, and, more recently, the joint top Groenendael for 1999, Ch. Woodlyn Cointreau. Another granddaughter, Sabrefield New Story, became the foundation of the well-known Story line in the Sabrefield Malinois.

MALINOIS

THE ORIGINAL PAIR
All the Malinois in the UK stem from the first pair imported by Jane Lane and Liz Richardson in 1973. The female, Venue de la Grange aux Cerfs, and the male, Vidock du Clos des Ondes, both came from France, both carrying lines to the well-known Ventadour kennel.

Sabrefield Ask For Me.

SABREFIELD BREEDING
The Sabrefield 'A' litter was born in 1974, producing the bitch Sabrefield Ask for Me, and dogs Sabrefield Aiming High and Sabrefield Ace is High. Ace is High was exported to Sweden, to begin the variety over there. Sabrefield Ask for Me began a line of selective breeding that is still to the forefront of the British Malinois today. It has also spread across various countries, including Sweden, Australia, and the US.

As a brood bitch, Ask for Me reproduced her type and character. Her most notable litters were to the imported stud Ben de Maugre. From the 'F' litter came the bitches Sabrefield Fall for Me and Sabrefield Follow Me, the latter becoming a Swedish Obedience Champion. The repeat mating, in 1980, produced Sabrefield Here I am, Sabrefield Hope for Me (one CACIB and four CCs in Sweden), and Sabrefield Here's Harriet.

SABREFIELD HERE I AM
Sabrefield Here I Am became the next dam in the breeding programme. She was mated in 1987 to the Tervueren, Ch. Questenberg Masai. This was a superb joining of lines and the 'N' litter arrived, with the grey dog Sabrefield Near the Marque (Best of Breed winner), and, in Australia, Ch. Sabrefield Novel Idea.

SABREFIELD NEW STORY
Liz kept the bitch Sabrefield New Story. She was a bitch of outstanding quality who became the first Malinois Junior Warrant Winner, was Belgian Shepherd Dog of the Year in 1989, and did much to promote the Malinois before the breeds

Sabrefield New Story.

were amalgamated in 1994. However, it is as a brood bitch that her true worth lies.

Her first litter, in 1991, at four years old, was to Peejay Dancing Brave, and produced some great male dogs: the red dog Sabrefield Over the Page, who won multiple Best of Breed titles, Sabrefield Overleaf, an excellent Agility dog, and Sabrefield Over the Sea, the first Malinois police dog in Sweden.

MANON DE LA BELLE EDITA AT SABREFIELD
At the same time that New Story was having her first litter, another bitch was imported from Belgium by Liz Richardson. Manon de la Belle Edita at Sabrefield went on to have two litters to New Story's son, Sabrefield Over the Page. The resulting 'Q' litter, born in 1993, produced Sabrefield Quite a Story (three RCCs), Sabrefield Qee Dee (Senior Agility qualifier), Sabrefield Quire Master (went to the Ministry of Defence), and, in Canada, Sabrefield Qurack of Klaar (Reserve Best of Winners).

Their second litter produced the bitches Sabrefield Sky's the Limit, and Sabrefield Sequelle, both top Agility and Championship show winners. The 'S' litter also produced Sabrefield Shout for Me, a Reserve CC winner as well as an Agility and Flyball winner.

THE 'R' AND 'T' LITTERS
Sabrefield New Story was also mated to her grandson, Sabrefield Qee Dee, and the marvellous 'R' litter arrived, a litter of great conformation, all with wonderful characters. The bitches included Sabrefield Right Answer for Bonvivant (one CC and three RCCs), and Sabrefield Raring to Go (CDEx, Open UD, one CC, two RCCs), Sabrefield Right on Cue (CDEx and Agility winner), and, in Sweden,

Sabrefield Reach for Me (Korad and CACIB).

New Story's next and final litter was to another grandson, Sabrefield Quire Master. Again, this produced good-looking dogs, although these were more work-oriented. Sabrefield Time Traveler became the first Malinois police dog in the UK, with Thames Valley Police. The grey male, Sabrefield Time Will Tell, excelled in Obedience. His sister, Sabrefield Tell Me A Story, was a Best of Breed winner as well as an Agility dog, and Sabrefield Top Story went on to produce working/show litters to Janice Tyer's Brown Warrior, a son of Gwashleas Dale (the only Malinois to win Reserve in the Working Group at Crufts, in 1991).

RECENT SABREFIELDS
The influence of New Story did not stop with her own litters. Her granddaughter, Sabrefield Quite a Story, produced another police dog, this time for West Mercia, in Sabrefield Vortex. Her second litter, to her nephew Sabrefield Right on Cue (CDEX), produced a Championship show-winning trio of bitches: Sabrefield What A Story (one RCC), and Sabrefield Way With Words and Sabrefield Wild Words (both Class winners and Agility winners).

Another New Story daughter, Sabrefield Right Answer For Bonvivant, produced Taz, the Aldershot police dog that went to the finals of the Police Dog Working Trials. Also produced was a bitch, Bonvivant Arc en Ciel (RCC).

From this small kennel have come the foundation stock for other well-known kennels in the UK: Peejay, Gwashleas, Tiffany and Bonvivant. Other kennels to produce Malinois using Sabrefield breeding include Leircote, Zodannta, Windetta, and Chievele.

LAEKENOIS

TWIES V. LIMBURG STAM OF ZHALE
Born in 1984, Twies V. Limburg Stam of Zhale was purchased as a puppy by Hazel Pond. Bred by Mme Gencijen V. Mill in Holland, she was out of Cesar and Elza. Her first litter, to the Malinois Sabrefield Aiming High, produced Zhale Nell Gwynn. Her next litter was to Oud Sabbinge Flint V. Donald of Zhale, another dog imported by Hazel Pond with Ann O'Shea. Oud Sabbinge was a lovely dog, winning many Best of Breeds, including Reserve Not Separately Classified at Crufts. This mating gave the Zhale Rough litter, with Zhale Ragged Muffin and Zhale Rough N Ready winning well in the UK. Both Zhale Rough Justice and Rough Diamond were exported to Sweden. Zhale Rough Justice was owned by Carina Wallin and gained the title of International Champion, having won his Swedish, Norwegian, Danish, and Finnish titles. Rough Justice also became a search and rescue dog.

Her third litter, again to Oud Sabbinge, produced Zhale Wishing Well Of Kelflyn, a Best of Breed winner. Her daughter, Zhale Ragged Muffin, also mated to Oud Sabbinge, produced Zhale Werewolf and Wily Fox. Special mention must go to Mr and Mrs Ralph's Zhale Melissa, who gained her stud book numbers – one of the few Laekenois in the UK to do this. She was the only representative of the breed at Crufts 2000, and now, as a veteran, she is the last of the Laekenois bitches in the UK.

12 *EUROPEAN PROFILES*

There are many excellent European Belgian Shepherd Dogs, of all varieties. This chapter focuses on some of the more influential.

TITLES

The reader may find the various European titles bemusing.

In France, any dog that is graded Excellent must pass a character test consisting of three parts: the first two are mandatory for any dog with this grading, while the third part is optional, and dogs taking part in it are trained for it. Any male dog that has won CACs (Championship Certificates) or Reserve CACs is unable to gain his title without passing this character test.

Throughout this chapter, dogs' names appear with the affix RE or Re. In short, the terms stand for Reproducteur Elite – Category A in the case of RE, and Category B in the case of Re.

GROENENDAELS

RE ONIX DU CHEMIN DES DAMES

Bred in 1965 by Jacqueline Aubry, out of RE Krack du Chemin des Dames and RE Mick de Iamara, Onix was an extremely popular stud dog of that era in France. He achieved his RE status through his offspring, SR Quelange de Mavoureen (by RE Jasmine de Iamara), SR Qualif de Mavoureen, SR Sardes de Mavoureen (by RE Noren de Mavoureen), RE Ringo du Donjon de Vincennes, RE Ch. Int. Ch. Ranke du Donjon de Vincennes, SR Ralf du Donjon de Vincennes, SR Thierry du Donjon de Vincennes (by RE Ozo du Chemin des Dames), and SR Terek des Trois Fleuves (by RE Loris de Marquisere).

RE OZO DU CHEMIN DES DAMES

This bitch was another bred by Mme Aubry. She was born in 1965 out of RE Jerry de Iamara and Lily du Chemin des Dames. She was sent to the Donjon de Vincennes Kennel of Mlle Annick Couasmet.

Her first litter, to Karl van Nekkerberg ter Leie, produced Quintin, Quella, and Quetty du Donjon de Vincennes.

The second, to Onix du Chemin des Dames, produced the R litter that included Re Ch. Int. Ch. Ranke du Donjon de Vincennes, SR Ralf, RE Ringo, and Swiss and Int. Ch. Ruxi du Donjon de Vincennes.

A second litter with Onix produced SR Thierry du Donjon de Vincennes, who became stud for the Forges Monceux kennel in Belgium.

RE VEGA DU CHEMIN DES DAMES

Vega was born in 1972 out of Rex du Parc d'Emonville and Quitta du Chemin des Dames. She was an outstanding brood bitch and produced many Champions and top-winning Groenendaels of her time. She was mated to the famous International Ch. Louky des Severiers on a number of occasions, each time with great success. Most Groenendael and Tervueren pedigrees include Vega, at least once. Not only was she a beautiful bitch, but she has passed on these qualities to her following generations.

RE CH. AND INT. CH. LOUKY DES SEVERIERS

Louky was born in 1975 out of Ch. and Int. Ch. Ranke du Donjon de Vincennes and Vesta de la Fontaine du Bois. He was shown eight times only, winning Best Belgian Shepherd in all varieties each time. He was an extraordinary producer – 332 puppies to 41 bitches. In the first generation, 32 dogs became recommended subjects (SR), and there were nine French Champions and eight foreign Champions (Italy, Luxembourg, Holland, Spain, Germany and Canada).

Louky's offspring were also influential in the working field, including the well-known Olympe de Chateau de Mirabeau, O'Nack de Chateau de Mirabeau, Naidia de Chateau de Mirabeau and Siva de la Piste de Damerjog.

In the second and third generation, his influence is still strong, most notably with the lovely grey Ch. Ares du Bois du Tot, and the Groenendael Ch. Kadour de la Quievre. Louky will be found in the pedigree of many of today's dogs, both Groenendaels and Tervueren.

RE CH. PERETTE DU CHEMIN DES DAMES

Born in 1979, out of RE Fr. and Int. Ch. Louky des Severiers and RE Vega du Chemin des Dames, Perette was sold to the Perigord Vert kennel of Mme Alain Rudeaux. She was bred to RE Fr. Ch. Clark de la Pouroffe, producing Silene du Perigord Vert. A 1986 litter with RE Fr. Ch. Sam de la Douce Plaine produced Nl. Ch. Bellman du Perigord Vert, RE Fr. Ch. Betsy, Fr. Ch. Braise (later belonging to the Clos du Cher kennel), and Danish Ch. Black Boy du Perigord Vert. The following year, Perette was bred to Ch. Int. Ch. Grimm van de Hoge Laer, and produced Carry du Perigord Vert, Re Cartoon du Perigord Vert, Cartouche du Perigord Vert, and Canelle du Perigord Vert. Carry was used at the van Lana's Hof kennel in Holland, Cartoon was

Ch. Perette du Chemin des Dames.

exported to Belgium, Cartouche entered the van de Hoge Laer kennel in Belgium, and Canelle entered the Grande Lande Kennel.

RE FR. CH. ROMY DU CHEMIN DES DAMES

Romy was born in 1980, from RE Fr. Int. Ch. Louky des Severiers and RE Vega du Chemin des Dames. Bred to RE Fr. Ch. Clark de la Pouroffe, Romy produced the T litter in 1982, which contained: Tito du Chemin des Dames, exported to Mme Bossi in Switzerland; RE Toasty du Chemin des Dames, the Tervueren that entered Mme Renee Demillier's Hauts de Bievre Kennel; and SR Toumai du Chemin des Dames. A repeat breeding in 1983 produced: Fr. Ch. Ukine du Chemin des Dames, entered to the Reserve des Princes Noirs Kennel in France; Un-Vision, exported to Belgium and influential in the van de Hoge Laer breedings; and Une Dame, entered to the de la Quievre Kennel in Belgium.

RE FR. BELG. NETH. LUX. CH. KADOUR DE LA QUIEVRE

Born in 1986, at the well-known de la Quievre Kennel in Belgium, and owned by Mr and Mrs Deschuymere, this great producer was a winner of CACs and CACIB. He won Best Dog at the French Specialty show in 1987, and was Champion of Europe in 1988.

Kadour goes back to the historical Belgian kennel of Forges Monceux, and to a Groenendael male, Vadis des Forges Monceux – son of Thierry du Donjon de Vincennes (RE Onix du Chemin des Dames ex Ozo du Chemin des Dames) – as well as to Quiette des Forges Monceux.

Vadis, mated to his daughter Asta des Forges Monceux (Vadis des Forges Monceux ex Unna de Forges Monceux),

Fr. Belg. Neth. Lux. Ch. Kadour de la Quievre. Photo Ritta Tjorneryd.

produced International Ch. Brigand de la Quievre. Brigand was mated to Oka de Iamara (Val de Mavoureen ex Volga de Iamara), and they produced the Groenendael male Ch. Int. and Nat. Ego de la Quievre. Ego was, in turn, mated to Gitane de la Quievre (daughter of Rendal de la Douce Plaine and SR Ch. Rhetie de Iamara), which produced Kadour.

Like his father, Ch. Ego, Kadour became one of the most successful producers of his generation. Kadour and Ego will be remembered not only for their excellent expressions, but also as producers of excellent temperament, which was characteristic for them.

RE BRISCAR DU SART DES BOIS

Re Briscar du Sart des Bois was born in Dr Denis Descamp's kennel in 1986, out of the Groenendael James du Clos de Raze and the red Tervueren Shawaz du

Sart des Bois. He entered the Douce Plaine kennel. His sire, James, was rarely used at stud, and was one of the rare Groenendael to successfully compete in Ring Sport 3. His list of SR offspring include Irish de la Grande Lande, Tayrha van't Belgisch Schoon, Figi de la Douce Plaine, Nelson de Kenatier, Ilene and Lison de Brunalines, Orlane des Tereres Bergeres, and Ceres Lynn and Jason de la Douce Plaine, a Groenendael that achieved third place in the class of best producers in 1999. The combination of James and Shawaz has been repeated, and produced Re Birdy du Sart des Bois.

RE FANDY BLACK DE CONDIVICNUM
Fandy was the only Groenendael son of Brennie du Sart des Bois, and was undoubtedly the finest of her offspring. He was the 'star' of his generation, and will remain in memory as the Groenendael

Fandy Black de Condivicnum.
Photo: Chris Fandy.

of the 1990s. With his irreproachable character, impressive coat, and his exceptional expression and chiselling, he had all the qualities that a breeder hopes one day to produce.

Fandy Black began his show career at 11 months, in great style, winning more than 20 Specialties in France and abroad under all the great judges. Towards the end of his show career, he won an impressive series of CAC and CACIBs – at Valladolid 1997 and 1998, Specialty of Marseille 1997, then the CAC French National Specialty 1998, where he also went Best in Show. This was followed by the CACIB at the Specialty of Orléans 1998, and his last show at Amiens 1999, where he won the CACIB and Best of Breed. An experienced show dog, he coped easily with the six-hour duration of a show and was always in super form in the final. Reproducteur Elite Category A, Fandy Black did not sire a great many litters, but his offspring are as appreciated as they deserve to be, and they, in turn, are reproducing well in the second generation.

TOSCA VANT GALE MAT
Tosca was born in 1974, for breeder H.A. Brandenburg, of Nijeveen in the Netherlands. Out of Wodan v.d. Adelweelde and Ric, she was purchased as a puppy by Bertus and Angela Barbe. Mated to Zoupy de la Baraque de Planches, she produced Ch. Athos and Akbar van't Belgisch Schoon. Her second litter, to Clark de la Pouroffe, produced SR Nl. Ch. Honey Black van't Belgisch Schoon.

Honey Black quickly gained her title. Her first litter, to Felix des Cinq Coquilles, produced the Z litter. When mated to Engel du Domaine Ponti, she produced SR Nl. Lux. Ch. Othiz, and Ch.

Romy van't Belgisch Schoon. Her next litter, to Dan de la Douce Plaine, produced the Y litter and Nl. Ch. Ylva van't Belgisch Schoon.

Honey Black's grandchildren continued in fine form. From Zantha Zarka came UK Ch. Alycon Parisien Prince at Vanistica, sire of several Vanistica Champions. Other well-known grandchildren include UK Ch. Gydo (see Chapter Eleven), Nor. Dan. Ch. Hurry Berry, SR Vendor, Am. Ch. Uniquest, SR Nl. Ch. Gaily van't Belgisch Schoon, Nl. Aaron de Palaemon, RE Gypsie de Mas de la Galandie, SR Gwendy de la Prairie de la Sommerau, SR Jami von den Schgaerwaard, US Ch. Mi-sha-ook Aquila, Mexican Ch. Mi-sha-ook Aspen O'Mawrmyth, and US Ch. Hailstorm Marajuyo.

WORLD CH. DUTCH LUX. EUROPEAN GER. CH. BUDDY VAN LANA'S HOF

Buddy was born in 1991 for breeder M. Scheepers, out of Mistyk van de Hoge

World Ch. Buddy van Lana's Hof.
Photo Ritta Tjorneryd.

Laer and E'Blackie de la Grande Lande. Reared with children, he really was a friend for owners Mart and Mia Scheepers, from Holland. A natural showman, he won his first title at the age of two and went on to win many awards, including his SR RE Elite A gradings. He produced several well-known Champions.

Mated to Wendy van Lana's Hof, he produced Am. Dan. Can. Dutch Ch. Jarl Wendy van Lana's Hof, and his sister Dutch, Ger. Lux. and European Ch. Bonnie Wendy van Lana's Hof. Mated to Jessie van Lana's Hof, he produced German Ch. Rebel Jessie van Lana's Hof. Mated to Nightrunners Windy Girl, he produced Dan. Sw. and Obedience Ch. Nightrunners Good as Gold. Buddy's influence continues with his grandchildren: UK Ch. Verona van de Hoge Laer at Belkanti, Am. Ch. Vienna van de Hoge Laer, Am. Ch. Sarron Sumerwynd Giovanni, Am. Ch. Touxi van de Hoge Laer, Int. Ch. T'Sisco van de Hoge Laer Schutzhund 3, and Dutch Ch. Chantryile Canadian Minister JW98. His untimely death occurred just as his influence was becoming acknowledged.

TERVUEREN

RE MILKO DU PARC DE L'HAY

Milko was born in France in 1963, out of the Groenendaels Harlem du Clos Rosny and Gaiety du Parc de l'Hay. A handsome grey with minimal masking, Milko was bred to both Groenendael and Tervueren, producing such outstanding offspring as the Groenendael SR Opale du Chemin des Dames, SR Poilu du Chemin des Dames, and RE Quilou du Chemin des Dames, out of Re Javotte du Chemin des Dames.

Bred to the grey Mira van Nekkerberg ter Leie, Milko sired the greys RE Quarry van Nekkerberg ter Leie, another outstanding producer, and his littermate Quito van Nekkerberg ter Leie, used in Belgium by the du Maugre and Champs du Bois Kennels. Bred to the Tervueren Manon des Bonmoss, Milko sired RE Pistache du Clos Briselet, entered to the Bois du Tot kennel.

CH. QUOWBOY DU LONG SPINOY
Born in 1967 for breeder Mme Bottemanne, out of the Groenendael Ogam de d'Artamas and the Tervuèren bitch Kinnie de la Ferme Termunt, Quowboy had an excellent show career and quickly gained his title. Selected as a recommended stud dog in 1969, he was of excellent all-round type, and went on to win 57 CACIB, and 26 CAC. He was at stud in Belgium on Groenendael, Malinois, and Tervueren, and was top stud in 1976. His most famous offspring are Lux. Ch. Tarass de la Pouroffe, and, from the same litter, Am. Ch. Tacou de la Pouroffe, SR Titan de la Pouroffe, Nl. Ch. Vibrato de la Pouroffe, and Urop de la Pouroffe.

RE LUX. WORLD CH. TARASS DE LA POUROFFE
Tarass was born in Belgium in 1970, out of RE Quowboy du Long Spinoy and Riquitta du Val des Aubepines. He was a tall, very red and masculine-looking male, with a long and elegant neck, a large mane, medium, well-set ears, good black masking, a majestic silhouette, a willing-to-please temperament, and an outstanding level of showmanship. Tarass had a long and successful show career, but it is as an outstanding sire that he has left his mark on the breed. Many of the best lines stem from the combination of Vici des Hauts de Bievre, with his exquisite head and expression, and Tarass de la

Pouroffe, for his beautiful outline and structure.

RE FR. CH. BEGGY OF THE TWO
Born out of RE If du Puits d'Ombelle and SR Juby des Trois Fleuves, Beggy was born at Erik Desschan's kennel in 1977, and purchased by Jean-Louis Vandenbemden. Beggy became the foundation bitch for Jean-Louis's van de Hoge Laer Kennel in Hoeilaart, Belgium. An elegant, feminine bitch, with excellent masking and tiny, well-placed ears, Beggy had an outstanding show career that included winning the CAC and Best Tervueren at the 1980 French National Specialty. However, it was as a valuable producer that she became most known. Through her descendants, Beggy of The Two is found in numerous Tervueren and Groenendael pedigrees worldwide.

RE BELG. FR. NL. CH. LUX. INT. CH. GRIMM VAN DE HOGE LAER
Produced by SR Zarka Of The Two crossed with RE Ch. Beggy Of The Two, Grimm was born in the back of a car

Belg. Fr. Nl. Ch. Lux. Int. Ch. Grimm van de Hoge Laer.

being driven from Mechelen to Hoeilaart, Belgium, on May 25th 1982. When he was old enough, he went to live with Firmin and Paula Aertgeerts in Holsbeek, Belgium, who also owned Grimm's sire, Zarka.

Those who knew Grimm described him as an extremely kind and confident dog, possessing not only good looks, but also working abilities, which earned him the CQN (Certificate of Natural Qualities) in Belgium, and the IPO I working title. His show wins, titles, and accomplishments were many, but it is as an outstanding producer that his name remains well known. Although no records were kept, it is estimated that Grimm sired at least 500 puppies, many becoming outstanding show, working, and foundation dogs for other kennels in a number of countries. Grimm passed away a few months short of his 13th birthday, and he is remembered as one of the outstanding Tervueren of modern times.

RE SWISS CH. VICI DES HAUTS DE BIEVRE
Vici was born in 1972, from RE Quarry van Nekkerberg ter Leie and Riane du Donjon de Vincennes. He was bred by Mme Renee Demillier and owned by Mme Delahaye in France. Vici was a lovely grey Tervueren who produced exceedingly well for a number of kennels. Among his many offspring were SR Zarka of the Two, Nl. Ch. Zultan of the Two, RE Maja du Bois du Tot, RE Nabor de la Noue St Eloi, and Fr. Ch. Priam du Castel des Biches. He was a major influence on Tervueren breeding in the mid 1970s, and many of today's dogs are still line-bred on Vici.

RE IF DU PUITS D'OMBELLE
Re If du Puits d'Ombelle was born in

France in 1973, for breeder Mlle Dusseau. Produced by Re Lux. Ch. Tarass de la Pouroffe and Re Tania du Chemin des Dames, he was sold to Mme Rochas in France. Mated to Juby des Trois Fleuves, If sired Fr. Ch. Beggy of the Two, the foundation bitch for the van de Hoge Laer kennel in Belgium. He also sired Lux. Ch. Bagheera Of The Two, dam of the British import Fanfare Of The Two, and British import Boris Of Thee Two. A repeat mating produced Danish Ch. Don Quichotte Of The Two, and Dundee Of The Two, the foundation bitch Of The Questenberg kennel. Mated to Morgane de Mas des Terribles, If produced Fr. Ch. Sheriff du Mas des Terribles, sire of Thibaud du Puits d'Ombelle, a dog imported into Britain. Also sired was Thalie de Puits d'Ombelle, the foundation bitch for the Clairiere aux Louves kennel in France.

MIRABELLE DU CHEMIN DES DAMES
Bred by Jacqueline Aubry, and born in France in 1976, Mirabelle was produced by the Groenendael SR Vaour du Mas de Sevre and Judy du Chemin des Dames. Mirabelle was noted not only for the titles she earned, but also for the dogs she produced, and what her offspring, in their turn, produced.

Mated to Vici des Hauts de Bievre, she produced Opale du Sart des Bois, the dam of RE Fr. Ch. San de la Douce Plaine, and Orex du Sart des Bois, ancestors of the British Champions France and Ferry de la Douce Plaine.

Mated next to Neron du Sart des Bois, she produced Phantome du Sart des Bois, the grandsire of RE Briscar du Sart des Bois. Mated to the Groenendael Fr. Ch. Orlick du Chemin des Dames, Mirabelle produced the T litter that contained: RE

Tiakie; RE Teksa du Sart des Bois, entered to the Bois du Tot kennel; and Tomrick du Sart des Bois, the sire of UK Ch. Leyla vant Wouwenhof. Mated to RE Int. Ch. Grimm van de Hoge Laer in 1984, Mirabelle produced SR Vrac du Sart des Bois, the sire of Jolie Canelle du Domaine Ponti, who entered the van de Lamar kennel in Holland.

FR. CH. SAM DE LA DOUCE PLAINE

Sam was bred by Martine and Pascal Tartare, and he was born in 1981. He had a very successful and distinguished career, both as a show dog and as a stud dog. He was by Barox de la Pouroffe (brother of UK Ch. Bandol), and his dam was Opale du Sart des Bois, a daughter of the famous Vici. Sam's illustrious show career included Best in Show at the French BSD Specialty.

Sam sired numerous Champions around the world, including two Groenendaels. He was a prepotent stud, often reused by the same breeders. Marcelle King, of Belamba Tervueren, saw photos of Sam in a French magazine and fell in love. On meeting him in the flesh, she found he was even better. She imported three of his children and was not disappointed as all three became British Champions, also inheriting Sam's exceptional temperament. Sam epitomised the Tervueren, with a beautiful head and expression, fabulous body shape, and, above all, a superb temperament. He died, aged 11, from throat cancer – a great loss.

RE FR. EURO AND LUX CH. ARES DU BOIS DU TOT

Ares was born at Dr Surget's kennel in Eu, France, in 1985, from SR Samour de la Javottierre de Corberon and RE Teksa du Sart des Bois. He was owned by Mme Fouquier. A beautiful grey, Ares not only

Fr. Euro and Lux Ch. Ares du Bois du Tot. Photo Ritta Tjorneryd.

had a highly successful show career, which included winning the French Championship four times, but he also dominated French long-haired breeding for almost a decade. He was awarded the title of Best Producer in France for 1991 and 1993, and he has sired more than 30 SR dogs, including Re Day-Dreem de Condivicnum, RE Daphnee du Castel d'Argences, RE Delphes du Castel d'Argences, RE Fidji du Castel d'Argences, RE US and Mon. Ch. Gourou du Crepuscule des Loups, and the black RE Fr. Ch. Gylson de la Fureur du Crepescule.

BRENNIE DU SART DES BOIS

Born in November 1986, Brennie was descended from exceptional bloodlines, the result of a long-term breeding programme by the Sart des Bois Kennel. Homed at two months by her breeder Denis Descamps, Brennie was taken back at one year because her owner was no longer in a position to keep her. She was placed again with a breeder wanting a bitch from the Sart des Bois Kennel, but the breeder changed her mind after a month and Brennie was returned once more.

Christophe Pichon had seen a photo of Brennie at 11 months of age, and, when Denis Descamps told him about the setbacks he was having with this bitch, Pichon immediately asked if he could take her and show her. Three days afterwards, at the end of July 1998, he collected Brennie at the Belgian Shepherd Day in Lille.

Brennie's arrival at Christophe's house was a great event, and she quickly formed an attachment to his two-year-old son, Landry. A month later she was mated, for the Sart des Bois Kennel, to SR Akim de Condivicnum. However, Brennie was too young for motherhood, overprotecting her puppies to an extent that they grew up somewhat timid, despite the sire's super character.

Brennie took a long break from maternal duties and became acclimatised to her new environment. She started her show career in 1989 and finished it as a veteran at the Spanish National Specialty in Valladolid 1996, where she won the title of Best Veteran in Show, with her granddaughter I Kiss You de Condivicnum winning the CAC from the Open Class.

For her first litter for the Condivcnum Kennel, permission for an intervariety

Brennie de Sart des Bois. Photo: Yan.

breeding was obtained and she was mated to the Groenendael RE Dandy du Chemin des Dames. The only Groenendael dog in the litter was RE Ch. Fandy Black de Condivicnum, the biggest Groenendael winner of the decade. Brennie was Top Tervueren Bitch in France for eight consecutive years, a record that is unparalleled. Of her many offspring, 31 obtained Excellent gradings at French Specialties, 16 have won placings at the French National Specialty, and, between them, they have won at 50 regional Specialties in France and Specialty shows abroad, as well as winning 6 times at the French National Specialty.

Brennie was a bitch of good size, with a well-chiselled head of perfect proportions. She had small, typical ears, black eyes, excellent pigmentation, and was short in body. Her only imperfections were that she was slightly straight in the shoulder, her feet were a little long, and her croup sloped slightly. A bitch of enormous class, she had great presence, and the harmony of her silhouette complemented her remarkable head type.

Eden de la Clairiere aux Louvres.

DAY DREEM DE CONDIVICNUM
Day Dreem was born in 1988, from a mating between Ch. Arës du Bois du Tot and Adena de Condivicnum. He started his stud career in 1990, and his influence was phenomenal, particularly given the small number of litters he sired before he went to live with his owners on the Pacific island of Reunion, in 1993. After their return to France in 1997, he was again at stud until 1998.

The extent of Day Dreem's influence can be seen in many pedigrees, both in France and beyond. He produced short bodies with very typical heads, good masks and very black eyes. His lovely reach of neck, his expression, his class, and his beautiful coat are qualities that are very evident in his offspring. He had the capacity to produce 'stars' in almost every litter he sired throughout his short career as a stud dog. Although he was not the most outstanding dog of his generation, the combination of his personal qualities and his exceptional pedigree made him a very prepotent stud dog.

RE EDEN DE LA CLAIRIERE AUX LOUVRES
Born in 1989 for breeder Michele Griol, Eden was out of Re Ch. Grimm van de Hoge Laer and Altesse de la Clairiere Aux Louvres. She was bred four times to Re Femto du Bois du Tot and produced 10 SR dogs and two Champions, SR Happy Dream, SR Horry, SR Ch. Fin Halloween Bre, SR Ch. Lane, SR Lutin, SR Liberty, SR Lynx, SR Lutece, SR Milton, and SR Mandy. There were also several quality offspring from this mating that have not been shown at the French Specialty: Heden, at the Prarie de la Sommerau Kennel; Morae in the US; and Montana, at the van de Hoge Laer Kennel in Belgium. However, Magnum, owned by the Corsini Kennel in the UK, went BIS at the French Specialty 2000.

MALINOIS

CESAR DE L'ASSA
Cesar was born in Belgium, at M. Hantson's kennel, on August 22nd 1953. Produced by Burgos and Vala de Mahyfaut, he became the most well-known Malinois of his era. Shown successfully for eight years, Cesar was the winner of numerous CACs and CACIBs. It was as a sire, however, that he has left

an indelible mark on the breed. Some of his offspring include the CAC winners Filou de l'Assa, Harie de l'Assa, LeBeau de l'Assa, and the beautiful Fabine de l'Assa. A carrier of the long-haired gene, Cesar also sired the Tervueren Jimmy and Kiou de l'Assa, both of which were exported, to the French kennels of Clos Saint-Clair and Clos Saint-Jacques respectively. There are few Malinois or Tervueren today that cannot be traced back to Cesar de l'Assa

RE BELGIAN CH. QU'RACK DU BOIS D'EMBLISE
Born in Belgium on September 19th 1967, Qu'Rack was originally known as Juan du Monastre Antique – Qu'Rack was the name he carried when he became famous. Entering the Boscaille Kennel in Belgium, Qu'Rack earned his Working Certificate in trials, competed in Working Championships in Belgium. He was a finalist in the 1971 and 1972 Championships, earning his CQN in conformation showing in Belgium, and produced litters for the Ventadour and Fontaine du Bois Kennels in France, the du Maugre, Boscaille and van Bouwelhei Kennels in Belgium, and the Colombophile Kennel in Switzerland. Some Qu'Rack offspring include International Ch. Vainqueur du Boscaille, RE Jams de Ventadour, and Am. Ch. Iakie de Ventadour, UD, Sch H 3. A carrier of the long-haired gene, Qu'Rack produced a number of Tervueren, including RE Xosie du Maugre, whose offspring include UK Ch. Bandol de la Pouroffe, Barox de la Pouroffe, and Dali and Darras de la Pouroffe.

RE CH. STEED DU HAMEAU ST. BLAISE
Born in Belgium in 1994, from RE

Maubray du Maugre and Re Purdey de la Casa du Barry, Steed became the most titled Malinois of the last 25 years. During the four years he was shown, he was the winner of 40 CAC/CACIBs under 22 judges in 7 countries. He is the father of more than 70 puppies all over Europe, and some of them already have very successful careers in the show ring. After the French Speciality 2000, Steed became an RE – a consecration for an exceptional dog.

RE RANIE DE VENTADOUR
Ranie and her brother, SR Fr. Ch. Raky de Ventadour, were born in France on July 27th 1968. They were double grandchildren of Cesar de l'Assa, out of RE Fr. Ch. Ogar de Ventadour and RE Lady des Chenevelles. Ranie became the foundation bitch for the Mas des Lavandes kennel of Mme Auriant. Ranie was noted for her beautiful head, and she is the Malinois head in Luc Goosen's four-head study of the varieties. She produced exceptionally well.

RE CH. LADY DE LA CASA DU BARRY
Lady was born in 1987, from Ch. Ino de la Casa du Barry and SR Ch. Fanny de la Casa du Barry. She was produced from an inbreeding on RE Ch. Raky de Ventadour and RE Ch. Qu'Rack du Bois d'Emblise. Her show career did not start until she was nearly five.

Noted for her exceptional head and expression, she was drawn by F. Aertgeerts. Bred to Ch. Markos de la Casa du Barry, she produced two males that have an influence on the variety. Lady was also bred to SR Ch. Pedro de la Casa du Barry and two males were exported, one to the USA and the other, Ch. Twice du Hameau St. Blaise, best young male at the

Ch. Lady de la Casa du Barry.

French Speciality 1996, became the foundation male for Malinois breeding in Russia.

LAEKENOIS
This rough-haired variety of the Belgian Shepherd has its origin in the park area at the castle of Laeken, where the shepherd family Janssen lived with their sheep and dogs. The dogs, which were known as hard-biting dogs, were not used for herding, but for guarding the laundries against theft. The family spoke only Flemish, and, therefore, they had very little contact with other breeders. J.B. Janssen had, for a long time, bred these rough-haired dogs, and he knew the exact pedigree for each of them. Some of Janssen's dogs were short-haired while others were rough-coated. Janssen himself

said: "The quality of a dog has nothing to do with its length of coat, neither its colour."

One of the males, Vos I de Laeken, was red-yellow and rough-haired. Mated with the grey-brown, short-haired female, Liske de Laeken, he produced the male Tom and the bitch Spitz, the foundation of the rough-haired variety. In the same litter were two other females, Diane and Mouche, which count as the 'origin-mothers' of the Malinois. Diane became mother of the famous Malinois Tjop and Mouche of Dewet. The combination of Vos/Spitz (daughter of Vos and Liske) produced Moor, a black, rough-haired bitch. Tom, red-brown and rough-coated, became father of Vos II (out of Belle). Vos II, together with Mira, produced the male Bazoef. He, in turn, was mated to

Multi Ch. Opium van Kriekebos: One of the most influential Laekenois of all time.

Representatives of the vom Fleosserdorf kennel in Switzerland.

his own mother, Mira, and produced the well-known rough-haired male, Boer Sus. This inbreeding fixed the coat quality and the colour of today's Laekenois. Vos I de Laeken died in 1897, aged 12.

The Laekenois sometimes show very differing types, but, according to the Standard, there is only one that is correct. Laekenois must carry the same elegance as the other varieties, being neither too heavy, nor too light, in construction. One of the most important breed points is the correct roughness of the coat. The colour should be red-brown, with traces of overlay, mainly on the muzzle and the tail. The length of coat must be the same all over the body, and the tail must not have any plume. In temperament, the rough-haired Belgian has to be the same as the other varieties of Belgian Shepherd.

SOME IMPORTANT LAEKENOIS KENNELS
Kennel names such as v.d. Middachten, Of the Orchid's Home, V. Elina's Home, V. Limburg Stam, vant Brugske, Van Verdediger and de Vlaamsche Scheper, are some examples of famous Dutch

Laekenois kennels, which will be found in many pedigrees, but there are, of course, many more.

Well-known Belgian kennels are Van Kriekebos, Van Balderlo, Du Bois Chablis, Van de Duvetorre, and Des Fauves de Saline. D'Eroudur, owned by Christine Bouchat, split from Des Fauve de Saline in 1999, and now standing on its own with independent breeding.

Switzerland has the Von Venus Kennel and also the Vom Floesserdorf. In Finland, there is a very successful Kennel with the prefix Valkohaampan (which also breeds Groenendaels), from where some dogs have been exported to the country of origin, Belgium. In Denmark, the Oud-Sabbinge and Pelsens Kennels stand for many typical and prize-winning individuals, and both of them have exported several Laekenois.

The Swedish Kennel, Fannyhill's, was a pioneer in Sweden, when it imported Cilli vom Floesserdorf from Switzerland in 1984. Fannyhill's Kennel (also breeders of Tervueren and Groenendael) have, at present, bred the most litters in Sweden.

Norwegian kennels that breed, or have bred, Laekenois, are Fakaiser's and Zagal's. The former is perhaps better known for its Groenendael and Tervueren breeding, while the second for its Malinois, but both have bred many Champions.

HOLLAND
Influential Laekenois in Holland include the fauve male Nl. Ch. Marcoo (Donald ex Adage), born in a litter of seven on April 21st 1957. Marcoo sired many Champions and is still present in many pedigrees. A famous daughter of Marcoo and Minkah was Nl. Ch. Int. Ch. de Vlaamsche Scheper Skivari, born in 1966, and mother to many other well-known

Laekenois. Marcoo sired 23 litters from 12 different bitches between 1960 and 1967.

In 1966, another important male, Arno Van Het Roosterbos (De Vlaamsche Scheper Robert ex Genovita), was born. Arno sired 12 litters, which gave 8 different combinations. Many line breedings have been done from his lines. His last litters were born in 1972.

Another important male is Nl. Ch. Ezer Van De Middachten, born on May 27th 1983 (Nl. Int. Ch. VH I Bart v.d. Middachten ex Nl. Lux.Ch. Nova v.d. Middachten). Ezer sired six litters with six different females, and a great number of his offspring have influenced the type of today.

A well-known Dutch female is Nora Van Limburg Stam (Caspar v. Limburg Stam ex Beertje). She has produced 24 puppies; two litters with Mendo v. d. Middachten and the third with Ezer v. d. Middachten. From the combination with Mendo (in 1984) came the famous Dutchman of The Orchid's Home, but she has also produced other typical and beautiful dogs.

BELGIUM
Evelyn and Dany Comeine are breeders at the Van Kriekebos Kennel in Belgium. In 1983, they bred a litter from Max v.d. Schepershoeve and Floride de l'Apache, which produced two males, Hussard and Hassan v. Kriekebos. Both matured into beautiful dogs with correct type, and both gained their Champion titles. SR Lux. Ch. Hassan v. Kriekebos Losh became an influential sire, producing successful children and grandchildren in Belgium, France, South Africa, Germany, Holland, Finland and Sweden. At the age of 6, he was exported to Anita and Hans Nirholt, at Fannyhill's Kennel in Sweden, and

became very important for the Scandinavian breeders.

When Hassan arrived from Belgium, he had already gained 21 CCs and 15 CACIBs. Together with Jody van Kriekebos, a half-sister to Hassan (out of Ch. Ego du Maugre, a Malinois crossed with Floride de l'Apache), he produced the famous and prize-winning SR Max van Kriekebos Alsh. Max is credited with improving many lines – SR Lux. Ch. Opium van Kriekebos Losh (Max v. K. ex Lux. Ch. SR Kanelle v. Kriekebos), for example.

When the Journée Internationale et Amicale du Laekenois was held in Moscron in September 1997, 120 Laekens, from many different countries, were represented. Each one was shown and given a written critique. The one that follows is for the beautiful Opium: "Excellent head, very typical, correct stop, excellent parallelism, ears of medium length, well carried, excellent coat texture, good dry hair, good attachment of the neck, good back, good chest, nice feet, angulations in forequarters and hindquarters, good covering gait, moves a little narrow behind, very good Belgian type." Opium has some promising offspring and has sired many Champions.

SWEDEN
The Swiss import, Cilli vom Floesserdorf, was the very first Laekenois in Sweden. Cilli was imported by Anita and Hans Nirholt at Fannyhill's. Unfortunately, she died in an accident after only a year. Fannyhill's then imported her sister, Dizza vom Floesserdorf (born in 1985 from Fedor v. Sisgau ex Nicole Poretta). Kennel El-Jo-Mi's also imported her litter-brother, Dingo. In 1987, the first Laekenois litter in Sweden was born. The mother was Dizza, and the sire was Dutchman of the

Multi Ch. Zhale Rough Justice: A record-breaking dog in Sweden.

Orchid's Home. From this litter came the first Finnish Laekenois. The Fannyhill's kennel has produced a total of five litters.

In 1987 Kennel El-Jo-Mi's produced Sweden's second litter. Dingo was crossed with the Danish-imported female, Oud-Sabbinge Holly v. Ezer. The offspring from this mating developed into successful working and show dogs. In 1988 two Laekens from the same litter came to Sweden, Zhale Rough Justice, and his sister, Rough Diamond. Zhale Rough Justice remains one of the highest prize-winning Laekenois in Sweden, and has passed the highest level of character tests and the rescue dog title. One of his sons, Lacken-vacken d'Artagnan (out of Int. Nordic Ch, TJH Fannyhill's Chantal), has also achieved considerable success, carrying the titles Sw. Norw. Int. Ch. Norw. Korad Tjh LP.

Other Swedish breeders are the kennels of Vajert, Hund's and Humlan's. The brood bitch at Vajert is Korad Paradise Lady, known as Effie (Ch. Hassan v. Kriekebos ex Ch. Zagal's Felissia), and Vajert Qinza (daughter of Effie and Multi Ch. Pelsens Scirocco). Effie was imported from Norway. At Kennel Hund's the brood bitch was Ch. SR Fakaiser's Hacy de Hexagone (Ch. Hassan v. Kriekebos ex Ch. Nouchka v. Kriekebos). Hacy had two litters with Belg. Ch. Quichot v.d. Duvetorre, but, unfortunately, she died unexpectedly in the springtime of 2000, leaving her last litter at five weeks of age. Hacy won many shows, including the French Specialty, where she gained the SR title.

Humlan's Kennel breed from their lovely female Vajert Quindy, a sister to Qinza, at Kennel Vajert. Quindy had a litter with Multi Ch. Opium v. d. Kriekebos, from which one dog has been exported to Belgium and another to the US.

THE BELGIAN SHEPHERD IN NORTH AMERICA

The status of the four Belgian Shepherd varieties continues to rise in the US, thanks to the efforts of some particularly influential kennels.

NORTH AMERICAN TITLES

Throughout the text, dogs are named with their achievements listed after their names. To avoid confusion, definitions of those achievements are given here.

- Ch.: Conformation Champion.
- UDT: Utility Dog Tracker. This title is earned after a dog completes his third level of Obedience work at American Kennel Club trials, plus a title earned at a tracking test.
- OA: Open Agility. This title is earned after a dog completes his second level of Agility work at AKC trials.
- AD: A Schutzhund title earned at an endurance event that requires the dog to trot next to a bicycle for 12 miles, and to perform some simple Obedience exercises.
- SchH3: A title earned after a dog completes his third level of competition in the sport of Schutzhund, requiring the dog to demonstrate, in a one-day trial, competence in tracking, Obedience, and protection work. This is the highest title awarded.
- IPO1: The first level of the international

version of Schutzhund. It is similar to the TDX title in the AKC.
- ROM: Registry of Merit, awarded by the BSCA, based on how many Champions and performance-titled offspring a dog or bitch produces. The dog or bitch must have the Companion Dog title, and pass various health clearances. He or she must also earn points (100 for dogs, 50 for bitches) based on their titled offspring.
- HOF: Hall of Fame. This is also awarded by the BSCA, based on points awarded for various group placements and best of specialties.
- SR: Recommended Subject. This title, the only French title to be included in this section, is a highly prestigious award given at the Nationality Speciality Show.

GROENENDAEL KENNELS

CADRE NOIR

The Cadre Noir kennel was established by Mary-Linda Adams, who became involved with Belgian Shepherds in 1974. Her first dogs were American Groenendaels. She moved to Europe in 1977, started buying and showing dogs under the affix Loup Noir, and was fortunate to have excellent mentors such as Jacqueline Aubry, Jean

Am. Ch. Boris de la Pouroffe, owned by Mary-Linda Adams.

Renard, and Raoul Godeau. She owned Lux. Ch. Baraka de la Baraque de Planches, from the kennel of Leon Bottemanne, a bitch defeated only once in her European show career. She also purchased Am. Ch. Boegna de Domaine Ponti, one of the top ten males in Belgium in 1978.

Later, Mary-Linda acquired the top-winning Am. Lux. Ch. Boris de la Pouroffe, and imported many other dogs to the US, notably Ch. Devon and Ch. Drakkar de la Pouroffe, Paola del Lago Nero, Ch. Desirée de la Pouroffe, and Ch. Celte de la Pouroffe CD. However, the increased travel required by her work made it difficult to continue with the dogs, and she formed a partnership with Katherine John.

Veterinary technician Kathy bought her first Belgians from Mary-Linda in 1988. When Mary-Linda relocated to the West Coast, Kathy offered to assist with the dogs. In 1994, Mary-Linda moved back to the East Coast and the partnership was formed.

Continental dogs have completely dominated this kennel's breeding programme. Mary-Linda's most successful dog was Boris de la Pouroffe. He was almost flawless, with the rare qualities of a long head, tiny, well-set ears, a long neck, and a short back. His front was perfect, with a prominent prosternum, equal length scapula and humerus, and perfect alignment of the front and rear. He influenced Tervueren and Groenendael lines the world over.

SUMERWYND
Since 1986, Rick and Dennette Cockley have shared their home and hearts with Belgian Sheepdogs. However, it was not until 1989 that they established their New Hampshire-based kennel. Two bitch puppies, who grew up to become Group placing Ch. Rolin Ridge Mystique Ete, bred by Jan Manuel and Carolyn Kelso, and BISS, five-times Select Am. Can. Ch. Johnsondale's Windsong CD, HIC, HOF, became the foundation for SumerWynd Belgian Sheepdogs, and provided the kennel with a name.

The turning point in the SumerWynd breeding programme came with the litter produced by Den. NL Ch. Kevin From Black Home and Ch. Johnsondale's Windsong. Although the litter was of good quality, the offspring from the pups in that litter, Kevin and Windsong's grandchildren, have achieved more success in the breed ring.

LISWYN
Lisa Leffingwell acquired her first Belgian in 1978 as a present from her mother. At that time she was almost too old for junior showmanship competitions, and she wanted a dog she could show in both Conformation and Obedience. Her first dog, Ch. Pistol's Son of a Gun of Geka CD, bred by Dottie Lee, gave her a taste for the breed, and she has been devoted to Belgians since.

Lisa believes that the best dog to

emerge from her Dallas-based kennel is Ch. Liswyn's Firefly of Geka UD, produced by Ch. Liswyn Augustus McRae of Geka and Ch. Liswyn's Candlefire of Geka UKX, ROM. European dogs have influenced Lisa's breeding through the sire of her foundation bitch Ch. Mawrmyth Nadia Mika at Geka UD, ROM, bred from the import Vicomte du Parc de l'Hay. Lisa is currently campaigning Mawrmyth Mallo Mar O'Liswyn, progeny of a sire and dam from Holland.

Lisa hopes that, in the future, the current trend towards extremes of type will be tempered by an emphasis on structure. Her ambitions are to retain the breed's intelligence, by not focusing too hard on the physical features to the detriment of temperament.

ROLIN RIDGE

Linda McCarty, from Virginia, was an experienced dog owner and exhibitor when she saw a male Belgian at a show and began enquiring about the breed. She has owned, handled, and bred some truly extraordinary dogs, which have won two All-Breed Best in Shows and five National Specialty Best in Shows. Her most famous individual, and, in her opinion, the best dog she has owned, handled and bred, Ch. Rolin Ridge's Fourteen Karat CD, HIC, CGC, HOF, ROM, was the first Belgian Sheepdog to win three National Specialty Best in Show awards and also the first to be placed in the Group at the prestigious Westminster Kennel Club. To date, he remains the breed's top-producing sire, with 95 Champions to his credit.

European dogs have always influenced Linda's breeding programmes. Her foundation bitch, Ch. Endymion's Charisma CD, HIC, ROM, was doubled on a top-producing import, Ch. Quivala

de la Baraque de Planches. Her second litter was to S.R. Boegna de Domaine Ponti. Since then, her pedigrees show the influence of some of the most well-known European lines and kennels.

ISENGARD

Lorra Miller purchased her first Belgian, a Groenendael from the Siegestor Kennel, in 1977. She had admired the versatility of the Belgian breeds for some time, and she wished to compete in both Obedience and Conformation. Am. Ch. Brenna v Siegestor UDT, ROM WD-C was a wonderful Obedience dog, very sound in temperament and structure.

In 1995, Lorra finally found more time to devote to dogs and managed to book a puppy from a bitch she had always admired, BISS five-times Select Am. Can. Ch. Johnsondale's Windsong CD, HIC, HOF. The puppy lived up to expectations and has become the Multiple group winning BISS three-times Select Am. Can. Ch. Sumerwynd's Dana of Isengard HX, AX, AXJ, CDX, TD, WD-X, HOF. She has exceeded her owner's expectations, and, in Lorra's opinion, she is the best dog she has owned to date.

Lorra's kennels, based in Washington State, have long been influenced by European dogs. In 1999 she flew Dana to the Netherlands to be mated to Angela Barbe's R.e. Greco de la Grande Lande. The subsequent litter, although still young, are proving themselves in the ring.

KUPENDA

Sonja Ostrom, from Denver, Colorado, has owned Groenendaels since 1957, although she did not start competing with them until 1985. Sonja's daughter has travelled and taught in Kenya, which explains the kennel affix Kupenda – Swahili for love.

In the 1990s, Sonja began importing Laekenois from Norway, France and Belgium, and she works constantly towards not allowing this variety to die out.

In terms of temperament, the best dog Sonja has owned was her Groenendael Ch. U-CD Kupenda's Machachari CD, PT, NA, TT. He is the sire of several working service dogs, including wheelchair dogs, a seizure-alert dog, hearing dogs, and dogs working with brain-damaged children. He epitomises the character and temperament of a Belgian. Her prettiest dog is her Groenendael U-Ch Erin's Venot de'Loree Cygne HT, JHD, TT, a beautiful dog with an excellent temperament and working ability, as well as excellent herding abilities.

Sonja is attempting to focus on health in the breed, establishing a health registry and promoting performance events. She was the founding president of the American Belgian Laekenois Association, and she hopes to see the Laekenois variety once more recognised by the AKC in the United States.

MAWRMYTH
Marcy Spalding established her Mawrmyth kennel in Houston, Texas, when she acquired her first Belgian in 1972. This dog won his Championship title along with Obedience titles.

Since her first dog, Marcy has produced more than 50 Champions, either directly from her breeding, or through dogs she has bought in for her breeding programme. Some of Marcy's dogs have also gained Obedience titles, although she has not recently exhibited in this activity. Instead, her attention has moved on to breeding, judging, teaching conformation classes, publishing the Belgian Sheepdog

Handbooks, and being active in local and national dog clubs.

Early on in her breeding programme, Marcy began using European dogs to improve type in head, coat and outline. She has imported several dogs, and also sent bitches to be mated in Europe. Her goal has been to breed Belgians with more of a European type, as opposed to the structure and movement seen in the US.

Her favourite Belgian is Am. Can. Ch. Mi-Sha-Ook's Wonita, her foundation bitch. In the future, Marcy would like to see the AKC recognise Belgian Shepherds as one breed with four varieties. She is also eagerly awaiting the development of DNA testing for health problems in the breed.

MI-SHA-OOK
In 1959, students Skip and Elsie Stanbridge married and acquired their first Belgian Shepherd Dog. Although their choice was not the result of a strong desire to own a dog of this breed, Belgians have influenced their lives ever since. Obedience competitions followed, and they developed an interest in breeding and showing.

Skip and Elsie acquired another two bitches, and established their Mi-Sha-Ook Ontario-based kennels in Canada in 1961. However, they quickly realised that no amount of socialisation, training or feeding would change the basic genetic make-up of the dog. Several trips to Europe in the late 1960s and the early 1970s, and their friendship with Mme Aubry of Chemin des Dames fame and Mme Demillier of Hauts de Bievre, helped them to develop a concept of the Belgian that is still apparent today.

They have continued to breed Belgian Shepherd Dogs for the past 40 years. Primarily a Groenendael kennel, they have always introduced Tervurens when they think that the dog might contribute to what they want to produce. The issue of coat type and colour is, in their view, and from a genetic position, an easy one to deal with. The other genetic issues in the breed, such as temperament, epilepsy, hip dysplasia, eye problems, heart and blood disorders etc., are more important issues, and should never be overshadowed by the variety and coat debate.

With more than 40 years of breeding, it is difficult to isolate a few special dogs that have been most instrumental in the kennel. However, three spring to mind: Am. Can. Ch. Star de la Baraque de Planches, acquired from Mr and Mrs Bottemanne in 1969, went on to win an All Breed BIS – the first for a Belgian in North America – and several specialty BIS. He was instrumental in changing the direction of the breed in North America. Am. Can. Ch. Mi-Sha-Ook's Wista exemplified type and quality and possessed a wonderful temperament and character, while Am. Can. Ch. Mi-Sha-Ook's Annick was outstanding in type and soundness.

CHANTRYILE

Greg Storms and Eleanor Heagy have been involved with Belgian Shepherds since 1988. Both grew up with dogs and decided that they wanted a medium-sized dog that was intelligent, trainable, and protective, with a longer coat and no face hair or beard. Through research they came upon Belgians. Living in Ontario, Canada, Greg and Eleanor found breeders living nearby, Skip and Elsie Stanbridge, whose assistance and introductions were instrumental in establishing the Chantryile breeding programme. They purchased their first Belgian from Skip and Elsie in 1988 – Ch. Mi-Sha-Ook Tamarack.

The next Belgian to join Chantryile was Elysée de la Douce Plaine (Engel du Domaine Ponti ex Biesca de la Douce Plaine) from France. Since then, two other dogs have been imported from the Netherlands: Am. Can. Ch. Nicole-Blackie van Lana's Hof Am. Can. CD (Kimba van Lana's Hof crossed with Blackie de la Grande Lande), and Ch. Carry Jessie van Lana's Hof CD (Ch. Buddy van Lana's Hof crossed with Jessie van Lana's Hof).

Greg and Eleanor have always loved the European type; the elegance, gorgeous head, expression, and outline. They have tried to marry this elegance to correct structure and stable temperament, to produce a balanced dog with a strong character and an excellent temperament. In their opinion, the best dog to arise from their breeding programmes is Am. Ch. Chantryile Célébre Abigail (Ch. Buddy van Lana's Hof crossed with Ch. Johnsondale's Jolene). Abigail has excelled in the breed ring in North America.

In 2000, they produced their first litter of Tervuren from an English-French background. The dam, Belle Étoile de la Lune, is a recessive black from Questenberg Rheingold of Branock and Am. Ch. Domburg Talk of the Town. The sire is Neartic de la Grande Lande. Recently, they have also obtained a recessive-black puppy bitch, sired by Branock Rhythm 'n' Blues to the dam Domburg French Flair. This beautiful puppy will help to introduce some new blood to the black lines in North America.

Like many North American breeders, Greg and Eleanor hope the AKC will reclassify Belgians as one breed with four varieties. This will enlarge the gene pool and enable breeders to make choices that are, currently, unfeasible. Canada has no restrictions about intervariety breeding.

SANS BRANCO BELGIANS

Terri Ann Votava became actively involved in the breed in 1972. Her Sans Branco Belgians kennel was established in 1980, in Franklyn, Tennessee, with the purchase of the foundation dog Ch. Crocs-Blancs' Darth Vadir CD, bred by D. Daugherty and L. Halpin. He grew up to be an elegant dog with a beautiful temperament and a desire to work and please. His European outline was passed to his children. In 1982, Terri leased Ch. Sunsdown's Debut, from Mike and Marcy Fine of the Sunsdown kennels, and produced her first litter.

Terri is dedicated to producing a sound dog in both mind and body, with health and temperament being of the utmost importance. She believes that dogs must, first and foremost, be a member of the family; titles, whether performance or conformation, are secondary to the production of a dog that is a healthy, trusted, and reliable member of the family.

TERVUEREN

ARRIVEE

Lisa Bates met her first Belgian in 1988 and was fascinated by the breed. Shortly after, she obtained her first dog, Am. Can. Ch. Bon Chien Mercedes CD. In 1993, she established her Michigan kennels when she bred her first litter under the French affix of Arrivee. Her lines are founded on European kennels. She has a strong alliance with the De La Lune Kennels, owned by Cynthia Royal and Nikki Swap, and, with their assistance, she was able to obtain one of her foundation bitches Am. Can. Ch. Starbright Glory de la Lune. Mated to S.R. Lynx de la Clairiere aux Louves, this bitch produced Arrivee's Les Impressioniste, a BOS, WB, and BPIS at the 1998 National Canadian

UKC BISS opera de la Clairiere Aux Louves.

Arrivees Remy Van Gogh.

Regional Supported show. The foundations of Arrivee come from the offspring of Clairiere aux Louvres, Condivicnum, De La Lune, and other imports, including Branock Rhythm 'n' Blues from the UK.

SANROYALE

Sallyann Comstock has been involved with dogs since 1956, mainly with Dobermanns and Great Danes. In 1965, she saw a Belgian Tervuren at a dog show

166

and fell in love with the breed. She spent her next year researching the breed, and, in 1966, she purchased her first foundation bitch from Dorothy Hollister of Val de Tonnerre Belgians. This bitch became Ch. La Marie du Val de Tonnerre CD, C-BAR, and she helped to set the standard for Sallyann's Texan kennels. Sallyann's background of raising and training horses allowed her to understand and to recognise correct structure and movement, but La Marie opened her eyes to the incredible intelligence and versatility of this wonderful breed.

Her first stud dog, Am. Can. Ch. Rajah D'Antre du Louves CD, BAR, was out of a Canadian bitch bred to a French import, Kenny de Cledeville. She has always leaned toward the more 'one-piece' heads with the beautiful, dark, almond-shaped eyes and high-set ears, which come from the French.

She has been fortunate enough to have acquired or produced many outstanding Tervuren, including such greats as BIS Am. Can. Ch. Rajah D'Antre du Louves CD BAR, the breed's third Best in Show dog; Ch. Kajon's Kashmier of Sanroyale BAR; their son Multi-Ch. Int. Ch. Our Valiant du Sanroyale; and Rajah ex La Mariee son, Am. Bel. Ch. Sanroyale's The Hustler CD, BAR.

Sallyann believes that, without recombining the varieties in the US, Belgians will suffer. She feels Groenendaels are losing substance and structure, and Tervurens are losing head planes; all could benefit from the larger gene pool that recombination would allow.

TOUCHSTONE
Carol Creger has been involved with Belgian Shepherds since 1980. She met Paul in 1990, when he wanted to purchase a dog from her Touchstone kennels in Michigan.

Initially, Carol had a Great Dane, with which she was attempting to compete in Obedience. Her Obedience instructor had a Tervuren. After one frustrating night in class, she remembers approaching her instructor and bursting into tears. Pointing to her instructor's dogs, she said, "I want a dog that works like that!". Several months later, she purchased her first Tervuren, a male named Seafields Stonewall. Tragically, Stoney was killed by a car a few months later.

Carol and Paul's outstanding dogs include Ch. For Askin de Loup Noir CGC, TT, a dog that finished with three five-point majors. Ch. Winjammers Buck Shot, also ranked in the top ten in conformation, achieving multiple Best in Show Specialty Show wins. As a sire, Buck Shot was very influential. Ch. Neartic de la Grande Lande was imported from France in 1997. His wins include going best in Sweepstakes at the 1998 ABTC National Specialty show, and Best Male of all varieties at the 1999 UKC National Specialty show.

European dogs have had significant influence on this kennel. The increased exposure to European dogs has meant that they have been able to develop a real appreciation for breed type.

BONHEUR
The Bonheur kennels in Virginia have existed since 1962, run by Faye, Carole and Alleyne Dickens. Their first Tervuren was Ch. Kriquette de Fauve Charbonne. They bred the first Belgian Best in Show winner, Ch. Bonheur D'Artagnan UDT, the first Tervuren to earn a perfect score in Obedience. Other famous dogs from this kennel include Tishanimga de Weeping Pines CDX, and the first dog of any breed

to go Best in Show from the newly created Herding Group, Ch. Bonheur Star Treader CDX, TD.

One of the kennel's lowest points came when they bred a beautiful litter without knowing the sire was a carrier of epilepsy. The line had to be discontinued, which made the Dickenses committed to complete openness regarding the health of their Belgians. It is their hope that more breeders will disclose health problems, as silence hurts everyone.

The best dog they have owned or bred is AKC, UKC Ch. Arlequin Bonheur Buccaneer. He fitted the Standard for the breed more than any other dog they ever had, being elegant, square with a beautiful head, and with a wonderful expression. He was an outgoing, effervescent character, and a wonderful companion.

BLACKWATER

Dr Linda Fung has owned Tervuren since 1982. She acquired her first dog from Judy Smith (Frostfire) and Carol Hein Creger (Touchstone). In 1994, she imported a bitch, Juby de la Prarie de la Sommerau, from Francis Rauner's kennel in France. Since then, they have gone into partnership in many breeding programmes and acquisitions.

The first time that Linda saw an import was in 1982. Having seen Dali de la Pouroffe, a Belgian import, she decided she wanted that 'look', consisting of great head structure and a beautiful expression. Her foundation bitch, Am. Ch. Winjammers Clean Sweep HIC, was his daughter. Linda prefers the look of a beautiful, well-balanced dog, with correct Belgian type, and a good expression.

The best dog Linda's Michigan-based kennels have produced is Ch. Blackwater's Silverstreak. For his time, he was one of the most influential dogs in the US for the acceptance of greys. He was the only grey ever to go select at the ABTC National Specialty. Another of Linda's favourite dogs is Olim de la Tangi Morgane, an import from Brigitte Ouhlem in France. He was the only grey dog to ever go WD at an ABTC National Specialty, and he is proving himself as the best producer she has ever owned. She is excited about his young offspring and feels he will be one of the most influential dogs from Blackwater kennels.

BEAUGENCY

This is a fairly new kennel, established in California in 1997 by Lee Jiles and Joanne Thielen. The kennel name is the same as the small village along the Loire River where the kennel owners can be found enjoying the food, wine and scenery when they are in France. Originally, both were Groenendael owners from the mid-1970s, although they eventually switched to the Tervuren variety, attracted by the beauty

Nicole (left) and Louves de la Grande.

of the imports. The foundation bitches for their kennel were from the French Grande Lande kennel, Louve and Nicole de la Grande Lande, with the males being Northwind de la Grande Lande and Ystatis van der Hoge Laer. The objective of their kennel is to maintain the quality of Belgians, by producing healthy, happy puppies that will live long and pleasant lives in loving homes.

Having kept Belgians for almost a quarter of a century, there have been a number of highs. Success in conformation shows, tracking, Obedience and Schutzhund, as well as being founders of the United Belgian Shepherd Dog Association, are high on the list. In the future, they hope to see the abolition of the division of the four varieties into separate breeds within the American Kennel Club.

BAR-K BELGIANS
In 1951, Bob and Barbara Krohn of Fauve Charbonne, Los Lunas in New Mexico, decided to get a medium-sized family dog. They purchased an eight-month-old female, imported from Belgium by Rudy Robinson in Wheaton, Illinois. Zamorane, out of Ubro of the Country House and Xivlette, came to live with them.

Their breeding has always been directed towards the use of imports and dogs with immediate imported parentage. Their outstanding dogs have included Ch. Mars du Fauve Charbonne UDT, a talented dog and a fine producer, Ch. Nugget de Fauve Charbonne CDX, TD, and Ch. Scorpio du Fauve Charbonne CD, TD, noted for his beauty and his fine stud dog record. Barbara says that the best dogs they have had were their original foundation bitches Zamorne, and the Tervuren Jasmine de Cledeville. Through their puppies, these

two bitches formed the foundation stock for many other kennels in the US.

CHATEAU BLANC KENNELS
Janina Laurin arrived in the US from Germany, with her husband Walter, her daughter Janina, and her German Shepherd. When her German Shepherd became gravely ill, she searched for another breed and the Chateau Blanc Belgian Tervuren kennel was established in 1960 in Connecticut, with Edeltraud Laurin.

The first Tervuren to arrive was Viv de la Moulin Rouge. While she was a beloved pet of the family, the next two Tervuren were to set Chateau Blanc on an upward spiral for breeder achievement in all venues of the sport. Ch. Flair de Fauve Charbonne CD, BAR was acquired as a five-year-old male from an acquaintance of the family. Ch. Kandice de Fauve Charbonne CDX, BAR was acquired as a puppy from the Krohns in New Mexico. Janina and her sister, Gerlinde Hockla, travelled to more than 60 dog shows all over the US with these two animals, in search of sufficient points to finish their Championships. The dogs were mated three times, and dogs and bitches from these three early matings went on to become major influences in Tervuren breeding programmes across the United States.

The philosophy of the kennel for the last 40 years has been to breed Belgian Tervuren that meet the AKC American Belgian Tervuren Standard. It has always sought out dogs or bitches to improve aspects of its breeding programme based on the merits of the potential breeding pair, their pedigrees, and checks into their health background. Dogs on both sides of the ocean have a great deal to offer one another. A blending of the strengths that meet the Standard in the countries in which they reside will bode well for the future of the Belgians. While some US dogs would improve from importation, some European and English lines would benefit likewise from the strengths of the American-bred Belgians.

CACHET NOIR

This New Hampshire kennel began in 1972 as Sunburst Kennels, and four Tervuren litters were born under this prefix. Three litters were produced by Ch. Luba vom Gebirge CDX, the foundation bitch. Luba was the daughter of Ch. Chateaubriand CD, BAR, one of the most influential of the early Tervuren in the US. The fourth litter was produced by Ch. Apache of Sunburst CD, a daughter of Luba and the kennel's first home-bred Champion. Both Luba and Apache can be found in many pedigrees and were particularly influential in structure and temperament, especially when bred back to Chateau Blanc males.

In 1979, Apache produced their fifth litter, but this was the first under the kennel name Cachet Noir, which came from the old Belgian translation of cachet, meaning a seal affixed to important documents. This seal was often a crest or a whimsical mask, so a loose translation was adapted to mean 'seal of the black mask'. This was also the first litter produced by a young male that proved to be a turning point for this kennel, Ch. StarBright Bonne Chance CDX Am. Can. TD, HIC, PD1, PD2, BAR specialty select, known as Banner.

Soundness of mind and body is the most important characteristic that founder Dana MacKoni looks for in her breeding programme, but Banner's influence in type and work ethic gave Cachet Noir a different direction in breeding. This was a dog that was ahead of his time in type. However, several kennels used him, and, in only 11 litters, he sired BIS, BISS, group winners, high in trials winners, herding winners, specialty winners, and many other dogs with superior temperaments. His influence will remain in many kennels, as it has in Cachet Noir.

WINJAMMER

In 1971, Pat Morgan was an instructor at a local Obedience class. This led to dog show involvement and the desire to have a top-performance breed of dog. Her first Belgian was soon purchased, and she was hooked. The foundation bitch for her Winjammer kennels in Michigan was Am. Can. Ch. HTCH Hi Times Top of the Crop Am. Can. UDT, STDc, OTDds.

Pat enjoyed finding truly beautiful dogs with excellent temperaments. She was especially taken with French dogs. They influenced her sufficiently to make her start again, with the exception of one dog from her previous line. Her first French import was UKC Ch. U-AG I Jenny du Crepuscule des Loups STDds, PT. She was also most impressed with the Bois du Tot dogs, and began importing many dogs from that kennel.

SEAFIELD

Judith Specht has been involved in Tervuren since the early 1970s, when her family moved to several acres in Malibu, California. She wanted an intelligent, beautiful, rustic family dog that would accompany her on long horseback rides in the mountains behind her house.

In her opinion, the best dog she ever owned was Ch. Seafields Loup-Varrou, Best dog and Select at the National, Select the following year, and Best of Breed the year after. Varrou went on to earn his BAR award for having produced

BISS Ch. Seafields Loup-Varrou.

Champions in the conformation ring, as well as in Obedience and performance events.

Judith thinks that Belgians will become more and more popular as people find out how devoted, intelligent, and fabulous they are. She says, "As breeders, we need to be very careful in placing these dogs because, as we know, they are not for everyone". Judith also believes that, because of the dedication of the breeders, many health problems are currently being addressed, which will benefit all in the future.

DE LA LUNE
In 1986, Nikki Swap's sister, Cynthia Royal, got her first Belgian puppy, Am. Can. Ch. Starbright Full Moon Shadow CD, TD. Nikki was so impressed she decided to get one of her own. Kay Maves introduced her to Linda Collins in England, and, shortly after, Am. Can. Ch. Domburg Talk of the Town TD was imported from England. A very different type from the American Tervurens, she quickly gained her title.

Nikki founded her Michigan-based kennels with Talk of the Town, and she looked to England to find a suitable dog with which to mate her. Questenberg Rheingold was chosen, but attempts to

use artificial insemination using his frozen semen were unsuccessful. Through Linda Collins, Nikki eventually purchased the dog, and he went to live with Cynthia. The first litter from these two dogs produced a surprise, as four of the puppies were Groenendael. Due to the AKC ruling, they had to be registered as Black Tervuren and could not be shown in AKC competition. This is one of Nikki's greatest disappointments, although the dogs can be shown in Canada and in United Kennel Club competitions.

One of the black dogs from the litter, Belle Étoile de la Lune, was mated to UKC Ch. Neartic de la Grande Lande, producing a litter of red puppies that look promising. These lines will be of great use to the Tervuren breeders of the future.

Nikki hopes that, in the future, the American Kennel Club will succeed in recombining the varieties so they again become one breed with four varieties, allowing Belgians to be registered by variety, not parentage.

KLAAR
The Canadian Klaar kennel was founded in the late 1980s, beginning with a male and female Tervuren bred from local lines. Christine Reed and Dermott Young had both been brought up with Border Collies in their native Ireland and England, and had chosen Tervuren because they were herding dogs. They worked their Tervs in Obedience with much success, but were not sure as to the quality of the pair for breeding. The decision was taken out of their hands when both Tervuren developed epilepsy. This horrible experience almost put them out of the breed. They neutered the original Tervs, rehomed them as pets, and began again.

They researched the breed carefully and found some old lines in Belgium and

France that they liked. In 1991, they imported Tervuren Can. Am. Ch. Perfect of the Two C-Bar, and Tervuren Ch. Gabelle de la Douce Plaine, and the Malinois group-winning BISS, BPIS, S.R. Can. Am. Ch. Gildas du Mas des Lavandes CDX. Gabelle was mated to Multi Ch. Kouros of the Two in Belgium and produced a triple Champion and three-times Specialty winner BISS, U Ch Am. Can. Ch. Klaar Altesse la Foi V. Kouros. They are the first North American kennels to win an S.R. on a locally bred dog, with S.R. Ch. Klaar Elda, a Malinois bitch, now resident in Australia.

European dogs have totally influenced the breeding programmes of this kennel. They have imported several quality bitches including Ch. Udine de la Maison du Bois CD, Ombre de la Quiviere, and several from Van de Hoge Laer.

MALINOIS

DIADEM
Antonia Diamond has been in the breed her whole life. Malinois were first kept by her family generations ago, in the early 1920s, as working sheepdogs on her grandfather's ranch. As a child, Toni acquired her first Malinois in 1947, and entered her first dog show in 1953. She went on to purchase her first show dog in 1954, Sabre Bassanio, out of the de Mahyfaut and the du Chaos lines from Belgium. Sabre obtained his CD award and was the last living AKC-registered Malinois in the US, until Toni imported Ladesiree Diadem Regio Semine, in 1962, from Belgium.

It seemed to Toni a grave injustice that a breed with so much to offer was unappreciated. Fortunately, when she married her husband Dale, he agreed and

Am. Ch. Diadem Paragon Paladin.

they sought the assistance of F.E. Verbanck, who assisted them with their selection of dogs, realising that these dogs were being imported for the purpose of establishing the breed in the US. He selected Ladesiree Diadem Regio Semine, the first CDX Malinois and Ch. Lagardaire de la Mascotte Royale CD, the true trailblazer for the breed that consistently won miscellaneous classes. After the reinstatement of full show status by the AKC, he consistently won Best of Breeds all across the US and Canada, including being shown three times and winning three Best of Breeds at the Westminster Kennel Club shows, as well as producing many top-quality offspring.

Toni is convinced that, without the influence of European dogs on her California-based kennels, there would not be the great Malinois that now exist in the US.

SOUVENIR
In 1973, Donna Haworth of Washington State had reached a point in her life when she knew she wanted another dog, and

she was impressed by the Malinois. The favoured bitch turned out to be a Malinois bred from Uline du Maugre and Diadem Le Brigand Du Coeur. Her first Malinois became Souvenir O'Crocs-Blancs, and gained her breed Championship title and her Utility Dog title. Mated to Zaf du Boscaille CDX, TD, SchH3, owned by Wade Campbell, she produced Ch. Souvenir Accent CD. Another bitch of her breeding, Ch. Souvenir Harmony CD, owned by Barbara Peach, has produced offspring that will be figuring in the breeding programmes of many hobby breeders.

DE L'FERME
Dorothy Kutlik has been in Malinois since 1974, when she received a Tervuren puppy as a gift. She was impressed with the Belgian intelligence in Obedience and herding, and she began to research the breed. The shorter coats appealed to her, being easier for country living. Over a period of 15 years, she bred or co-bred 16 litters, each time looking to improve the breed.

For 10 years the de l'Ferme dogs have made up three generations of top Belgian Malinois, Ch. la Beau Berger de l'Ferme, his son Am. Mex. Ch. Mr Mighty Mo de l'Ferme CDX, and his son, Ch. Hugo von Heinrich de l'Ferme. Mighty Mo was the first Malinois to earn Best in Show, doing so twice.

The gene pool in the US was very small, so importing Malinois of sound temperament was of great importance; beauty and work ability were also very important. Dorothy has used males with different working backgrounds, trying to achieve the 'perfect' dog, or trying to correct at least one particular fault, so she is now looking forward to the future generations of lineage.

Am. Ch. Tri Sorts Solitaire, aged six months.

TRI SORTS
Carol and Frank Knock, and their daughter Lisa, have been involved in the world of pure-bred dogs since 1965, when Carol and Frank founded The Civilised Dog Obedience and Breed Handling School. To date, they have trained more than 32,000 dogs and people.

Carol and Frank obtained their first Malinois in 1979, Diadem Gemma de Charleroi. Gemma quickly gained her title, and the Knocks' passion for Malinois took over. By using a combination of European and American bloodlines, their Virginian kennels have produced more than 62 conformation Champions, along with numerous Obedience, Agility and herding titles. In addition, they have bred search and rescue dogs, as well as therapy dogs.

173

Am. Ch. Avonlea Queen Anne's Lace.

AVONLEA

European dogs have also influenced Ann MacKay's breeding programmes at her Michigan kennels. Her first litter was from an import from the la Terre Aimee kennel, four of which are now dual titled in conformation and Agility including U-AG1 BISS Gr. Ch. Am. Can. Ch. Avonlea Forget-Me-Not, a dog that has won both AKC and regional Specialties. Forget-Me-Not also travelled to France, where she gained her S.R. grading, the first US Malinois to earn this honour. Ann has also travelled to Europe and used other well-known stud dogs, including R.E. Maubray du Maugre, and a grandson of Maubray, S.R. Orwell du Domiane de Vauroux.

LAEKENOIS

It is difficult to predict the future of this variety in the US, given the different types of Laekenois in Europe and America. There is also the additional problem that Laekenois are not recognised by the American Kennel Club. At present, in the US, all Laekenois have European influences, with most of them bred from European imports. Breeders will have to continue to import from Europe in order to expand the gene pool and to continue to improve their dogs. Much depends on the European breeders to ensure that Laekenois continue to develop well in health and temperament.

In the US, there is a great deal of interest in the Laekenois, but, unfortunately, not many places where they can be shown. However, they can now compete in the American Kennel Club performance events like Obedience, tracking and Agility. This will be of great benefit for the variety. Many people like the Laekenois' cute, funny look, but it is difficult to make people understand that this is a working dog with a great deal of drive and an intelligence that needs to be directed. The next few years in the US will be very exciting indeed.

MIDDLE-EARTH

Cindy Fitzgerald, based in Ithaca, New York, acquired her first Malinois in 1979, and, in 1995, her first Laekenois was imported from France. Her original Malinois, Ch. Bowell's Aragorn of Gondor, was the third top Malinois in the US, and many of today's dogs trace back to him. After researching Laekenois lines she imported Lalique du Mas de Turco, whose brother, L'Emir du Mas de Turco, went to live with Sonja Ostrom.

Although Cindy says that her original Malinois, Aragorn, was very special, his daughter Ch. Middle-Earth Arien Gil-Gilland, CD HIC, TT was probably her best dog. In Laekenois, her original bitch, Lalique, has an outstanding temperament and has won the breed many fans.

SPRINGWOOD LAEKEN
Brigitte and Bill Walkey joined the Belgian Sheepdog Club of Canada in 1986. They had always admired the rarest Belgian, the Laekenois, since Brigitte's mother had grown up with them in Holland. Through the breed club, they had hoped to learn more about the variety and who might be raising them in Canada. To their dismay, no one was actively breeding any and there were less than half a dozen in the country at the time. They then began a long research period, which culminated in a visit to Holland in 1992. There, they saw their first Laekenois and made definite plans to import a female puppy.

Aicha v Ijsselvliedt, born in 1993, came to the Walkeys at nine weeks old. She attained her Canadian Championship at two years old. This was a major accomplishment as only three other Laekenois have ever won Championships in Canada (in Canada, the four varieties

Can. Ch. Haicha v' Ijsselvliet.

must be shown together as one breed). This is hard to do, as many judges have never seen a Laekenois in the flesh and can become quite confused when they see a rough, wiry, unkempt-looking dog standing in front of them. More experienced judges knew the variety and praised it.

At this point they started searching for a mate for Aicha, importing the nine-month-old male, Blackroyal's Famous Filemon, from Finland. Together, these dogs have produced two litters; the progeny are now young adults and are spread across North America, competing in shows, trials and working events. They are an excellent combination of their parents and should have a very good influence on future Laekenois.

KHABARET
David and Rhonda Smiley from Virginia have been involved in the breed since 1981. With their first dog, a Shetland Sheepdog, they joined an obedience class. The teacher owned a Tervuren and this was their introduction to the breed, but they later settled on the Laekenois as their chosen variety.

As a result of the small gene pool of Laekenois in the US, the Smileys were almost completely dependent on continental dogs. They took their Laekenois bitch, Laekenhuset's Anny, to Belgium to be mated. Currently, they are campaigning a promising male from the subsequent litter.

AVOIR DU CACHET
In 1989, Diana Fisher imported to her North Carolina kennels one of the first Laekenois to enter the US since the 1950s, SK Ch. Etamine des Seigneurs du Plessis HCT, from France. She was the first Laekenois to earn her Championship

title in the US. She also earned her herding instinct certificate. In 1991, Diana imported a male, SK Ch. Noble van Balderlo, and he also gained his title. These two dogs were successfully mated, and produced Avent Avoir du Cachet. Sadly, this dog was killed by a car at a young age. However, he had been used at stud before he died, producing Badin Avoir du Cachet, currently the only Laekenois in the US to have earned two UKC Grand Championship points. A puppy from the following generations, Blackfeathers Flint, has been successfully shown. Due to the size of the gene pool in the US, Diana has recently imported a further bitch from the Nature's Best Kennel in Belgium.

Diana says that it was very hard in the beginning to get any help. No one in the US really knew anything about the variety, so she had to learn by experiment how to groom. It was hard to compete in any shows because the judges also did not know about Laekenois. One judge commented on another Laekenois that was in the ring with her and asked her why her bitch had less beard hair than the other; not wanting to offend anyone, Diana replied that all dogs were different. What she wanted to tell the judge was that this was not a Bouvier and the other dog was incorrect to have so much hair. Usually, in the US, people think that more hair is better, so the other dog won that day. At the time, Etamine rarely competed against a Laekenois, and all her wins came in the Group, against many other unusual breeds.

Diana is concerned for the future, because of the limited Laekenois gene pool. Her vision for her kennel is to provide soundness of temperament, looks, and health. She plans to add Malinois bloodlines and also to import bloodlines that differ from those currently available in the US. Although some of those dogs may not meet her vision for a good-looking Laekenois, hopefully, with careful choices, their offspring will.

BLACKFEATHER

Melinda Hughes from Colorado has been in Laekenois since 1994. She had wanted one ever since she had seen a picture of Sapho de l'Orchidee Noire. At this time there were only two breeders in the US, and Melinda, in conjunction with Diana Fisher, eventually placed a deposit on a female puppy. The puppy was obtained in 1994. UKC Ch. Badin Avoir du Cachet HIC, CGC, TT, TDI, also known as Bad Dog, had a wonderful temperament, had started in Schutzhund, had two legs on her CD, and had started in drug detection, when, due to kennel jealousy, she had to be rehomed. Badin produced one litter only, but most of the puppies have achieved some competition success.

Melinda won the first American Belgian Laekenois Association National with Badin and then repeated the win with her son four years later. She also works her Laekenois on sheep, and loves seeing them settling down and thinking about what they are doing.

Her original bitch, Badin, was a great first Laekenois to own, and her temperament and charm won her many friends in the breed. Her import, Uriah Fauves de Saline, was the "easiest-going and the sweetest dog" she has owned, although he did not care for showing and would rather be at home. In the long term, she thinks that her home-bred Blackfeathers Alibi will be the best; she is prettier than her mother and more impressive than Badin.